The Invention of the Eastern Question

The Invention of the Eastern Question

Sir Robert Liston and Ottoman Diplomacy in the Age of Revolutions

Ozan Ozavci

I.B. TAURIS
LONDON · NEW YORK · OXFORD · NEW DELHI · SYDNEY

I.B. TAURIS

Bloomsbury Publishing Plc, 50 Bedford Square, London, WC1B 3DP, UK
Bloomsbury Publishing Inc, 1385 Broadway, New York, NY 10018, USA
Bloomsbury Publishing Ireland, 29 Earlsfort Terrace, Dublin 2, D02 AY28, Ireland

BLOOMSBURY, I.B. TAURIS and the I.B. Tauris logo are
trademarks of Bloomsbury Publishing Plc

First published in Great Britain 2025

Copyright © Ozan Ozavci, 2025

Ozan Ozavci has asserted his rights under the Copyright,
Designs and Patents Act, 1988, to be identified as Author of this work.

This work was supported by the FP7 Ideas: European Research Council,
(grant number n.615313).

Cover design: Adriana Brioso
Cover image © *View of Istanbul from the Dutch Embassy at Pera* by
Jean Baptiste Vanmour. Courtesy of Rijksmuseum, Amsterdam

All rights reserved. No part of this publication may be: i) reproduced or transmitted in any form, electronic or mechanical, including photocopying, recording or by means of any information storage or retrieval system without prior permission in writing from the publishers; or ii) used or reproduced in any way for the training, development or operation of artificial intelligence (AI) technologies, including generative AI technologies. The rights holders expressly reserve this publication from the text and data mining exception as per Article 4(3) of the Digital Single Market Directive (EU) 2019/790.

Bloomsbury Publishing Plc does not have any control over, or responsibility for, any third-party websites referred to or in this book. All internet addresses given in this book were correct at the time of going to press. The author and publisher regret any inconvenience caused if addresses have changed or sites have ceased to exist, but can accept no responsibility for any such changes.

A catalogue record for this book is available from the British Library.

A catalog record for this book is available from the Library of Congress.

ISBN: HB: 978-0-7556-3861-1
       ePDF: 978-0-7556-3863-5
       eBook: 978-0-7556-3862-8

Typeset by Integra Software Services Pvt. Ltd.

For product safety related questions contact productsafety@bloomsbury.com.

To find out more about our authors and books visit www.bloomsbury.com
and sign up for our newsletters.

For Elizabeth

Contents

List of Illustrations	ix
Note on Transliteration	x
List of Abbreviations	xi
Prologue	1
1 *Philosophe* and diplomat	11
An airy phantom	11
The folds of deceit	17
Objects of ambition	24
2 'Now everything has changed'	31
Battle for the Crimea	31
The rise of the Romanovs	37
Alarming intentions	42
3 Forbidding obstacles	49
'Barbarians of the Bosphorus'	49
Diplomacy and reform	55
4 The spirit of treaties	63
The capitulations	63
Selling security	70
The Mykonos affair	75
5 Intermission	81
Henrietta	81
The Ottoman Napoleonic Wars	89
Revolutions	93
Peace	97

6	A peace worse than war?	105
	The sultan's fears	105
	The Treaty of Bucharest	111
	Voyage to Istanbul	116
	The diversion plan	122
7	Either war or plague	129
	A 'very strange' government	129
	The Serbian question revisited	133
	The conundrum	137
	'Another victory over France'	144
8	The Vienna moment	151
	Two proud nations	151
	The proposals	157
	The most valuable fruit of civilization	164
9	The phantom of Pera	173
	Journey homewards	173
	Spectral illusions	180

Select Bibliography	190
Index	199

Illustrations

Maps

1 The Crimea and the Black Sea, Source: NLS MS 5579   33
2 'Turkey in Europe: According to New Observations by the Gentlemen at the Royal Science Academy', by Pieter van der Aa, 1729, Source: Library of Congress   106
3 Mingrelia and the Phasis River, Source: NLS MS 5579   115
4 Liston's Map of Georgia, Source: NLS MS 5579   139

Figures

1 Robert Liston by Gilbert Stuart, 1800, National Gallery of Art, Washington DC, Public Domain   52
2 Henrietta Liston by Gilbert Stuart, 1800, National Gallery of Art, Washington DC, Public Domain   85

Table

1 Greek losses during the Mykonos affair, NLS MS 5579   76

Note on Transliteration

This book draws on primary and secondary sources in English, French, Dutch, Russian, Ottoman and modern Turkish. All translations are my own. Ottoman Turkish is transliterated using modern Turkish orthography, while Russian follows the Library of Congress system. For names in Ottoman Turkish, I retain their Turkish forms (e.g. Mahmud instead of Mahmoud, Mehmed rather than Mohammed). City names are used in their contemporary versions, such as Edirne instead of Adrianople, Istanbul instead of Constantinople, Russian form Ochakov rather than the Turkish Özi and Shumen instead of Shumla.

Abbreviations

AMAE	Archives Ministère des Affaires étrangères et du Développement international, La Courneuve, Paris
AVPRI	Arxiv vneshnej politiki Rossijskoj imperii (Foreign Policy Archive of Imperial Russia), Moscow
BL	British Library Manuscripts, London
BOA	Başbakanlık (now Cumhurbaşkanlığı) Osmanlı Arşivi (Ottoman State Archives), Istanbul
Dépêches	Dépêches inédites du Chevalier de Gentz aux Hospodars de Valachie pour servir à l'histoire de la politique européenne (1813 à 1828), I, ed. Anton Prokesch-Osten
EUL	Edinburgh University Library
HETNA	Nationaal Archief (Dutch National Archives), The Hague
HHStA	Österreichisches Staatsarchiv, Haus-, Hof- und Staatsarchiv, Vienna
NLS	The National Library of Scotland, Edinburgh
TNA	The National Archives, Kew, London
TSMA	Topkapı Sarayı Müzesi Arşivi (Topkapi Palace Museum Archives), Istanbul
VPR	Vneshnyaya politika Rossii XIX i nachala XX veka. Dokumenty rossijskogo Ministerstva inostrannyx del. (Russian Foreign Policy Nineteenth until early Twentieth Century. Documents of Russian Ministry of Foreign Affairs) (VPR)

Prologue

'To be noble is to defend the weak not to assist the strong.'
Sir Robert Liston, n.d.[1]

The young Robert Liston (1742–1836) was only twenty-three when he confided to his best friend Andrew Dalzel that '[f]ame, distinction, all that, is but an airy phantom'.[2] At that time, working as a private tutor in Paris, he saw himself as an unremarkable figure, unacknowledged and unnoticed amidst the vibrant throng of the city. Liston was torn between ambition and contentment, uncertain whether to pursue lofty achievements or settle for a respectable if modest life back in his native Scotland – cherishing the love of a beautiful young woman, starting a family and tending to the land.

The allure of fame and distinction proved irresistible. He decided to shake off his 'hindrances' and 'follow the phantom'.[3] And follow it he did, from the learned clubs and universities of London, Edinburgh and Glasgow – where he dreamt of becoming a *philosophe* and professor – to the diplomatic stage, posted to Munich, Regensburg, Berlin, Turin, Madrid, Stockholm, Istanbul, Philadelphia, The Hague, Copenhagen and, finally, Istanbul again. It was in this profession that he shone, appointed to the Privy Council in 1812 and knighted in 1817. In his obituary, Sir Robert was referred to as 'the father of the diplomatic body … throughout Europe', in recognition of his decades of service and wise counsel.[4]

This book follows Liston's relentless pursuit of the phantom. Every phase of the life and career of this significant, yet often overlooked, figure warrant

---

[1] Volume of Poems, Notes and Extract from Books, Robert Liston Papers, NLS MS 5720, f. 21.
[2] Robert Liston to Andrew Dalzel, 19 September 1765, NLS MS 5517, f. 17.
[3] Ibid.
[4] 'Death of Sir Robert Liston', *The Scotsman*, 23 July 1836.

and still await careful study, to understand the subtleties of British and global diplomatic politics, as well as the life of a diplomat in the late eighteenth and early nineteenth centuries. But my focus here will be on Liston's two embassies in Istanbul – first in 1794–5, and then between 1812 and 1820, his longest time in post. He spent a decade of his career in the Ottoman imperial capital, residing in the city's diplomatic quarter, Pera.[5]

Liston's postings to Istanbul – known to contemporaries (and to Liston) as Constantinople – coincided with the onset of the Eastern Question, the most perilous, complex and enduring issue in nineteenth-century international politics, stretching into the 1920s. The Eastern Question had deep and diverse roots, but strained relations between the Russian and Ottoman Empires lay at the heart of its semantic coinage in the early nineteenth century.

Only a few decades prior to Liston's first Istanbul embassy, Russia had occupied the Crimea, driven by imperial ambitions and security concerns. It established a satellite khanate and then, in 1783, annexed the once Ottoman peninsula outright. As Russia's borders crept south to the shores of the Black Sea, Empress Catherine II found herself in a position to threaten the heart of the sultan's empire. Her squadrons could potentially seize Istanbul before the news reached the nearest European capital.[6] This represented an existential and lasting threat, and not only to the Ottomans. Russian control over strategically crucial dominions such as the straits could disrupt the European power equilibrium. It could plunge the continent, and indeed the entire world, into a catastrophic war. The risk of Russian domination, combined with fears of the fall of the Ottoman Empire, among others, shaped the course of international relations down to the 1920s. This said, the Eastern Question continued to influence events long after it itself became part of history.

British historian Tim Blanning cites the Eastern Question among the underlying causes of the Revolutionary and Napoleonic Wars (1792–1815).[7] Paul Schroeder posits that it was the most dangerous issue in European international politics in the long nineteenth century.[8] Indeed, differing interpretations of the Eastern Question ignited the next major conflict among the so-called Great

---

[5] P.W. Schroeder, 'The 19th-Century International System: Changes in the Structure', *World Politics*, 39, no. 1 (Oct. 1986), 1–26.
[6] Karl A. Roider Jr. *Austria's Eastern Question* (Princeton, NJ: Princeton University Press, 1982).
[7] T.C.W. Blanning, *The Origins of the French Revolutionary Wars* (London and New York: Longman, 1986), 53–7.
[8] Schroeder, 'The 19th-Century International System', 6.

Powers post-1815: the Crimean War of 1853–6, a brutal inter-imperial clash that claimed nearly a million lives.⁹ In the Balkans, the Eastern Question planted the seeds of the First World War, seeds that began to germinate in the 1870s, if not earlier. It lingered until at least the Treaty of Lausanne in 1923, which marked the end of both the 'Greater War' of 1911–22 and the Ottoman Empire, ushering in a new global imperial order.¹⁰

Since its inception, several conferences convened to resolve the Eastern Question. Time and again, it was purportedly solved, only to resurface again, challenging both regional and global stability.¹¹ So persistent was its influence that, in 1841, the French author and political scientist Alexis de Tocqueville declared it 'the question of the century'. 'It dominates all others,' he wrote. 'All others must be subordinated to it.'¹² In a similar vein, the prominent Ottoman writer Namık Kemal described the Eastern Question as 'the most perilous of all issues' in nineteenth-century international politics.¹³

During two of its crucial phases, in the 1790s and the 1810s, Robert Liston played a central role in brokering peace between Russia and the Ottoman Empire. He acted as arbitrator between the 'two proud nations', as he once described them, offering counsel to imperial representatives on both sides and organizing special missions to prevent inter-imperial tensions from erupting into an open conflict. He also strove to settle the disputes around the commercial and legal agreements signed between the Ottomans and the major European powers since the sixteenth century. His diplomatic efforts triangulated between the differing Ottoman, Russian and British perceptions of the Eastern Question.

A study of Liston's career allows us to trace how the Russian invasion of the Crimea and the subsequent Russo-Ottoman tensions changed the course of world history at the turn of the nineteenth century. Although Liston's diplomacy helped to secure the fragile Russo-Ottoman peace temporarily, his relative

---

[9] Candan Badem, *The Ottoman Crimean War (1853–1856)* (Leiden: Brill, 2010).
[10] Jonathan Conlin and Ozan Ozavci (eds.), *They All Made Peace – What's Peace? The 1923 Lausanne Treaty and the New Imperial Order* (London: Gingko Library, 2023).
[11] Ozan Ozavci, *Dangerous Gifts: Imperialism, Security, and Civil Wars in the Levant, 1798–1864* (Oxford, New York: Oxford University Press, 2021), 118, 167, 286.
[12] Cited in Andrew Arsan, '"There is, in the Heart of Asia, … an Entirely French Population": France, Mount Lebanon, and the Workings of Affective Empire in the Mediterranean, c. 1830–1919', in *French Mediterraneans: Transnational and Imperial Histories*, Patricia Lorcin and Todd Shepard (eds.), (Lincoln, NE: University of Nebraska Press, 2016), 76–100, at 88.
[13] Namık Kemal, 'Yunan meselesi üzerine mütâlaât', *Hürriyet*, 11 January 1869, cited from Alp Eren Topal, *Sürgünde Muhalefet: Namık Kemal'in Hürriyet Gazetesi* (Istanbul: Vakıfbank Kültür Yayınları, 2018), 379.

success proved instrumental in the emergence of the Eastern Question. War was averted during both embassies, but underlying issues continued to fester and intensify, posing risks to global peace and security for decades to come.

§ § §

A nineteenth-century dictionary defines the Eastern Question as '[i]n modern times, a so-called mainly political problem about the future of the Ottoman Empire and countries that are closely tied to it'.[14] Notwithstanding this definition, historians, as well as historical actors, have found little consensus on what exactly the Eastern Question meant and where it originated.[15] Ahistorical and tendentious interpretations usually trace its roots to the early crusades of the eleventh and twelfth centuries, or to the arrival of the Slavs and the Turks in the Balkans during the sixth and fourteenth centuries, respectively, associating it with a civilizational clash and the 'retreat of Islam in Europe and Asia'.[16] More commonly, if equally misleadingly, the Eastern Question is linked to the contentious and anachronistic 'Ottoman decline thesis', centred on the debate over what the European powers should do about the power vacuum they anticipated in the wake of the Ottoman Empire's seemingly inevitable demise.[17]

In her seminal analysis of major nineteenth-century questions, Holly Case argues that '[h]istorians have generally assumed there is a real essence to questions that can be historicized … There is some truth in such general assessments, but it is also true that one essential feature of questions is that they have been chronically, indeed almost reflexively redefined'.[18] Indeed, the Eastern Question was repeatedly redefined in the course of the long nineteenth

---

[14] *Nastol'nyj slovar' dlja spravok po vsěm otrasljam znanija (Spravočnyj ènciklopedičeskij leksikon)*, vol. 3, 1863, 520.

[15] Matthew S. Anderson, *The Eastern Question, 1774-1923: A Study in International Relations* (London, Melbourne: Palgrave Macmillan, 1966); Alexander L. Macfie, *The Eastern Question 1774-1923* (London, New York: Longman, 2013); Stephen Pierce Hayden Duggan, *The Eastern Question: A Study in Diplomacy* (Unpublished Doctoral Thesis, Columbia University, New York, 1902); M.A. Luchaire, *La Question d'Orient* (Paris: Libraire Hachette, 1911); René Pinon, *L'Europe et l'empire ottoman: les aspects actuels de la Question d'Orient* (Paris: Libraire académique, 1917); Philip E. Mosley, *Russian Diplomacy and the Opening of the Eastern Question in 1838 and 1839* (Cambridge, MA: Harvard University Press, 1934).

[16] Macfie, *The Eastern Question*, 2–4.

[17] Alexander Bitis, *Russia and the Eastern Question: Army, Government and Society, 1815-1833* (Oxford: Oxford University Press, 2006), 21.

[18] Holly Case, *The Age of Questions or, A First Attempt at an Aggregate History of the Eastern, Social, Woman, American, Jewish, Polish, Bullion, Tuberculosis, and Many Other Questions over the Nineteenth Century* (Princeton, NJ, and Oxford: Princeton University Press, 2018), 12.

century. It acquired different meanings across different contexts and periods, at the hands of diverse stakeholders.[19] As with most questions of security, it was intersubjective.[20]

Still, this need not prevent us from pinpointing a core puzzle that transcended the Eastern Question's successive reimaginings. An in-depth, longitudinal and inclusive reading of the decades surrounding the turn of the nineteenth century – when the term was coined – through the experience of Liston and his associates permit us to identify a complex constellation of issues that led to the spontaneous invention of the Eastern Question as a semantic category. By contextualizing each of its episodes serially and examining their intersectional and cross-sectoral undertones, one can argue that the Eastern Question essentially pertained to an uncertainty around how to deal with the perceived and relative weakness (but not necessarily 'decline') of the Ottoman Empire – relative both to the other Powers of the time and to its own past grandeur.

The following pages will explain how this puzzle emerged and burgeoned into an urgent security issue, casting its dark shadow over more than a century. Even though the Russian annexation of the Crimea, a land predominantly populated by Muslims, was not typical of other episodes of the Eastern Question, it transformed a regional security concern into one of history's most enduring dilemmas. To understand the impact of this event, it is important to consider the often-overlooked 'Ottoman' link in the historical narrative of the Revolutionary and Napoleonic Wars (1792–1815) and their aftermath.[21] Although anglophone scholarship on the Eastern Question is extensive, the period encompassing the Russian invasion of the Crimea, Ottoman responses to the Revolutionary and Napoleonic Wars, and the 1814–15 Congress of Vienna receives very little attention in that literature.[22]

---

[19] Ozavci, *Dangerous Gifts*, 9.
[20] Beatrice de Graaf and Cornel Zwierlein, 'Historicizing Security: Entering the Conspiracy Dispositive', *Historical Social Research*, 38, no. 1 (2013), 52. There is a budding revisionist literature that considers the Eastern Question as a dynamic process. See, for instance, Christine M. Philliou, *Biography of an Empire: Governing Ottomans in an Age of Revolution* (Berkeley, CA: University of California Press, 2011); Lucien J. Frary and M. Kozelsky, *Russian-Ottoman Borderlands: The Eastern Question Reconsidered* (Wisconsin: University of Wisconsin Press, 2014). Also see, Michelle Tusan, 'Britain and the Middle East: New Historical Perspectives on the Eastern Question', *History Compass*, 8, no. 3 (March, 2010), 212–22.
[21] Few studies consider the Ottoman Empire as an integral part of the Napoleonic Wars. See esp., Alexander Mikaberidze, *The Napoleonic Wars: A Global History* (Oxford: Oxford University Press, 2020); Virginia Aksan, *The Ottomans 1700-1923: An Empire Besieged* Second Edition (London and New York: Routledge, 2022).
[22] J.A.R. Marriot, *The Eastern Question: An Historical Study in European Diplomacy* (Oxford: Clarendon Press, 1940), 64–72; For the Vienna order, see esp. Beatrice de Graaf, Brian Vick and Ido de Haan, *Securing Europe After Napoleon: 1815 and the New European Security Culture* (Cambridge: Cambridge University Press, 2019), 'Introduction'; Beatrice de Graaf, *Fighting Terror after Napoleon: How Europe Became Secure after 1815* (Cambridge: Cambridge University Press, 2020), and Glenda Sluga, *The Invention of International Order: Remaking Europe after Napoleon* (Princeton, NJ, and Oxford: Princeton University Press, 2022).

This book is a modest attempt to address this gap, taking as its point of departure the life of Robert Liston and his wife Henrietta (neé Marchant) Liston (1751–1828) whom he married in 1796. Through Robert's pursuit of the elusive phantom of distinction and Henrietta's new life as an ambassadress, I will seek to reveal the connections and continuities that historical actors saw among the different episodes of the Eastern Question. The temporal biographical focus of the book will interweave these episodes, at once tracing how historical developments altered the Listons' lives and perspectives.[23]

The Invention of the Eastern Question builds on previous work in which I have considered the emergence of this major puzzle in the context of Russo-Ottoman relations at the turn of the nineteenth century.[24] I was unable to do justice to some of the issues such as the roles the capitulations – the legal and commercial privileges accorded to the European subjects by Ottoman sultans – and the corrupt *berat* system played in kindling tensions among the Powers (particularly Russia and the Ottoman Empire), and the Serbian revolution and its crucial role in the making of the Eastern Question.

In what follows I reconsider these subjects and propose two main arguments. First, that the 'Eastern Question' centred on the challenges related to the (mis-) interpretation and (non)implementation of the unequal treaties signed between the Ottoman Empire and its western and northern neighbours, particularly Russia, in the eighteenth and early nineteenth centuries. These treaties had implications for commercial competition among the Great Powers, the protection of European protégés in Ottoman territories and, related to this, the quest for autonomy on the part of Serbians, Greeks and others in a revolutionary era.

While traditional international law, or the law of nations as it was called in the eighteenth century, aimed to establish order among *sovereign* states and prevent war and aggression, the unequal treaties that the Ottoman elites were compelled to sign further compromised the empire's sovereignty.[25] This was especially apparent in commercial and capitulatory privileges, the exploitation of the *berat* system, the protection of the non-Muslim communities and Ottoman neutrality in European conflicts. European and Ottoman statesmen alike employed international law selectively, to navigate the murky waters of inter-imperial

---

[23] Laura Almagor, Haakon A. Ikonomou and Gunvor Simonsen (eds.), *Global Biographies: Lived History as Method* (Manchester: Manchester University Press, 2022).

[24] Ozavci, *Dangerous Gifts*; Ozavci, 'A Priceless Grace? The Congress of Vienna of 1815, the Ottoman Empire and Historicizing the Eastern Question', *The English Historical Review*, 136, no. 583 (December, 2021), 1450–76.

[25] Antony Anghie, *Imperialism, Sovereignty and the Making of International Law* (Cambridge: Cambridge University Press, 2005), 5.

relations at the time, as the political and economic sovereignty of the Ottoman Empire hung by a thread. International law evolved into a tool of indirect control – a form of legal and security imperialism – and a deficient shield for vulnerable semi-sovereign polities and subjugated peoples within imperial domains. During his embassies, Liston was keenly aware of the inequitable nature of these treaties and their exploitative implementation. At times, he chose to remain silent. Sometimes he took unprecedented steps, intervening in ways that ran counter to his immediate material interests.

Second, the Eastern Question embodied an importunate array of threats and interests that Ottoman imperial elites and subjects alike wrestled with, sought to address and occasionally manipulated in their favour.[26] In the end, the future of the very empire they ruled or inhabited was at stake, as well as their more immediate political, strategic, economic, financial, cultural (religious) and health interests. This is why, although the focus of this book centres on the Listons, it will not lose sight of the Ottoman experience of the Eastern Question. Through a 'contrapuntal' lens, it will bring the threat perceptions, interests and corresponding practices of both European and Ottoman and both imperial and subjugated historical actors under the same analytical grid, placing their histories into one narrative.[27]

Adopting such a perspective reveals that the Eastern Question was far more than a European concern – it was also a story of those labelled as semi-civilized or 'barbarians' within the overt and implicit hierarchies of the international order. It equally encapsulates the history of subjugated and imperialized peoples, such as the Serbs and Greeks, who faced horrendous mass killings, violence, economic and financial losses, and other tragedies, while also mounting significant resistance and struggle for independence.[28]

As such, the temporal lens of the Listons' lives will permit us to peel away some of the key layers of the Eastern Question. These include rivalries and joint-action by major European powers of the time, the unequal interactions between European powers and the Ottoman imperial authorities and the subject peoples

---

[26] Ozavci, *Dangerous Gifts*, 42, 253, 356.
[27] Edward Said, *Culture and Imperialism* (New York: Vintage Books, 1993), 50; Geeta Chowdry, 'Edward Said and Contrapuntal Reading: Implications for Critical Intervention in International Relations', *Millennium: Journal of International Studies*, 36, no. 1 (2007), 101–16; David Bartine, 'The Contrapuntal Humanism of Edward Said', *Interdisciplinary Literary Studies*, 17, no. 1 (2015), 59–85; Pınar Bilgin, '"Contrapuntal Reading" as a Method, an Ethos, and a Metaphor for Global IR', *International Studies Review*, 18, no. 1 (March 2016), 134–46.
[28] Donald Bloxham, *The Great Game of Genocide: Imperialism, Nationalism, and the Destruction of the Ottoman Armenians* (Oxford: Oxford University Press, 2007); Mark Mazower, *The Greek Revolution 1821 and the Making of Modern Europe* (London: Penguin Press, 2021).

under Ottoman rule, the (violent) relationship between Ottoman rulers and their subjects, and the role of non-state actors in risking or preventing conflict.

§ § §

My analysis here draws primarily on Robert Liston's private and public writings. Acquired by the National Library of Scotland from the Liston-Foulis family in 1936, the Liston archive consists of some 177 volumes that include Robert's official and personal correspondence, as well as maps and passports.[29] These volumes also contain his wife Henrietta's diaries and correspondence. Unlike the writings of an earlier ambassadress in Istanbul, Lady Mary Wortley Montagu (1689–1762), whose work posthumously gained great fame, Henrietta's papers have long remained 'virtually unknown'.[30] *The Invention of the Eastern Question* capitalizes on the invaluable insights they offer into contemporaries' thoughts, emotions and experiences of the Ottoman world.

Robert's first embassy in Istanbul and tenure in Philadelphia have previously garnered attention in the works of Alan Cunningham, Mehmet A. Yalçınkaya and Bredford Perkins.[31] While I was working on this book portions of Henrietta's Istanbul diaries were published in an edition with commentary by Patrick Hart, Dora Petherbridge, Valerie Kennedy and F. Özden Mercan.[32] My narrative here builds on this previous scholarship, but stakes out new ground by drawing on additional British, Ottoman, Russian, French, Austrian and Dutch archival sources, as well as other primary and secondary literature in English, French, Russian, Turkish and German. I do so not only to verify and cross-check information from the Liston papers, but also to offer a contrapuntal and dialogical analysis of the Eastern Question.

---

[29] Patrick Hart, '"Out of Your World": Liston's Turkish Travels', in *Henrietta Liston's Travels: The Turkish Journals, 1812–1820*, Patrick Hart, Valerie Kennedy and Dora Petherbridge (eds.) (Edinburgh: University of Edinburgh Press, 2020).

[30] Hart, "Out of Tour World", 4–5.

[31] Allan Cunningham, *Anglo-Ottoman Encounters in the Age of Revolution: Collected Essays*, vol. 1, Edward Ingram (ed.) (London: Frank Cass, 1993); Mehmet A. Yalçınkaya, 'Robert Liston'un İstanbul Büyükelçiliği (1794–1795) ve Osmanlı Devleti Hakkındaki Görüşleri', Osmanlı Araştırmaları, 18, no. 18 (1998), 187–216; Bradford Perkins, 'A Diplomat's Wife in Philadelphia: Letters of Henrietta Liston, 1796–1800', *The William and Mary Quarterly*, 11, no. 4 (October, 1954), 592–632; Louise V. North, *The Travel Journals of Henrietta Marchant Liston: North America and Lower Canada, 1796–1800* (London: Lexington Books, 2014); James C. Nicholls, 'Lady Henrietta Liston's Journal of Washington's "Resignation", Retirement and Death', *The Pennsylvania Magazine of History and Biography*, 95, no. 4 (October, 1971), 511–20.

[32] Patrick Hart, Valerie Kennedy and Dora Petherbridge (eds.), *Henrietta Liston's Travels: The Turkish Journals, 1812–1820* (Edinburgh: University of Edinburgh Press, 2020).

I must admit that the research for this book, which began to be written amid a pandemic, faced further disruption when Russia launched yet another campaign in 2022, unlawfully invading eastern Ukraine following its 2014 occupation of the Crimea. All these developments severely hindered my plans to conduct archival research in Moscow and Saint Petersburg, among other locations, which I had hoped would lend further empirical support to some of the arguments presented here.

Finally, in the slipstream of the burgeoning sub-field of new diplomatic history (NDH), I adopt an 'actor-oriented approach through the study of individuals and groups who perform diplomatic roles, rather than [focusing on] international relations as a whole'.[33] NDH represents an expanded, extended and deepened history of diplomacy. It explores dynamics that move beyond the narrowly defined political and strategic realms. This multi-actor and multi-sector approach forms the methodological core of this book, aiming to provide a fresh and nuanced understanding of the multifarious web of diplomacy woven around the Eastern Question.

The Invention of the Eastern Question consists of nine chapters. Chapter 1 introduces Robert Liston, exploring his early life, his aspirations, experiences and career prior to his arrival in Istanbul. Chapter 2 offers an overview of the onset of the Eastern Question down to Robert Liston's first embassy in 1794, tracing the history of Russo-Ottoman tensions, the ebb and flow of war and peace, and explaining how their struggle over the Crimea and the legal and commercial privileges Russia acquired along the way presaged the Eastern Question. Chapter 3 documents Liston's observations of the Ottoman world and diplomatic corps in Pera during the 1790s.

In Chapter 4, we plunge into the impact of the commercial and capitulatory agreements signed between the major European powers and the Ottomans in the eighteenth century on decision-making processes in 1794–5, and how these nearly sparked a new Russo-Ottoman War. This chapter outlines the venal *berat* system that placed Robert in a moral quandary, torn between generating revenue for his impoverished embassy and maintaining cordial relations with Ottoman ministers.

We meet Henrietta in Chapter 5. This chapter explores her relationship and unexpected marriage to Robert, and her new life as an ambassadress in North

---

[33] Houssine Alloul and Michael Auwers, 'What Is (New in) New Diplomatic History?', *Journal of Belgian History*, 48, no. 4 (2018), 112–22, at 114; Stefan E. Amirell, 'New Diplomatic History and the Study of the Global Nineteenth Century', *Global Nineteenth Century Studies*, 1, no. 1 (2022), 27–36.

America, Western Europe and finally the Ottoman Empire. It also covers the historical developments that transpired between Robert's first and second embassies in Istanbul. During this period the Ottomans were drawn into the Revolutionary and Napoleonic Wars, most notably when Napoleon Bonaparte's army invaded Egypt from 1798 to 1801. Three successive Ottoman sultans subsequently engaged in a prolonged war with Russia, lasting from 1806 to 1812. The chapter documents the onset of the Ottoman Napoleonic Wars, which coincided with Robert's retirement from, and eventual return to, diplomacy.

Chapter 6 considers the complex dynamics surrounding Robert Liston's 1811 appointment to Istanbul and the broader implications of the Russo-Ottoman conflict. The chapter examines the strained negotiations between the two empires, set against the backdrop of Napoleon's massive Russian campaign in 1812. It highlights the tensions between Tsar Alexander I's demands and Sultan Mahmud II's resistance, ultimately leading to the Treaty of Bucharest in 1812 – a peace agreement fraught with unresolved issues and mutual dissatisfaction. Through Liston's role, the chapter illustrates how the treaty, though averting war, sowed the seeds for future instability.

Chapter 7 captures the harrowing period of 1812–13 in Istanbul, as the city grappled with devastating fires, a severe plague and mounting political tensions. The chapter documents the hardships faced by the Listons at the time as well as Sultan Mahmud II's efforts to consolidate power amid domestic unrest and international turmoil. As Robert Liston observed the Ottoman government's internal power struggles, he found the empire caught between factions that sought raproachment with Russia or France, each vying for influence over the sultan. The chapter also revisits the Serbian question, exploring how unresolved Russo-Ottoman disputes led to further instability, ultimately setting the stage for mass violence.

The penultimate chapter looks into the endeavours to involve the Ottoman Empire in the concluding act of the Congress of Vienna of 1814–15, which marked the end of the Napoleonic Wars, but left Russo-Ottoman disputes unresolved. The last chapter revisits the post-1815 lives of the Listons, tracing at once connections between lingering Russo-Ottoman disputes, the outbreak of the Greek Revolution and the enduring legacy of the Eastern Question.

1

Philosophe and diplomat

An airy phantom

The private correspondence of Robert Liston with one of his closest and oldest friends, Andrew Dalzel, paints a vivid picture of his life and ambitions prior to his arrival in Istanbul in 1794. The two knew each other from an early age, attending the same school in Kirkliston, to the west of Edinburgh, a village originally known simply as Liston. Born on 6 and 8 October 1742 respectively, both lost their fathers at a tender age, Andrew at nine and Robert at seven.[1] Their paths continued in tandem as they both went on to the University of Edinburgh to study for the kirk, reading classics and theology. For the first two years, they shared rooms in the house of a certain Mrs Wilke, as Robert fondly recalls, 'in a close to the north of the College and of the High Street, with our window looking to the Firth of Forth'.[2] They lived a 'simple, cheap life', with plain meals of potatoes and eggs, and would walk home together on weekends whenever the weather permitted.[3]

Even though their paths diverged widely after university, the friendship between Robert and Andrew continued lifelong. It inspired those around them. 'Bob is quite the beau but a gentleman for whom I have (&indeed always had) a great regard,' Andrew's brother Archibald once wrote, 'I have often known the want of such a friend.'[4] Dalzel and Liston never lost touch, corresponding fairly regularly until Dalzel's untimely decease in 1806.[5] They closely followed each

---

[1] *Memoir of Andrew Dalzel, Professor of Greek in the University of Edinburgh*, Cosmo Innes (ed.) (Edinburgh: T. Constable, 1840), 5.
[2] Hardy Bertram McCall, *Some Old Families. A Contribution to the Genealogical History of Scotland* (Birmingham: Watfon & Ball, 1890), 87.
[3] *Memoir of Andrew Dalzel*, 5.
[4] Archibald Dalziel to Andrew Dalziel, 28 March 1771, EUL DK.7.52, f. 18. Andrew's family surname was spelt as 'Dalziel' until 1784. However, for consistency, I use Dalzel throughout the body text.
[5] Ibid., 6.

other's ambitions and steady progress in their respective careers, which saw both rise far above their humble origins.

The son of a carpenter, Andrew Dalzel became professor of Greek and Classical Literature at the University of Edinburgh, co-founder of the Royal Society of Edinburgh, and a renowned figure of the Scottish Enlightenment. The son of a tenant farmer, Liston became a prominent diplomat, representing Britain in several European courts and in the United States.

Robert's parents were Patrick Liston (d. 1749) and Christian Dick (d. 1790). Both his elder brother James and younger brother Alexander died at an early age. His sister Henrietta married Alexander Rammage, captain of the Port of Leith, and gave birth to five sons before she passed away in 1778.[6] In 1762, while still a student at Edinburgh, Robert Liston accepted an invitation from Sir Gilbert Elliot, later third baronet of Minto, to serve as travelling tutor to his sons Gilbert (12) and Hugh (10). Liston presumably hoped to acquire a patron as well as the polish that came with foreign travel.[7] Prior to departure he was expected to 'perfect himself in classics, law and dancing'. He moved to Twickenham near London, receiving a salary of £25 a year (equivalent of around £6,000 today), plus bed, board and laundry.[8] Liston formed a deep attachment to the Elliot family, admiring Sir Gilbert's learning and 'oratorical ability'. He found Mrs Murray-Elliot to be a 'very graceful woman'. Though 'too lusty for a beauty', she managed her children and household 'very thoroughly'.[9] Robert, Gilbert and Hugh departed for Paris at the end of 1764, where the boys enrolled in Abbé Choquart's academy at the Barrière St. Dominique.

Acting as travelling tutor to young aristocrats was a common avenue to preferment among bright Scotsmen born to middling families. In 1765, an older Glasgow graduate from a similar background, Adam Smith (1723–90) was also in Paris, acting as tutor to the young duke of Buccleuch. Britain's recent victory over the French in the Seven Years War (1756–63) had surprised many in France, fostering *Anglomanie* among fashionable Parisian *salonnières* and the *philosophes* they patronized. Along with his noble charges, curiosity about Britain and particularly Scotland, viewed as a land of ancient bards and other noble savages, gave Liston an *entrée* to this world, which included yet another Scot, Smith's close friend David Hume.

---

[6] McCall, *Some Old Families*, 87.
[7] Robert Liston to Mr. Dick, 31 July 1771, NLS MS 5517, f. 45.
[8] The Countess of Minto, *A Memoir of the Right Honourable Hugh Elliot* (Edinburgh: Edmonston and Douglas, 1868), 4.
[9] Robert Liston to Henry, January 1763, NLS MS 5517, f. 11.

A confidant of Sir Gilbert Elliot, Hume moved to Paris in 1763 as personal secretary to the earl of Hertford, the new British ambassador.[10] Hume was a 'reigning lion of the Parisian *salons*', impressing his locutors with not only his philosophical ideas, but also his views on politics and international affairs.[11] He often visited Gilbert and Hugh to oversee their studies and acted as official advisor to Liston, commending the latter for his tutelage of the Elliots as well as for his open mind.[12]

During his first sojourn in Paris the young Liston proudly published his first literary essay and attended several salons. He was eager to share his 'astonishing accomplishment' with his family and friends back in Kirkliston, yet remained grounded. 'Many to be sure are the things I have seen and heard and done in this great city, enough to turn the head of any ordinary man,' he wrote. Despite these flattering accomplishments he vowed to 'remain the same in every Place, in every station: in every nation & in every alternation of Life: firm as a rock on the seashore, against which the stormy winds and boisterous waves wreck all their rage in vain'.[13]

Liston also became acquainted in Paris with the French novelist Marie-Jeanne Riccoboni (1713–92), perhaps through Hume. Stuck in a failed marriage to the ill-tempered and impulsive actor Antoine François Riccoboni (1707–72), Marie-Jeanne developed a deeply passionate and maternal affection for the young Robert, twenty-nine years her junior, attracted by 'his good nature, his neat dress, an underlying strain of conservatism, and above all, his *"petite sauvagerie"* and *"sensibilité"*'.[14] Robert spent a good deal of time in Marie Jeanne's apartment, giving her English lessons as well as little gifts, while she prepared his 'favourite dishes and knitted him scarves'.[15]

This relationship appears to be an *amitié amoureuse* – a form of a platonic affection Marie Jeanne harboured for Liston. But Liston was enamoured with another woman, possibly in Scotland at the time, described as a 'nymph maid',

---

[10] James A. Harris, *Hume: An Intellectual Biography* (Cambridge: Cambridge University Press, 2015), 409.
[11] Ernest C. Mossner, 'Rousseau Hero-Worship', *Modern Language Notes*, 55, no. 6 (June, 1940), 449–51, at 450.
[12] David Hume to Sir Gilbert Elliot of Minto, 14 April 1765, cf. Patrick Flood, '"Liberty Man and Great Reformer"? A New Analysis of a Scottish Enlightenment Emissary Abroad and the Expansion of British Diplomacy in the Early American Republic' (Unpublished Bachelor's Thesis, University of Sydney, 2022), 21–2.
[13] Robert Liston (Paris) to Henry, 18 February 1865, NLS MS 5517, f. 13.
[14] James C. Nicholls (ed.), *Mme Riccoboni's Letters to David Hulme, David Garrick and Sir Robert Liston: 1764–1783* (Oxford: The Voltaire Foundation at the Taylor Institution, 1976), 20–1.
[15] Nicholls, *Mme Riccoboni*, 22.

in Liston's letters. Her identity remains unknown. As he confessed to his friend Dalzel, Liston had strong fondness for the 'nymph maid' to the point that he would never be able to get over it: '[I] must certainly give up over my ambitious schemes, and content myself with a professorship, the pleasures of a family and the sweet obscurity of a country life.' Yet even as he entertained such thoughts of a more modest future, he felt it 'impossible for me to live without distinguishing myself in some way or other that may perhaps be in publishing'.[16]

Robert's emotions were unsettled. With each person he met and each experience he had in Paris, the tone of his letters changed. 'I have an infinity of things to say to you,' he wrote to Dalzel two months later, 'had I time and paper.'[17] He was thrilled when his essay was read at a public session of the Academy of Sciences in Caen, and proud to claim the title of 'philosopher'. As he modestly observed: '[T]hey did not speak contemptibly of my essay.' After attending a 'rustic' country wedding, he was captivated by the 'unambitious happiness of the married pair' and imagined a simpler life. 'I could wish to spend my life, in cultivating the soil and adding to the riches of my native country. So long as I continued in the country all objections to this *aurea mediocritas* were banished from my mind.'

But each time he returned to Paris, the scene changed, and so did his ambitions:

> I walk the streets, unheeded, unregarded, while others draw the attention of all that pass. I go to the play. I mingle unseen and undistinguished with the crowd in the pit, while Mr Elliot is invited to one of the boxes by a lady of the greatest rank and learning in Paris. I dine at home, or in a shilling ordinary. ... I take a walk after dinner in a public garden, with who, *Solus*. I meet Sir J. Macdonald with Mr Dalmbert [sic] or with the prime minister. What does all this signifie [sic]? Says you: Fame, distinction, all that, is but an airy phantom ... Yes, it is a phantom. But I see it beckon to me, like the Ghost to Hamlet, and its call is irresistible. I'll follow it. I must follow it.[18]

As for the 'nymph maid' who 'hinders' him, Robert wrote to Andrew that he decided to 'shake himself loose' and, instead, 'follow the phantom', for there would be 'no infidelity in it, for I never made any promises to her'.[19]

---

[16] Robert Liston to Andrew Dalzel, 18 July 1765, NLS MS 5517, f. 15.
[17] Robert Liston to Andrew Dalzel, 19 September 1765, NLS MS 5517, f. 17.
[18] Ibid.
[19] Ibid.

§ § §

Among the many individuals Liston encountered in Paris, he was undoubtedly most eager to meet the *philosophe* Jean-Jacques Rousseau. Unable to remain in France after publishing *Émile* (1762), Rousseau had sought refuge in his native Switzerland, only to find himself persecuted by the 'over much righteous' pastors (as Liston called them) of Geneva.[20] The Comtesse de Boufflers persuaded Hume to offer Rousseau sanctuary in England. Liston met the Swiss philosopher at a café shortly before Hume and Rousseau departed Paris on 4 January 1766.[21] A few months later, in March, as the Elliot boys and Liston returned to Britain, Liston continued his correspondence with Rousseau. This correspondence was cut short after the spectacular falling-out between Rousseau and Hume, which became widely publicized.

Upon arriving back in Britain, when Gilbert and Hugh Elliot resumed their studies under Professor George Stuart in Edinburgh, Liston's tutorship came to a halt. He swopped the fashionable world of Paris for the family farm in Kirkliston, helping his widowed mother and looking for teaching jobs. David Hume recommended him for a professorship in Parma to teach modern literature and the English language, but Liston soon discovered that only Roman Catholics were eligible.[22] In the meanwhile, he continued his *amitié amoureuse* with Marie-Jeanne Ricobonni, who wrote that she 'never, can forget you'.[23] Liston went back to France in December 1768, when he set off for Paris again – this time in the role of bear-leader, accompanying the Welsh aristocrat Thomas Johnes (1748–1816) on a grand tour of Europe that lasted until the end of 1770.[24]

In his second Paris sojourn, Liston made the acquaintance of Colonel Robert Ainslie (1730–1812), who later served as British ambassador to Istanbul (1775–93), where Liston succeeded him.[25] From Paris, Liston returned to London. There he worked for a time as assistant to Gilbert Stuart, editor of the

---

[20] Robert Liston to Henrietta Ramage, 13 January 1766, NLS MS 5517, f. 21.
[21] Mossner, 'Rousseau', 451; Robert Liston to Henrietta Ramage, 30 December 1765, NLS MS 5517, f. 19.
[22] David Hume to Sir Gilbert Elliot, 24 May 1768, NLS MS 5513, f. 85; Sir Gilbert Elliot to Robert Liston, 11 July 1768, NLS MS 5513, f. 98.
[23] [Jeanne] Marie [Riccoboni] to Robert Liston, 30 October 1767, NLS MS 5513, f. 63.
[24] Robert Liston to Earl Poulet, 15 January 1767, NLS MS 5517, f. 24; Robert Liston to Alex Ramage, 17 July 1769, NLS MS 5517, f. 37.
[25] Robert Ainslie to Robert Liston, 25 June 1783, NLS MS 5536, f. 176.

London Magazine.²⁶ He remained 'very much alive to literature', but also anxious that condescending to 'write to the magazines' might harm his dwindling chances of obtaining a professorship in Scotland.²⁷

In 1771, Liston declined offers to return to private tutoring. He had no desire to go back to the 'drudgery and solicitude' of that role. His hopes that tutoring might lead to preferment, rather than yet more tutoring, had not been realized. 'After many years of faithful service', he wrote to his uncle, 'I did not find myself advanced a single step as to fortune, not even able, in any kind of independence, to wait for employment of a different nature.' Accepting another tutoring position would be a step backward. Instead, Liston set his sights on securing a more favourable position in London.²⁸

Despite assurances from influential contacts no significant progress was made for some time, and he turned his attention further afield. In January 1772, he offered his services as secretary to James Harris (1746–1820) – the future first earl of Malmesbury, recently appointed envoy extraordinary to the court of Berlin. This was Liston's earliest documented expression of interest in diplomatic service.²⁹ 'With regard to the qualifications necessary to fill this office', he acknowledged, 'all I have to boast of is that I have had regular education, that I [have] paid some attention to composition, and that I [have] spent more time than is common in the study of the French language.' Though he admitted that his French was still imperfect, he emphasized his dedication: 'However easy it may be to meet with persons of more experience and greater ability, it is impossible you should ever find one that will serve you with more ardour or with more attention.'³⁰

When this offer of service was refused, Liston returned to Kirkliston for another year, continuing his pursuit of a professorship. His prospects seemed to improve when George Stuart, the father of Gilbert Stuart, decided to retire from his chair of Humanities at Glasgow and sell it for £500, though Stuart intended to retain the accompanying salary. Liston recognized the terms as 'a little hard' and began exploring how to secure the necessary funds.³¹ He could obtain the sum from his mother at once. But he scrupled to accept of it from her, because

---

[26] Nicholls, *Mme Riccoboni*, 21.
[27] *Memoir of Andrew Dalzel*, 8.
[28] Robert Liston to Mr. Dick, 31 July 1771, NLS MS 5517, f. 45.
[29] Robert Liston to Mr. Harris, 13 January 1771, NLS MS 5517, f. 49.
[30] Ibid.
[31] Robert Liston to Andrew Dalzel, 8 September 1773, NLS MS 5517, f. 53.

in case we lose the farm ... which is more than probable, the interest of the money she may have laid up, is all she would depend upon for a living, and were any great part of it, in my hands, you know the event of my Death would deprive her at once of what she has so hardly earned.[32]

There were twelve other candidates vying for the professorship at Glasgow and Liston was prepared to 'apply to everybody I can think of that may be of any sort of service'.[33] At this point, he wrote to Sir Gilbert Elliot, the father of the Elliot brothers that he had tutored in Twickenham and Paris. Sir Gilbert's response would prove life-changing. Liston was invited to join his former pupil, Hugh Elliot, as his private secretary in Elliot's new role as minister plenipotentiary to the elector of Bavaria at Munich. Liston promptly accepted the offer and arrived in Munich in June 1774.[34] Thus began his new career, in the world of what would soon be termed 'diplomacy'.

The folds of deceit

At this point, a brief etymological digression is called for, to understand the diplomatic firmament of the time. The term 'diplomacy' came into common parlance only in the 1780s, with French foreign minister Charles Gravier de Vergennes (1719–87), himself a former ambassador to Istanbul, likely one of the first to employ it in its modern sense. The word originated from the ancient Greek *diploma*, which referred to official state documents written on double leaves (*diploo*) joined together and folded (*diplono*).[35] Initially, *diplomas* conferred specific rights to their bearers, as with the passports and way-bills used on imperial roads.[36] The Greek (and later Latin) term evolved different meanings over time, such as 'a papal letter of appointment to a mission' and precipitated new words. *Diplomatarius* meant 'the scribes in charge of writing *diplomas*', *diplomatica* came to denote the science of studying official documents, and *diplomaticus* or *diplomatique* described the study and knowledge of the relations between rulers and states.

---

[32] Ibid.
[33] Robert Liston to Andrew Dalzel, 10 September 1774, NLS MS 5517, f. 55.
[34] Robert Liston to Andrew Dalzel, 30 July 1774, NLS MS 5517, f. 57.
[35] Alexander Stagnell, *Diplomacy and Ideology: From the French Revolution to the Digital Age* (New York: Routledge, 2020), 61; Costas M. Constantinou, *On the Way to Diplomacy*, (Minneapolis, MN, London: University of Minnesota Press, 1996), 77.
[36] Constantinou, *On the way to Diplomacy*, 77.

By the end of the seventeenth century, the word *diplomat* had come to signify the people who dealt with the affairs of state and international treaties.[37] As Alexander Ostrower explains, it was towards the close of the eighteenth century that attention shifted from the documents and texts themselves to what they 'represented in international relations'. This shift in focus led to the coinage of the word *diplomacy* in its current sense, first in French, in the 1780s, denoting 'the art and business of the French *diplomate*', and then in English by the 1790s.

In the eighteenth century, before the term 'diplomacy' became part of common vocabulary, the diplomatic profession acquired a new character. Historian Lucien Bély observes that, as the number of legal treaties multiplied – defining the principles of the law of nations based on peace treaties signed over the centuries – there was a growing interest in outlining the qualities of a 'good negotiator' and the 'perfect ambassador'.[38] Bély argues that this shift coincided with the emergence of a new European order, beginning with the Congress of Utrecht that opened in 1712, though the chronology here might also include the Congress of Karlowitz of 1698–9, which will be discussed in the following chapter.

From the early eighteenth century onwards, diplomatic discussions extended over much longer periods – sometimes dragging on for years and often giving the impression of stagnation. The new diplomatic gatherings offered a unique opportunity to delve into the numerous conflicts that had troubled Europe, allowing for a comprehensive redrawing of its political map. These congresses did more than just settle disputes; they became symbols and promoters of peace.[39]

Negotiation grew ever more refined and became a sustained rather than intermittent practice. As a result, the diplomat's role evolved into something both extraordinary and impressive, though not without its risks. The art of negotiation transformed into a prestigious career, flourishing within well-structured institutions and clear, established protocols.[40] Diplomats – exclusively male until the early twentieth century – emerged as key figures in polite society. Although their work was crucial in maintaining peace across Europe, their lifestyle also

---

[37] Andrew F. Cooper, Jorge Heine, and Ramesh Thakur, 'Introduction: The Challenges of 21st Century Diplomacy', in *The Oxford Handbook of Modern Diplomacy*, Andrew F. Cooper, Jorge Heine, and Ramesh Thakur (eds.) (Oxford: Oxford University Press, 2013), 3.

[38] Lucien Bély, 'Un art de négocier', *Revue des deux mondes*, no. 4 (April, 2004), 91–102, there at 97. I should like to thank Jonathan Conlin for drawing my attention to this source.

[39] Bély, 'Un art de négocier', 97.

[40] Ibid., 99.

epitomized the values that captivated the Enlightenment world. They combined eloquence and poise, impeccable manners, an elegant appearance, a network of international connections and a passion for travel. Ambitious young men eagerly sought to join a diplomat's circle, hoping to travel abroad and catch the attention of influential ministers, aspiring to make their mark in this illustrious world. However, success in diplomacy was not solely determined by one's performance or ability. Influence and patronage were often more critical in determining who would be appointed to diplomatic roles.[41]

§ § §

As the diplomatic career became more professionalized, a lively discussion unfolded among French and British writers and *philosophes* on the art of diplomatic negotiation and how it should be practised.[42] Following in the footsteps of François de Callières' (1645–1717) diplomatic manual *De la Maniere de Négocier avec les Souverains*, French diplomat-theorist Antoine Pecquet (1704–62) argued that the ability to combine the 'qualities of the heart' and the 'qualities of the mind' makes an ideal negotiator.[43]

According to Pecquet, while the qualities of the heart – such as patience, courage and liberality – were paramount, they ought to be complemented by sagacity, judgement and flexibility. A successful diplomat had to balance firmness on the substance of issues with flexibility in managing relationships. Additionally, eloquence and ease of expression were essential, though not in the form of presumptuous or overly light rhetoric. Personal grace and charm played a significant role in diplomacy, as they helped create a favourable impression and foster goodwill.[44]

A good diplomat, Pecquet believed, embodied a combination of personal virtues and strategic skills that balance moderation, dignity and flexibility. Moderation and modesty were central to diplomacy, as these traits helped avoid the indiscretion, fear, or hatred that arose from excessive passion or arrogance. Modesty, however, ought not be mistaken for weakness – it maintained a distinct

---

[41] Raymond Jones, *The British Diplomatic Service: 1814–1914* (Waterloo: Wilfrid Laurier University Press, 2000), 30–48.
[42] Bély, 'Un art de négocier', 99.
[43] Antoine Pecquet, *Discours sur l'art de négocier* (Nyon: ESSEC IRÉNÉ, 2003).
[44] Aurélien Colson, 'Le Discours sur l'art de négocier (1737) d'Antoine Pecquet, ou l'esquisse d'une théorisation de la négociation', *Négociations* 1, no. 33 (2020), 151–60, there at 158–9.

sense of dignity without slipping into pride or ostentation. Pecquet stressed the importance of avoiding displays of erudition or obstinate firmness, as these were often perceived as vanity or inflexibility rather than true strength.[45]

In a similar vein, the likes of Gabriel de Mably (1709–85), Denis Diderot (1714–84), Victor de Riquetti, marquis de Mirabeau (1715–89) or Pierre-Paul Lemercier de La Rivière (1719–1801) criticized the principles that had shaped diplomatic action, particularly the idea of 'the balance of power', then the dominant system of thought. For these thinkers the idea of a 'balance of power' belonged to 'newspapers and coffee-house politicians' and reduced the 'whole science of politics to knowledge of a single word', thus pleasing 'both the ignorance and the laziness of the ministers, of ambassadors and their clerks'.[46]

In his venerable but still unsurpassed article, Felix Gilbert explains how the *philosophes* highlighted the vanity and perils inherent in this traditional understanding, contending that treaties were 'nothing but temporary armistices', and alliances merely 'preparations for treason'. Diplomatic activity, the *philosophes* claimed, was 'identical with double-dealing and pursuing different purposes for those it openly avows', necessitating a cloak of secrecy. It was an 'obscure art which hides itself in the folds of deceit, which fears to let itself be seen and believes it can exist only in the darkness of mystery', ultimately guided by 'the blind passions of the princes'.[47] The art of negotiation was actually 'the art of intrigue'.[48]

The *philosophes* advocated the 'establishment of a rule of reason'.[49] Pursuing a Physiocratic line of thought, they argued that politics and economics were intertwined and that diplomatic relations should be conducted with an understanding of the mutual interdependence of nations. And, in the slipstream of Charles Louis de Secondat, baron de La Brède et de Montesquieu (1689–1755), they proposed that 'the realisation that increase in one nation's wealth means increased wealth for all nations, and that the interests of all nations are identical ... there would be no advantage in enlarging one's own territory and combatting one's neighbour'.[50]

---

[45] Ibid.
[46] Felix Gilbert, 'The "New Diplomacy" of the Eighteenth Century', *World Politics*, 4, no. 1 (October, 1951), 1–38, at 8.
[47] Diderot, Paix, *Ouevres*, XVI, 188, cf. Gilbert, 'New Diplomacy', 8–10.
[48] Mably, *Oeuvres*, V, 17, cf. Gilbert, 'New Diplomacy', 10.
[49] Gilbert, 'New Diplomacy', 11.
[50] Ibid., 12.

For their part, two of Liston's acquaintances, Jean-Jacques Rousseau and David Hume, who also did time as embassy secretaries, shared the belief in the interconnectedness of states, through common historical experiences, heritage, tradition and interests. They maintained that new diplomatic activity should depart from traditional methods they associated with deceit and be grounded in moral principles.[51] However, Rousseau also believed that 'a flexible balance of power' was necessary to remedy the anarchic nature of inter-state relations. The magical formula was not merely 'free trade' but also a world federation, to which governments controlled by the people – republics – would be more eager to cooperate.[52] Hume, on the other hand, praised the balance of power as essential to 'prevent the domination of one big power', ensuring it could not pursue its own plans unopposed.[53] Contrary to Montesquieu, Hume was sceptical about free trade as a path to universal peace, fearing that it could also enable rulers 'to push forward bellicose plans'.[54]

Although Liston dismissed the 'balance of power' as an 'old hobby-horse' in a 1783 letter to Dalzel, he did not explicitly engage in discussions about diplomacy or free trade until later in life, making it difficult to determine his stance in these philosophical debates.[55] This being said, as we will see in the following pages, Pecquet's ideas on moral and ethical diplomacy appear to have left a lasting impression on him. In his later years, Liston explicitly recommended Pecquet's *L'Art de Negocier* as essential reading for the younger diplomats under his tutelage.[56]

§ § §

When he joined his former pupil and new patron Hugh Elliot, Liston entered a diplomatic service that increasingly relied on Scots of modest backgrounds. After the suppression of the Jacobite Uprising at Culloden in 1746, the integration of

---

[51] Ibid., 15.
[52] Genevieve Blanchet, 'Jean-Jacques Rousseau's Contribution to International Relations Theory', *Glendon Journal of International Studies (GJIS) / Revue d'études internationales de Glendon*, 2 (2002), 15–23, there at 17–19; Rousseau, 'Extrait du Projet de Paix Perpetuelle de M. l'Abbe de Saint-Pierre', I. 364–96, cf. Gilbert, 'New Diplomacy', 14–15.
[53] Edwin van de Haar, 'David Hume and International Political Theory: A Reappraisal', *Review of International Studies*, 34, no. 2 (April, 2008), 225–42, at 233.
[54] Ibid., 237.
[55] Robert Liston to Andrew Dalzel, 29 January 1783, NLS MS 5527, f. 123.
[56] 'Note for L.H.S.', n.d., NLS MS 5658, f. 64. I should like to thank Dora Petherbridge for drawing my attention to this source.

Scottish elites into the British Empire and military was one means of reshaping Scottish identity towards a broader British allegiance. This development was further encouraged by the perception that Scottish universities, where knowledge of the French language was more prevalent than in England, served as excellent training grounds for individuals suited to secondary diplomatic roles.[57] Consequently, a 'Scottish clan' seems to emerge within the British diplomatic body, with many Scots accompanying Liston in diplomatic service as patrons or protégés over subsequent decades.

Hugh Elliot was the first of them. He took up his new diplomatic role as minister plenipotentiary in Munich in the 1770s among a 'new crop of gentry sons and their dependents', such as James Harris, Joseph Ewart, Charles Whitworth and Morton Eden that would change the tone of the British diplomatic corps.[58] Elliot's father had bought him a commission in the army at the age of eight. After his studies at Oxford, he went to Metz to further his studies.[59] Changes in the political landscape in London, however, subsequently prevented him from taking up his commission. Frustrated and eager to embark on a military career, Hugh Elliot joined the Russian army in 1772, and was sent to the Ottoman front, in Moldavia.

When Elliot arrived, an armistice was in effect between Russia and the Ottoman Empire. His thirst for adventure led him to Istanbul in December 1772, accompanied by Lieutenant Colonel Robert Ainslie.[60] From Istanbul, Elliot wrote to his father, 'We have had in this jaunt the advantage of seeing an army of which Europeans in general have little acquaintance, and form very false conjectures: the people, the manners, the governments, seem to be as little understood.'[61]

When the Russo-Ottoman conflict recommenced, Elliot joined the campaign at Ruschuk on the Danube under the command of Piotr A. Rumyantsev (1725–96). But on receiving firm instructions from his father, who had secured him a diplomatic post to divert his son from a 'foolish' military career, Elliott returned to England. In 1774, just as the Russo-Ottoman War reached its denouement, Elliot and Liston took up their new posts in Munich.[62]

---

[57] Robert Liston to Andrew Dalzel, 1 December 1781, NLS MS 5573, f. 70.
[58] Jennifer Mori, *The Culture of Diplomacy: Britain in Europe, c. 1750–1830* (Manchester: Manchester University Press, 2011), 41.
[59] Hugh Elliot to Robert Liston, 17 December 1769, NLS MS 5513, f. 176.
[60] R.A. Cunning to Ainslie, 9 October 1772, NLS MS 12976, f. 11; Robert Ainslie to H. Elliot, n.d., NLS MS 12976, f. 26.
[61] Minto, *Elliot*, 21.
[62] Robert Liston to Andrew Dalzel, 30 July 1774, NLS MS 5517, f. 57.

In Munich, Liston felt 'less alone' than he had in Paris, and enjoyed the company of 'bigger' acquaintances. 'I must make the most of it, as it is … The business is exceedingly agreeable to me', he wrote to Dalzel. He also appreciated the way Hugh Elliot treated him with 'wonderful kindness and distinction'. Elliot himself 'succeeded here beyond all imagination. The men look up to him with admiration that has no bounds', while 'the women are in love with him even to indecency to madness.'[63]

Yet, despite his professional satisfaction, Liston's ambition remained undimmed: 'A secretary here is rather a low Character,' he complained, expressing dissatisfaction with his lack of access to the upper echelons of society. 'He has no *entrée a la Court*', and this exclusion from 'the highest company' clearly troubled him. Liston believed he was 'as good as the best of them'.[64] He was learning the language of the country. But he regarded it with disdain, calling it 'gibberish' and finding it 'much more pain than any other modern language' he was acquainted with.[65]

When Andrew Dalzel informed Liston that Gilbert Stuart's post at the University of Glasgow was still vacant and encouraged him to reconsider applying, Liston dismissed the suggestion. His current role, he felt, was 'much more to my taste, and perhaps also more suited to my genius, than a place in a college'.[66] Furthermore, he was still reluctant to ask his mother to provide the funds to secure the professorship:[67]

> I know my mother … will say there is no enjoyment she can have in this world equal to that of having me near her. She would give up everything, and almost live on bread and water, rather than forego this. My sister will add that she sees no necessity that her sons should be bred up gentlemen, that they may be as happy and as honest men, as common sailors, or soldiers or plough men. But I should think myself inexcusable were I to take advantage of these ideas however flattering and however kind.

There was no immediate prospect for Liston to become a plenipotentiary yet, but he believed that he would eventually become 'secretary to the Embassy to Holland, Vienna, Paris or Madrid' by continuing in the service of Elliot, whom

---

[63] Ibid.
[64] Ibid.
[65] Ibid.
[66] Robert Liston to Andrew Dalzel, 11 January 1775, NLS MS 5517, f. 67.
[67] Robert Liston to Andrew Dalzel, 23 March 1775, NLS MS 5517, f. 71.

he expected to be appointed to one of these positions in the future. In the meantime, he wrote, 'I live as happily as I can well do, and am much satisfied to feel myself in the situation in life which perfectly suits me (a thing which never happened me before) and to think that I am doing exactly what I ought to do.'[68]

Liston remained in Elliot's service, following him to Regensburg (Ratisbon) and Berlin.[69] In 1776, he visited Paris, where he was reunited with his 'good friend, Madam R[iccoboni]'. He noted that her 'friendship and affection' for him had 'not in the least abated' and that she looked upon him with 'the partial eyes of a fond mother' who embraced his projects 'with warmth'.[70]

While in Regensburg and Berlin, Liston often found himself in charge during Elliot's frequent absences on personal business.[71] When accusations against Elliot for his relationship (and eventual marriage) with Charlotte Kraut, the young daughter of a Prussian noble family, became rife in 1778, Liston stood by him, feeling a 'real attachment to Mr. E – an idea that I am now become almost necessary to him'. He dreaded the thought of disappointing Elliot's mother and other relatives if he were to part ways with Elliot.[72]

Objects of ambition

Alongside these loyalties, Liston also nurtured 'a small mixture of a hope and wish' to better his fortunes. Believing he had a strong chance at securing a consulship, he sought connections with influential figures such as Henry Howard, twelfth earl of Suffolk (1739–79), the secretary of state of the Northern Department. 'My knowledge of foreign countries would enable me to save money,' Liston confided to Dalzel.[73] By mid-1781 he had grown increasingly eager, even anxious, to see some results from the connections he had cultivated in Berlin, Paris and London. As he noted somewhat complacently to his childhood friend, 'nobody would be surprised [...] on the contrary, everybody seems to expect to see me one day a minister – you see, my dearest Andrew, I continue to speak to you with open heartedness of our youth'.[74]

---

[68] Ibid.
[69] Robert Liston to Henry, 24 July 1775, NLS MS 5517, f. 79.
[70] Robert Liston to Andrew Dalzel, 13 March 1776, NLS MS 5517, f. 89.
[71] Minto, *Elliot*, 45; Robert Liston to Andrew Dalzel, 12 April 1777, NLS MS 5523, f. 4.
[72] Robert Liston to Andrew Dalzel, 5 May 1778, NLS MS 5523, f. 15.
[73] Ibid.
[74] Robert Liston to Andrew Dalzel, 31 July 1781, NLS MS 5523, f. 60.

The offer Liston had long awaited finally arrived in 1781. He was invited to join the service of John Stuart, Lord Mount Stuart (1744–1814), who was envoy extraordinary at the Court of Turin and son of Lady Montagu.[75] However, this left Liston in a dilemma, because he feared he would take too big a step by moving to Turin. The British diplomatic service was structured into a clear hierarchy, dispatching the highest-ranking diplomats to the most prestigious and influential nations for imperial policy. By 1815, ambassadors were sent to major European capitals in France, Russia, Austria, Spain and the Netherlands, signifying the political weight these countries carried in European affairs at the time. A slightly lower classification (second rank) was given to the Ottoman Empire, which also received an ambassador. Envoys extraordinary and ministers plenipotentiary, who held less prestige than ambassadors, were assigned to countries like Prussia and Portugal, still significant but not on par with the Great Powers of Europe.[76]

Countries considered of even lesser influence were assigned lower-ranking diplomats. The Two Sicilies and the United States received fourth-class envoys, while Sweden, Bavaria, Denmark and Sardinia were handled by envoys of a fifth class. Further down the diplomatic chain, Wurtemburg, Tuscany, Switzerland and Saxony, all smaller states, had envoys extraordinary representing British interests.[77]

It is also important to note that before the establishment of the Foreign Office in 1782, British foreign policy was divided between the two departments: the Northern Department dealt with relations with Protestant states, such as northern European countries, while the Southern Department focused on Catholic countries and the Ottoman Empire. Liston's move to Turin would mean leaving the Northern Department while he believed that the Northern Department was 'the scene of business and bustle'. A few years more experience there in different courts would bring him 'so much forward as to make me be thought of for the acting part of the secretary of state's office'.[78] However, he also recognized that the move to Turin would tie his future to the 'fortunes' of Lord Mount Stuart, and he believed that 'nobody was likely to be so soon an Ambassador as His Lordship'.[79] His move would lead to his appointment as secretary of the Embassy some time soon.[80]

[75] Robert Liston to Andrew Dalzel, 1 September 1781, NLS MS 5523, f. 62; Mori, *Culture*, 43.
[76] Jones, *British Diplomatic Service*, 56.
[77] Ibid.
[78] Robert Liston to Andrew Dalzel, 30 October 1781, NLS MS 5523, f. 64.
[79] Ibid.
[80] Robert Liston to Andrew Dalzel, 1 September 1781, NLS MS 5523, f. 62

At the same time, Liston feared that attaching himself to a man (Mount Stuart) 'whose name alone is perhaps sufficient to exclude him from the first offices of the state, and whom a change of ministry or the death of his father [John Stuart, third earl of Bute, 1713–92] may probably send into retirement for the rest of his days'.[81] In such a case, Liston, as 'too credulous [a] secretary' would be left to exchange 'fond hopes for bitter disappointments'.[82] By leaving his position, he would lose his connections with figures like Lord David Murray (1727–96), the secretary of the state at the Northern Department, and 'even offend them by leaving a station in which they had been pleased to think I had distinguished myself'.[83]

In the end, after much hesitation and securing the approval of Hugh Elliot, whose reputation had suffered due to his 'scandalous marriage', Liston accepted the offer.[84] Although Liston still expected that Elliot might be appointed to St. Petersburg, 'the source of all snuff boxes & rings & sudden promotions', he did not wish to turn down a promising opportunity. His new position would provide him with a clear £1,000 per annum (£158,000 in today's values). As an unmarried man, he noted, 'I might support the necessary rank with about the half of that income, and save the other – a prospect surely extremely inviting'.[85]

Liston arrived in Turin in September 1782, passing through Vienna, where he had an audience with the state chancellor, Wenzel Anton, prince of Kaunitz-Rietberg (1711–94).[86] In Turin, the Scot continued to lead the typical life of a diplomat: 'dressing early and paying my Court to the King and Royal family, driving generally with some of the ministers or grandees, after dinner taking a short walk, and in the evening making one or two visit[s], or writing one or two letters or memorials'.[87] It was during this 'life without much variety' that Liston, along with many other political figures, turned his attention 'from the west to the East', as Russia's impending annexation of the Crimea became increasingly apparent.[88] He became better acquainted with the Eastern Question, *avant le mot*. He wrote detailed reports on the escalating tensions between Russia and the Ottoman Empire, observing that, for the Kingdom of Sardinia, the news

---

[81] Robert Liston to Andrew Dalzel, 30 October 1781, NLS MS 5523, f. 64.
[82] Ibid.
[83] Ibid.
[84] Robert Liston to Andrew Dalzel, 14 August 1782, NLS MS 5527, f. 1.
[85] Robert Liston to Ann Polson, 16 March 1782, NLS MS 5523, f. 82.
[86] Robert Liston to Andrew Dalzel, 14 August 1782, NLS MS 5527, f. 1; Robert Liston to Andrew Dalzel, 18 September 1782, NLS MS 5527, f. 3.
[87] Robert Liston to Christian Dick-Liston, 20 January 1783, NLS MS 5527, f. 73.
[88] Robert Liston to Andrew Dalzel, 29 January 1783, NLS MS 5527, f. 123.

Philosophe *and Diplomat* 27

was 'very alarming to the rest of Europe, and ought to be resisted by a general combination of the other Powers'.[89]

Only six months after his arrival in Turin, following in the footsteps of Lord Mount Stuart, Liston was appointed secretary to the embassy in Madrid. He now possessed full power and authority in the absence of the ambassador Mount Stuart.[90] Shortly after, on 14 May 1783, since Mount Stuart would not be able to move to Madrid immediately (he never did), Liston was promoted as minister plenipotentiary.[91] At last, at the age of forty-one, he had reached the long-desired 'object of his ambition'.[92] Even before leaving Italy, Liston wrote to Dalzel that he had become 'such a great and busy man', basking in the recognition and prestige of his new role.[93] He was already enjoying the distinction and fame he had longed for. But his pursuit of the 'airy phantom' was far from over.

§ § §

In Madrid, Liston's salary was '£900 clear money, besides a small extraordinary allowance for following the Court'.[94] This sum fell short of his expectations. Since 'money matters' held 'a critical nature' for him, during a visit to London prior to his arrival in Spain, Liston entered into a business venture with Dalzel. The pair drafted a 'Spanish contract for the sale of negroes', that is for the supply of enslaved Africans to the Spanish colonies.[95] The outcome of this venture remains unclear, owing to the lack of archival evidence. However, an examination of Liston's financial records indicates that he did not receive any income from this enterprise in subsequent years, suggesting that the arrangement did not materialize or yield the results he had expected.

Liston arrived in Madrid on 28 August 1783.[96] He relayed his first impressions of the country in a letter to Thomas Johnes. 'Of this country I have not much to

---

[89] Robert Liston to Sir James Harris, 18 January 1783, NLS MS 5527, f. 111.
[90] John Strange to Robert Liston, 19 March 1783, NLS MS 5526, f. 176; Robert Liston to Andrew Dalzel, 1 March 1783, NLS MS 5527, f. 187.
[91] D.B. Horn, *British Diplomatic Representatives, 1689–1789* (London: Offices of the Society, 1932), 138.
[92] Robert Liston to Andrew Dalzel, 1 September 1781, NLS MS 5523, f. 62; Robert Liston to Ann Polson, 16 March 1782, NLS MS 5523, f. 82.
[93] Robert Liston to Andrew Dalzel, 29 January 1783, NLS MS 5527, f. 123.
[94] Robert Liston to Andrew Dalzel, 1 March 1783, NLS MS 5527, f. 187; [London] to Robert Liston, 21 February 1783, NLS MS 5526, f. 124.
[95] Robert Liston to Andrew Dalzel, 24 April 1782, NLS MS 5523, f. 80; Andrew Dalzel to Robert Liston, 5 March 1783, NLS MS 5526, f. 148.
[96] Robert Liston Diary Entry for August 1783, NLS MS 5554, f. 43.

say,' he wrote, 'It is still nearly where we left it, two hundred years behind others.' This view was partially shaped by his distaste for the bullfights he attended near Le Palais du Buen Retiro, one of which made him 'sick at heart'.[97] He by contrast was content with his personal standing. As he remarked to Dalzel, 'I never shall be Ambassador in France, which would be literally, being at the top of my profession. But I am perfectly satisfied, and only wish my present happiness to last as long as I could wish it.'[98]

Following the establishment of the Foreign Office in 1782, which resulted in the merging of the Northern and Southern Departments, the former members of each department experienced a profound sense of insecurity. Liston observed that, in this restructured environment, he now felt 'pretty much out of the Ministerial instability, which I never thought myself till I crossed the Pyrenees'.[99] Indeed, Liston had secured a position where he would remain for half a decade.

With the arrival of Morton Frederick Eden (1752–1830) as the new ambassador to Madrid in 1787, however, it was time for Liston to move again. Eden was planning to bring his own staff, but he reassured Liston that he had 'established a character' as a trustworthy diplomat that would soon earn him a higher post, and the ministry in London had promising plans for him.[100] Shortly after, as France was rocked by the revolution, Liston was granted his own station as envoy extraordinary at Stockholm, where he stayed for nearly four years.[101]

In Stockholm, Liston was tasked with monitoring King Gustav III's relations with 'the other courts of Europe ... particularly those ... between ... Sweden and the Ottoman Porte who are essentially necessary for our immediate information'.[102] In alliance with the Ottoman Empire, Gustav III was seeking to draw the Triple Alliance – comprising Britain, Prussia and the Dutch Republic – into his war against Russia that had broken out in 1788. However, besides loans, his efforts yielded little.[103] The king's diplomatic endeavours required the British representative to communicate daily with the Swedish court and observe the unfolding Eastern Question.[104]

---

[97] Robert Liston to Mr. Johnes, 25 September 1783, NLS MS 5554, f. 131.
[98] Robert Liston to Andrew Dalzel, 30 October 1783, in *Memoir of Andrew Dalzel*, 41.
[99] Robert Liston to Mr Clement, 29 September 1783, NLS MS 5554, f. 157.
[100] Robert Liston to Christian Dick, 31 July 1787, NLS MS 5560, f. 193.
[101] Mr [Henry] Wesley to Robert Liston, 24 May 1793, TNA FO 73/14, no. 7; McCall, *Some Old Families*, 89.
[102] 'Instructions for Our Trusty and Well-Beloved Robert Liston, Esq', 30 June 1789, TNA FO 73/6, f. 1.
[103] Robert Liston to the Duke of Leeds, 19 February 1790, TNA FO 73/10, No 14.
[104] 'Note Confidentielle', 2 January 1790, TNA FO 73/10.

Liston reported that the Gustav III laid 'very considerable stress ... on his alliance with the Ottoman Porte' and was convinced that France had lost her sway in Istanbul, creating an opening for Sweden to assume a leading role there.[105] Though Liston found the Swedish king's claims 'overrated', in Stockholm, he could see how deeply entwined the 'northern and eastern affairs' were for Britain.[106]

During his tenure in Sweden, Liston received the sad news of his 'poor mother's death'. Unable to attend the funeral due to his diplomatic duties, he accepted the news with calm resignation:

> She had reached a good old age, she had lived to see the remain of her family prosperous, and she was no longer attached to this world. Yet I would have purchased a longer life for her at a great price, and I cannot help most sensibly feeling the loss.[107]

Margaret (Peggy) Liston, his aunt on the paternal side, remained at the family farm in Damhead, managing its affairs with guidance from Liston's trusted circle of friends. As she continued to work the land, Liston found himself increasingly drawn to thoughts of home. The prospect of retiring from his long diplomatic career and returning to the simple life of the farm began to appeal to him more seriously.[108] But, in the end, he decided to continue his diplomatic life longer. Shortly after, in September 1793, as Sir Robert Ainslie, the British ambassador to Istanbul, requested recall to Britain, Liston was appointed to succeed him at the Ottoman imperial capital.

With this appointment, Liston reached the pinnacle of his diplomatic career after almost twenty years of service, in pursuit of the phantom. He was a seasoned diplomat now, who had established key connections, amassed considerable experience, especially on eastern affairs, and he had learned the German, Italian, Spanish and French languages.[109] He set out for his new posting in the spring of 1794, prepared for a new chapter that would provide invaluable insights into the nascent Eastern Question from a vantage point.

---

[105] Robert Liston to the Duke of Leeds, 9 January 1790, TNA FO 73/10, no. 1.
[106] Ibid.
[107] Robert Liston to Andrew Dalzel, 21 January 1791, NSL MS 5566, f. 69.
[108] Ibid.
[109] Mr [Henry] Wesley to Robert Liston, 24 May 1793, TNA FO 73/14, no. 7; McCall, *Some Old Families*, 89.

2

'Now everything has changed'

Battle for the Crimea

Before we proceed to the story of Liston's first embassy in Istanbul, it is worth pausing for a moment to reflect on the empire he was dispatched to, which was gripped by anxiety, still reeling from successive defeats at the hands of Russian and Austrian forces. Throughout the eighteenth century, the Ottomans had been forced to sign a series of unequal treaties, and most notably, just a few years before Liston's arrival in Istanbul, they had officially ceded the Crimea and Ochakov to Russia. Although the balance of military power and diplomatic relations between the Ottoman and Russian Empires had shifted considerably by the 1790s, their contest over the Crimea, the Black Sea and the Balkans had only intensified.

This contest stretches back to the waning days of the Golden Horde in the fifteenth century. When the Ottomans brought under their sway the fragmented Crimean polities between 1475 and 1478, and the Tatars accepted Ottoman suzerainty in the 1520s, the frequent Tatar raids into Muscovite territory to capture slaves for Ottoman markets incited a long-standing hostility from Moscow.[1] During the so-called golden age of the Ottoman Empire under the illustrious sultans Selim I and Süleyman the Magnificent, interactions between these two powers were marked by a degree of friendliness and infrequency. In this era, Muscovite elites harboured aspirations of achieving equal status with the formidable Ottoman Empire, envisioning a balance of power that seemed within their grasp.[2] Their policy aimed to avoid conflict with the Ottomans. However, the emergence of a 'Muscovite imperial ideology' at the turn of the sixteenth century lent their struggle a new dimension.

---

[1] Alan W. Fisher, *The Russian Annexation of the Crimea, 1772–1783* (Cambridge: Cambridge University Press, 1970), 19.
[2] Adrian Brisku, 'Ottoman-Russian Relations', *Oxford Research Encyclopedia of Asian History*, 26 April 2019, accessed 1 December 2022.

This new ideology posited that Muscovy was the protector of Christendom and the successor of the Holy Roman Empire and Byzantium, with Moscow being the 'Third Rome': As the Russian monk Philotheus (Filofei) of Pskov (1465?–1542) declared in the early sixteenth century, 'two Romes have fallen, the Third stands and there shall be no Fourth'.[3] According to this account, the first Rome had fallen due to heresy, and the Second Rome, Constantinople, had fallen to the Ottoman Turks. Moscow, as the Third Rome, was 'the final bastion of true Christianity', and there would be no successor. This doctrine played a significant role in the Russian conception of their country's place in the world and its religious mission. By the mid-sixteenth century, it evolved into a state ideology. Muscovy, and later the Russian Empire, presented itself as the self-styled protector and liberator of Christians in the Caucasus and the Balkans.[4]

Meanwhile, Tatar advances and the tributes that the Muscovites were compelled to pay spurred Russian counteroffensives, leading to the conquest of the Kazan Khanate in 1552 and the Astrakhan Khanate in 1556. Such developments created a significant rift in Russo-Ottoman relations, resulting in their first major diplomatic clash. The Ottoman mission in 1569 perished in the Astrakhan steppes before any direct military confrontation occurred.[5] Russian campaigns directed towards the Tula, Bystraia and Tikhaia Sosna rivers aimed to prevent Tatar attacks on the Russian borderlands – the *okrainam* or the *ukrainy*, from which the word 'Ukraine' is said to have originated.[6] It is important to remark, however, that the inhabitants of these lands developed their own national consciousness and sovereign identity especially in the course of the nineteenth century.[7]

In 1637, Russian Don Cossacks captured Azov, a key outlet to the Black Sea/Azov basin. Four years later, following an Ottoman campaign, it was returned to the sultan's authority.[8] The first major war between Moscow and Istanbul erupted between 1676 and 1681, and ended without a decisive victory, while Muscovite campaigns in the Crimea in 1687 and 1689 culminated 'in total failure'.[9]

---

[3] R.O. Crummey, *The Formation of Muscovy, 1304–1613* (London and New York: Longman, 1993), 131–9; Bitis, *Russia*, 18.
[4] Bitis, *Russia*, 18.
[5] Ibid.
[6] S.F. Oreshkova, 'The Ottoman Empire and Russia in Light of Their Geopolitical Demarcation', *Russian Studies in History*, 57, no. 2 (2018), 125–45, there at 127.
[7] Serhii Plokhy, *The Gates of Europe: A History of Ukraine* (New York: Basic Books, 2021).
[8] Ümran Karadeniz and Alpay Bizbirlik, 'Azak Kalesi'nin İşgali ve İstirdadı (1637–1642)', *Akademik Bakış*, 14, no. 27 (Winter, 2020), 221–41.
[9] Bitis, *Russia*, 19.

A significant milestone in Russo-Ottoman relations was the battles during the War of the Holy League, also known as the 'Great Turkish War' (1683–99).

The conflict resulted in Russian reoccupation of Azov in 1696.[10] More importantly, swift victories on the battlefield whetted Peter I's appetite to gain access to the Black Sea and fulfil the 'long-standing dream of the Moscow tsars – the liquidation of the "Crimean Yurt," the last remnant of the Golden Horde'.[11] To this end, during his trip to Europe in 1698, Peter I sought to persuade the other countries in the Holy League (the Holy Roman Empire, Venice and the Polish-Lithuanian Commonwealth) to continue the war against the Ottomans. His efforts aimed to secure Russian control over the fortress of Kerch at the mouth of the Sea of Azov.

It was why Peter I instructed his chief plenipotentiary Prokofiey Bogdanovich Voznitsyn (1640–1702) to 'sabotage the work' of the Congress of Karlowitz that gather at the end of the 'Great Turkish War'.[12] From the opening of the

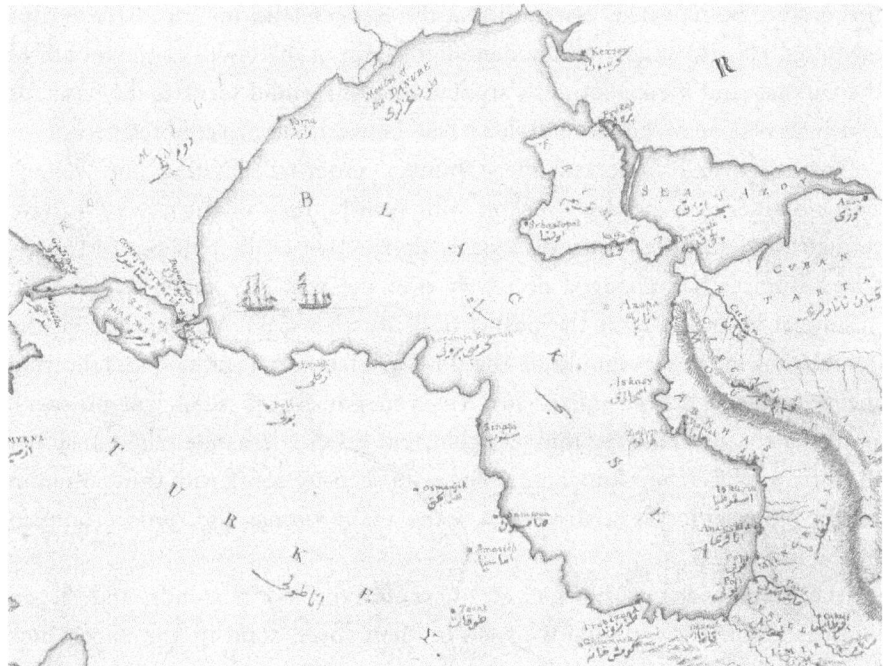

Map 1 The Crimea and the Black Sea, Source: NLS MS 5579.

---

[10] Oreshkova, 'The Ottoman Empire and Russia', 131.
[11] Andrey Guskov, 'Učastie Rossii v Karlovickom kongresse (1698–1699 gody): Russkaja diplomatija v rannee Novoe vremja', *Novaja i novejšaja istorija*, no. 3 (2018), 119–41, there at 121.
[12] Guskov, 'Učastie Rossii', 124–5.

congress on 9 November 1698 until shortly before the signature of its final act on 26 January 1699, Voznitsyn endeavoured to frustrate the peace by making uncompromisable demands to the Ottoman plenipotentiaries *Reisülküttab* Rami Mehmed Efendi (1654–1704) and dragoman Alexander Mavrokordatos (1636–1709).

This intention became evident from the very beginning of the congress during the opening remarks of the Russian and Ottoman plenipotentiaries. After exchanging ceremonial greetings and listening to the proposals of his Russian counterpart, Mavrokordatos opened with an intriguing account of the history of 'the world from the beginning', emphasizing the Ottomans' long-standing friendship with the Russians and asserting that this was something the whole world had long 'marvelled at'. He then addressed the Russian return of Azov in 1641, describing it as a 'praiseworthy act' on the part of the then Russian tsar Mikhail Fedorovich because he 'immediately gave [the fortress] back' to avoid 'damaging the friendship' with the sultan. Mavrokordatos proposed that this gesture be repeated, asserting that the Russians did not 'need [Azov] for anything'. He also suggested the demilitarization of the towns at the mouth of the Dnieper and their neutrality, arguing that this would serve as the basis for and guarantee of an 'honest and safe peace' between the two empires.

Voznitsyn flatly rejected the Ottoman proposal, inviting the sultan's plenipotentiaries instead to 'reckon with reality'. They ought not even 'have in their thoughts' the return of Azov or destruction of the Dnieper fortresses. Circumstances had changed decisively over the past fifty years. Rather than 'historical legends' about the past acts of Russian tsars, Voznitsyn said, the 'foundation for peace' should be the post-war territorial status quo, following the principle of *uti possidetis juris* ('as you possess, so shall you possess'). Immediately contradicting this very principle, he also demanded the transfer of the fortress of Kerch to Russia, as a pledge for security, along with compensation for the financial losses incurred due to the 'many wrongs and ruins' prompted by the Tatar raids.[13]

The sultan's agents blushed at these unexpected demands and began whispering furiously among themselves. Their voices soon rose in anger: how could anyone dare demand from the Ottoman Empire 'a great city, which holds the gates of the entire Black Sea and the Crimean peninsula … Did the

---

[13] *Pamjatniki diplomaticheskikh snoshenij drevnej Rossii s derzhavami inostrannymi*, IX (Saint Petersburg: Tip., 1868), 257–8, 280–81.

great and powerful ambassador mention [by any chance] a [wrong] name?'[14] Voznitsyn ignored Mavrokordatos's question, asserting that the days when the Crimean khans claimed tribute from Russia were long gone. 'Now everything has changed,' he declared. 'Now was the time for the Russian tsars to demand rewards for themselves, not to pay tributes.' Voznitsyn repeated his demand for Kerch and asked for a special treaty by which the Ottomans would guarantee not to support the Tatars in case of war.[15] Having begun inauspiciously with these heated remarks, the conference came to an abrupt end that same day.

By 13 January 1699, however, after nearly two months of negotiations, Voznitsyn found himself cornered by the mediating Austrian, German, Dutch and English representatives, all eager to bring an end to the war. The next day, he agreed to sign a two-year truce with the Ottomans.[16] 'For a long time I was perplexed, what was I to do,' he confessed to Peter I. He 'dared not' conclude 'a profitless peace', knowing the tsar's 'instructions and great preparation for war'. But in the end, he had done what he had to do 'for the most extreme need'.[17] Legally, there had 'remained no ground to stand on', he admitted.[18] The Ottoman plenipotentiaries promised Voznitsyn that the Crimean Tatar raids in Russian territories would be halted and tribute demands would no longer be made.[19]

Alongside the Russo-Ottoman truce, a twenty-five-year truce between the Habsburg and Ottoman Empires and an 'Eternal Peace' between the Polish-Lithuanian Commonwealth and the sultan were also signed in 1699. The next year, as Peter I's attention shifted to the conflict with Sweden over Pomeranian territories, the tsar hastened to sign a peace treaty with the sultan to ensure the security of his south-western borders.[20] On 3 July 1700, the truce was transformed into a peace treaty between the courts of Moscow and Istanbul. Azov remained under Russian control.

It is now commonly agreed that the Congress of Karlowitz radically altered the nature of diplomatic relations between the two empires. The truce that the tsar's representative reluctantly signed in 1699 became foundational to Russian imperial designs in the coming decades. Historian Andrey Guskov

---

[14] Ibid., 257–8.
[15] Ibid., 260, 283.
[16] Vladimir Degoev, 'Diplomatija Petra I na zaključitel'nom ètape Russko-Tureckoj vojny 1686–1700 Godov VI', *Rossija*, Vol. XXI, no. 6 (2016), 116–43, at 124.
[17] Ibid., 142.
[18] Guskov, 'Učastie Rossii', 140.
[19] Fisher, *Russian Annexation*, 22.
[20] Oreshkova, 'The Ottoman Empire and Russia', 132.

writes that the 1698–9 gathering was the first time in history that Russia had participated in an international congress as a full party. It emerged as a member of the pan-European international system.[21] Karlowitz also saw a pivot in Russian policy towards the Crimean Tatars and the Ottoman Empire, from defence to offense.

For the Ottomans, the cession of Hungary (to Austria), the Morea (to Venice) and Podolia (to the Polish-Lithuanian Commonwealth) were significant territorial losses, while the unprecedented payment of a tribute to the Christian Austrian king jeopardized the legitimacy of sultan Mustafa II.[22] As Abou Al-Haj tells us, the 1699 settlement demarcated a linear boundary between the Habsburg and Ottoman Empires, set a timetable for the implementation of territorial and other articles, and put in place guarantees for the territorial integrity of the signatory parties. Virginia Aksan emphasizes that it was a 'treaty among the equals', while Ali Yaycıoğlu argues that the 'Karlowitz moment' signalled the transformation from an expansive empire to a polity that sought 'peace, security and stability'.[23] Ottoman elites would nonetheless soon turn their attention to recapturing the strategically important Azov and the Morea.

Karlowitz also forged ties between Russo-Ottoman inter-imperial relations and non-Muslim subjects of the Ottoman Empire. The sultan was eager to make peace, Mavrokordatos explained, albeit 'in great grief and sorrow' because he feared that his Christian subjects would face terrible persecution, including the execution of their patriarchs, due to suspicion that they were secretly inciting Peter I to continue the war.[24]

For Russia, both the 'Polish question' and the 'Turkish question' had also come to a head at Karlowitz. During the congress, Russian plenipotentiaries reported that the 'malice of the Poles' had been fully revealed. The Poles had been involved in a struggle with Russia (and to a degree with the Ottoman Empire) over Ukraine. Now the Russians considered the Poles to be 'more enemies to us than any other nation', urging their superiors to be 'more careful of them than of the Turks and Crimeans'. They suspected that the Poles would never give up their claims to western Russian territories, and that those claims were leading them to encourage the Ottomans 'to go to war with Russia'.[25]

---

[21] Guskov, 'Učastie Rossii', 121, 141.
[22] Rifaat A. Abou-El-Haj, 'The Formal Closure of the Ottoman Frontier in Europe: 1699–1703', *Journal of the American Oriental Society*, 89, no. 3 (July-September, 1969), 467–75, at 467.
[23] Aksan, *The Ottomans 1700–1923*, 19; Ali Yaycıoğlu, 'Karlofça Anı: Osmanlılar 18. Yüzyıla Nasıl Başladı?' *Tarih ve Toplum*, 18 (2022), 8–56, there at 11, 15.
[24] Degoev, 'Diplomatija Petra I – III', 101.
[25] Degoev, 'Diplomatija Petra I – VI', 141.

A decade later, when a new Russo-Ottoman War broke out in July 1711, the Ottoman victory against the Russians at the Prut River turned Azov into a buffer zone under Ottoman rule, at least nominally.[26] But that was not all. The 1711 Prut Treaty resolved to terminate Russian dominance over the Polish-Lithuanian Commonwealth. That is, any Russian interference in the Commonwealth came to be regarded as a violation of the Russo-Ottoman agreement. From that point on, Ottoman statesmen came to be involved in the affairs of the Commonwealth with Russia as a means of asserting and testing their influence in European international politics. This would become a source of constant conflict between the courts of Istanbul and Moscow (soon to be moved to Saint Petersburg).

With hindsight, one might argue that the turn of the eighteenth century saw the Ottoman authorities realize the importance of adopting international law as a shield to ensure the security and territorial integrity of their empire.[27] The Eastern Question may have emerged as a semantic category more than a century later, but it owed its genesis to the Great Turkish War and to Karlowitz.[28] These events drew together the complex dynamics of the territorial integrity of the Ottoman Empire, the fate of the sultan's non-Muslim subjects, the Polish question, and, as I shall explain below, the capitulations as well.

The rise of the Romanovs

In 1720, an 'Eternal Peace' was proclaimed between Russia and the Ottoman Empire. Shortly after, however, Russian strategists proposed plans to partition the sultan's domains. This was in part due to mounting Tatar raids from the Crimea and to new Russian imperial ambitions, now developed in the new imperial capital Saint Petersburg under Empress Anna Ioannovna (r. 1739–40). Russo-Austrian interventions in the affairs of the Polish-Lithuanian Commonwealth triggered the outbreak of the Russo-Ottoman War in 1735, with Vienna supporting Saint Petersburg, and Paris backing

---

[26] *Abermahlige Confirmation von dem Moscowitisch- und Türckischen dreytägigen Treffen, und die nach derselben auf beyden Seiten bedungene Friedensarticul zu ewigen Zeiten:worüber aber der König von Schweden mit dem Gross-Vezier in einen scharffen Disputat gerathen* (Greifswald: Greiffswalde, 1711); Akdes Nimet Kurat, *Prut Seferi ve Barışı* (Ankara: AÜDTCF Tarih Enstitüsü Yayınları, 1951).
[27] Fikret Adanır, 'Turkey's Entry into the Concert of Europe', *European Review*, 13, no. 3 (2005), 395–417, at 397.
[28] Ivan Parvev, 'The War of 1683–1699 and the Beginning of the Eastern Question', in Colin Heywood and Ivan Parvev (eds.), *The Treaties of Carlowitz (1699): Antecedents, Course and Consequences* (Leiden, Boston, MA: Brill, 2020), 73–90.

Istanbul.²⁹ This time, Ottoman forces suffered heavy defeats at the hands of Russian armies.³⁰ The ensuing Treaty of Belgrade (1739) returned Azov to Russia.³¹ Thanks to the intervention of French agents in the peace-making process, especially the work of Louis Sauveur, Marquis de Villeneuve (1675–1745), the French ambassador to Istanbul, the treaty proved to be much less devastating for the sultan than it could have been. Russia was not allowed to fortify Azov, nor to have a navy in the Sea of Azov or the Black Sea, which remained an Ottoman lake.³²

The peace of 1739 brought relative stability to Russo-Ottoman relations for more than two decades. In 1762, however, 'Russian hawks' such as Mikhail Illarionovich Vorontsov (1714–67) argued that as long as the Crimea remained an Ottoman dominion, it would pose a threat to Russia, due to the unremitting Tatar raids.³³ The Crimea had to be either controlled by Russia or made independent so that Russian borders could be protected while Russia could exert greater influence in the Sea of Azov and the Black Sea.³⁴

Russia's incursions in the Polish-Lithuanian Commonwealth following the 1764 Russo-Prussian pact once again served as a pretext for another Russo-Ottoman War. The election of Stanislaus Augustus Poniatowski (1732–98), a 'protégé' of Empress Catherine II, as the king of Poland and the grand duke of Lithuania, along with the deployment of Russian troops to the Polish Confederation of Bar to quell local resistance, violated the treaties of 1711 and 1739.³⁵ Spurred by the French, sultan Abdulhamid I declared war on Russia, denouncing 'the Muscovite unbelievers' who, in their quest to seize Poland and subjugate the Poles, '[had] refused to recognize our repeated warnings that we would expel their troops from Poland'.³⁶

---

[29] Roider, Jr. *Austria's Eastern Question*, 196; Uğur Kurtaran, 'Marquis Louis Sauveur de Villeneuve'nin İstanbul Büyükelçiliği ve Faaliyetleri (1728–1741)', TAD, 41, no. 71 (2022), 276–323, there at 288.

[30] M.J.F. Scharffenstein, *Acten-mässige Deduction derer zwischen dem russischen und türckischen Hof, neuerlich entstandenen Irrungen und dadurch veranlassten Kriegs:nebst einer accuraten Charte und geographischen Beschreibung des türckischen Kayserthums und aller angränzenden Reiche und Länder, wie auch dem Diario der kayserlichen Armee in Ungarn* (Frankfurt, Leipzig: Bey Felseckers Seel. Erben, 1737).

[31] Fisher, *Russian Annexation*, 24.

[32] A.K. Bajov, *Russkaya Armiya v Tsarstvovanie Imperatricy Anny Ioannovny: Vojna Rossii s Turciej*, V, 1736–1739 (Saint Petersburg: n.p., 1906).

[33] Oreshkova, 'The Ottoman Empire and Russia', 135.

[34] Ibid.

[35] Virginia Aksan, *An Ottoman Statesman in War and Peace: Ahmed Resmi Efendi, 1700–1783* (Leiden: Brill, 1995), 115.

[36] Adnan Baycar (ed.), *Osmanlı-Rus İlişkileri Tarihi (Ahmed Câvid Bey'in Müntehabâtı)* (Istanbul: Yeditepe Yayınevi, 2004), 278–9; cited also in Fisher, *Russian Annexation*, 31. On French policy, see Sébastian Flynn, 'Franco-Ottoman Diplomatic Relations and the Secret du Roi, 1756–1774',

The war of 1768–74 proved catastrophic for the Ottomans.[37] By the end of 1771, Russia had seized control of Moldavia and Wallachia, and had invaded a considerable portion of the Crimea, securing peace with the Crimean khan Sahip Giray at Karasu Bazaar by offering him subsidies and support for independence.[38] The humiliating defeats suffered by the Ottomans on the battlefields and the de facto loss of a large portion of the Crimea culminated in the Treaty of Küçük Kaynarca after two years of protracted negotiations. Signed on 10 July 1774, this treaty has been aptly described as 'the most fundamental and the most far-reaching' of the agreements concluded between Russia and the Ottoman Empire.[39]

Under the treaty, the Ottomans ceded the fortresses of Yenikale and Kerch (article 19) as well as Azov (Article 20) to Russia. Saint Petersburg was placed in full control of the straits between the Sea of Azov and the Black Sea (Article 3). Its merchant vessels were granted free passage in the Black Sea, the Bosphorus and the Dardanelles (Article 11), ending Ottoman dominance there. Russian merchants were brought into the capitulatory system, enjoying the same rights and privileges as the British and the French (Article 11). Dragomans serving under Russian ministers in Istanbul were allowed to possess *berats*, the imperial patents, making them exempt from the Ottoman law (Articles 9 and 11).[40] Russia was accorded the right to have a permanent representative, a second rank minister, in Istanbul (Article 5) and act as the defender of the Orthodox Church there (Article 7), whose ministers were placed under the protection of the empress (Article 14).

In return, Russia ceded to the sultan all of Bessarabia with the cities of Akkerman, Chilia, Ismail and others, the Archipelago islands (Article 17), as well as Moldavia and Wallachia, on the condition their (Christian) law and dignity would be respected (Article 16). In Georgia, the fortresses conquered

---

Acta Orientalia Academiae Scientiarum Hungaricae, 75, no. 2 (2022), 311–26, at 322. Also see Yusuf Ziya Karabıçak, 'Enlightened Declarations: Ottoman and Russian Proclamations in the Ottoman-Russian War of 1768–1774', *Journal for Eighteenth-Century Studies* (2024), advanced online publication, accessed 20 June 2024; Michael Talbot, 'A Legal and Diplomatic Justification of the Ottoman Declaration of War against Russia, 1768: Legitimizing War within the Ottoman Empire', *Sharia Source at Harvard Law School*, https://portal.shariasource.com/documents/2924, accessed 15 March 2024. For the Russian declaration of war, see, *Abgenöthigte Kriegs-Erklärung Ihro Russisch-Kayserliche Majestät wider die Ottomannische Pforte, nebst den Berichten von den Operationen Allerhöchst Dero Armee wider die Türken* (Riga: bey Gottlob Christian Frölich, 1769).

[37] Brian L. Davies, *The Russo-Turkish War, 1768–1774: Catherine II and the Ottoman Empire* (London: Bloomsbury Academic, 2016); Aksan, *The Ottomans 1700–1923*, 59–60.
[38] Marriot, *The Eastern Question*, 150; Fisher, *Russian Annexation*, 44.
[39] Marriot, *The Eastern Question*, 151.
[40] See Chapter 3 for more on the history and effects of the *berat* system.

by the Russians were recognized by Russia 'as belonging to those to whom they have been from ancient times'. Should that be the Sublime Porte they would be returned to the sultan, provided that he would grant 'a perfect amnesty to the inhabitants' (Article 23). Sultan Abdulhamid I agreed to pay a massive war indemnity of about 7.5 million *akçes*. Most importantly, perhaps, '[a]ll Tatar peoples – Crimean, Budzhatsky, Kuban, Edisan, Zhambuyluk and Edichkul, without exception' were recognized 'as free and completely independent of any outside power' (Article 3).[41] However, in spiritual (religious) matters, the Ottoman sultan still retained his sovereignty as the caliph.

Historian David Fisher highlights that the 1774 treaty was far from being an outright surrender. The Ottoman diplomats were skilled and aware of the increasing domestic challenges facing Russia. They managed to secure concessions from the Russians, achieving a better outcome than initially expected, especially with regard to the Crimea.[42] Yet, these articles, along with the ambiguities surrounding their interpretation, laid the groundwork for numerous disputes that would constitute the Eastern Question in the ensuing decades. They initiated disagreements over the free passage of ships through the Bosphorus and Dardanelles, positioning Russia as a new commercial competitor within Ottoman dominions. Saint Petersburg's newly acquired right to act as protector of the Orthodox Church in Istanbul and overseer of the Christians in the Balkans dovetailed with the 'Third Rome' ideology wounding the pride of the Ottoman rulers. Furthermore, several issues regarding the Crimea were left unresolved. There were no measures established to define the processes for electing or removing the khans from office. No consideration was given to how the khan would be granted autocratic authority in a region composed of powerful factions unwilling to relinquish their influence.[43]

With a firm grip on the northern shores of the Black Sea and the disparities between Russian and Ottoman military and technological capabilities, Empress Catherine II would soon be capable of capturing the Ottoman imperial capital before the news reached Vienna, the nearest European metropole.[44] This posed a dire situation not only for the Ottoman Empire, but for the world. As a contemporary observer noted, potential Russian control over the straits could disrupt the balance

---

[41] 'Kjučuk-Kajnardžijskij Mirnyj Dogovor Zaveršil Russko-Tureckuju Vojnu 1768–1774 Gg' in *Pod Stjagom Rossii: Sbornik Arxivnyx Dokumentov* (Moscow: n.p.,1992); Baycar, *Osmanlı-Rus İlişkileri*, 490–1.

[42] Fisher, *Russian Annexation*, 55.

[43] Ibid., 56.

[44] Ozavci, *Dangerous Gifts*, 29–30.

of power in Europe, endangering global peace.[45] This is why historians of the Eastern Question regard the 1774 treaty as marking the onset of the Eastern Question.[46]

The 1774 treaty's articles on the independence of the Crimea and the fortresses in Georgia deeply perturbed Ottoman elites.[47] Despite reforms in the Crimean Khanate, Ottoman attempts to incite resurrections and khan Devlet Giray's attempts to play Russian and Ottoman interests off against each other brought further instability. This led to Catherine II establishing a second Crimean Khanate in 1775.[48] Russian troops repeatedly entered the Khanates to maintain order, leading, however, a massive exodus of the Crimean Muslim population to the Ottoman Empire, as occurred in 1777.[49] Meanwhile, two Ottoman naval missions in March and August 1778 ended in failure after their ships were shelled by Russian batteries in Aktiar (later named as Sevastopol).[50] A new convention was signed in Aynalıkavak in early 1779.

With this new convention, the Ottoman Empire once again recognized the Crimea as an independent Khanate. It stipulated that the sultan's approval, as caliph, would be required for the election of the khans.[51] Russian forces stationed in the Crimea were to withdraw immediately, while Russian merchants were once again granted rights in the Black Sea and the Mediterranean equal to those of Britain and France.[52] However, lingering instability within the newly independent Khanate, the Ottoman desire to reclaim the Crimea, and the Sublime Porte's unwillingness to fully implement the unequal commercial agreements in the Black Sea precipitated new clashes shortly after.

In 1781, Catherine II made a secret pact with Austrian emperor Joseph II to secure his support against the Ottoman Empire. Since the birth of her grandson Constantin in 1779, she had been contemplating the partition of the Ottoman Empire's European territories. Her grand ambition, known as the 'Greek Project', was to amalgamate Moldavia, Wallachia and Bessarabia into a new kingdom of Dacia under an Orthodox Christian and to resurrect a Byzantine Empire in Istanbul, where Constantin would ascend the new king when he came of age.[53]

---

[45] Thugut to Kaunitz, 3 September 1774, quoted in Roider, *Austria's Eastern Question*, 152.
[46] Anderson, *The Eastern Question*; Macfie, *The Eastern Question*.
[47] Baycar, *Osmanlı-Rus İlişkileri*, 492–3.
[48] Fisher, *Russian Annexation*, 61.
[49] Ibid., 75, 77.
[50] Ibid., 92–6.
[51] Ibid., 110.
[52] Baycar, *Osmanlı-Rus İlişkileri*, 503.
[53] Blanning, *The Origins*, 55–6.

The completion of permanent fortifications at Aktiar in 1782 allowed it, as it would the following year, to serve as the base for the newly established Russian fleet. In 1783, the hardliner Grigory Potemkin (1739–91) successfully persuaded Empress Catherine to annex the Crimean peninsula.[54] The entire world was holding its breath at this critical moment. Supported by Austria, the empress initially demanded from the Sublime Porte 'the renewal and confirmation of the independence of [the] Crimea, granting the khan the freedom to make treaties with other powers', which would more closely align the Crimea with the Russian Empire. Additionally, she called for 'complete freedom of commerce and navigation in the Black Sea and through the Dardanelles', along with the independence of the provinces of Moldavia and Wallachia.[55]

Alarming intentions

At this nadir, like much of the world, Robert Liston's attention fixated on the 'eastern affairs'. He regularly received intelligence from other British Empire stations and reported the views of the Court of Turin, where he represented London, back to Britain. He noted that Empress Catherine II was ready to realize her plan for 'the revival of the Empire of the East', as the Bourbon War (1778–83) provided her with 'an opportunity that might never arise again'.[56] The Anglo-French War, a part of the larger American War of Independence, had diverted the focus and forces of Britain and France – two powers that might have opposed Catherine – elsewhere.

The empress, together with Austria, was prepared to strike the Ottoman Empire, should the sultan's men refused her demands, planning to 'take the Crimea to herself' and annex Ochakov.[57] The intentions of the Russian empress and the Austrian emperor were 'very alarming to the rest of Europe', and many shared the belief these moves 'ought to be resisted by a general combination of the other Powers'.[58]

The Ottoman ministers' response to the Russian demands sought to maintain peace. They agreed on the empress's terms, though many observers

---

[54] Fisher, *Russian Annexation*, 135.
[55] Robert Liston to Sir Gilbert Elliot, 18 January 1783, NLS MS 5527, f. 93.
[56] Ibid.
[57] Ibid.
[58] Robert Liston to Sir James Harris, 18 January 1783, NLS MS 5527, f. 111.

at the time viewed this as 'more likely to attract than ward off' more serious Austro-Russian encroachments in the near future.[59] Liston recognized that the distant implications of these concessions were of 'the highest importance'. They would provide Russia with immense commercial advantages, and control over the navigation in the Black Sea would empower the empress 'to block up Constantinople when she pleases [and] to cut off its supplies'.

In a private letter to his close friend Dalzel, he remarked that the empress's moves would 'oblige the Infidels [Ottomans] to depart in peace and seen no more in Europe'. With evident satisfaction as a philhellene, he added: 'For my own private part, I wish them a good journey, and should be very happy', seeing it as a step forward 'the independence of Greece'.[60] Still, Liston was well aware that 'the political tètes-a-perruque of Europe will not be of this mind'. Both Britain and France, along with Prussia and Sardinia, had long tied their policies to preserving the Ottoman status quo, and none could 'see with indifference the aggrandisements of powerful neighbours'.[61] Yet, doubts lingered in Liston's mind:

> Whether our Ministry are sufficiently systematic to engage in new quarrels for the old Hobby-Horse of the Balance of Power; whether we shall be simple enough, after the experience we have recently had, to squeeze out the last shilling from our exhausted purse with a view to the future gratitude of natural allies; whether France is willing or indeed able, to make any considerable exertion, whether the King of Prussia may not be determined to end his days in peace, or whether he may not be bought off by proportionable accession of territory on the side of Poland; are question which a few months may possibly decide.[62]

The Sublime Porte adopted a strategy of delay, carefully watching to see what Russia and Austria's next move would be. But the sultan's worst fears materialized shortly after. Having already entered the Crimea the previous year to suppress Ottoman-sponsored rebels, Russian troops seized control of the peninsula.[63] On 8 April 1783, Russia formally declared the annexation of the Crimea.[64]

This prompted immense apprehension among Ottoman ministers. In an imperial council (*divan*) convened a few weeks later, Sheikh-ul Islam Dürrî-zâde Ataullah Efendi vehemently criticized the Ottoman silence in the face of

---

[59] Ibid.
[60] Robert Liston to Andrew Dalzel, 29 January 1783, NLS MS 5527, f. 123.
[61] Ibid.
[62] Ibid.
[63] S.F. Oreshkova, 'Osmanskaya imperiya i Rossiya v svete ix geopoliticheskogo razgranicheniya', *Voprosy istorii. Ezhemesyachnyj zhurnal*, 3 (2005): 34–6.
[64] Baycar, *Osmanlı-Rus İlişkileri*, 519.

Russian aggression and blatant annexation (*açıktan açığa zabt*). Grand Admiral Hasan Paşa opined that '[s]wallowing the Crimean annexation' would bring the end of the Ottoman Empire. Grand vizier Halil Hamid Paşa replied anxiously. The purpose of 'our labour day and night', he asserted, 'is to complete our mobilization preparations … [to] retaliate against Russia's arrogant violation' of previous agreements regarding the Crimea, and thereby 'reassert the glory of the Sublime State … [O]n such an issue, revenge against the enemy is a binding duty (*farîza-i zimmetdir*)'.[65]

At Liston's request, British ambassador to Istanbul Robert Ainslie reported to Lord Mount Stuart that the Sublime Porte was in the 'greatest alarm' and urgently sought to regain superiority in the Black Sea and it was exerting 'the greatest efforts for putting this Empire in the best posture of defence', especially against attack from the north.[66] Sultan Abdulhamid I and his ministers, especially grand vizier Halil Hamid, were acutely aware that the Ottoman army and navy, in their current state, were no match for their Russian counterparts. Their attempts at reform encountered domestic opposition. Furthermore, with France embroiled in a war with Britain over American independence, and the Habsburg endorsement of Russian plans, any major inter-imperial support for the Ottoman cause seemed unlikely. This was why the Porte endeavoured to bide its time and avoid a rupture, going so far as to recognize the Russian annexation of the Crimea with the second Aynalıkavak Convention on 9 January 1784. According to Liston, this was 'for the good of humanity', because if hostilities were to emerge between the two empires, 'the consequence would sooner or later be a general war'.[67]

Prior to this, Ottoman ministers had made concessions even to Austria relating to the boundaries of Croatia and Bosnia, and a sum of money was paid for depredations committed in their borders priorly. Furthermore, the court of Vienna was granted an unprecedented passport for its merchant ship to proceed from the Danube to Istanbul.[68] But most importantly, the Porte signed a Treaty of Commerce with Russia on 21 June 1783, in order to avert another war with Russia.[69] The eighty articles of this treaty delineated the prices and customs tariffs for numerous goods imported and exported by Russian merchants along

---

[65] Ibid., 525.
[66] R. Ainslie to Lord Mount Stewart, 25 June 1783, NLS MS 5536, f. 179.
[67] Robert Liston to Sir Robert, 23 February 1784, NLS MS 5555, f. 48.
[68] R. Ainslie to Lord Mount Stewart, 25 June 1783, NLS MS 5536, f. 179.
[69] İdris Bostan, 'Rusya'nın Karadeniz'de Ticarete Başlaması ve Osmanlı İmparatorluğu (1700–1787)', *Belleten*, 59, no. 225 (August, 1995), 353–94, there at 359.

the coasts of the Ottoman Empire – a matter left unresolved by the 1774 and 1779 agreements.[70] Most notably, Article 21 of the treaty stipulated that Russian subjects trading in the Ottoman Empire would pay only 3 per cent in customs duties.[71] As we shall see below, this article also became a reference point in subsequent Russo-Ottoman disputes.

As feared by many, Ottoman concessions did little to shelve the Greek project; instead they only incited further demands from the empress. After the end of the Bourbon War in 1783, France's reluctance to accept the invitation of Catherine II and Joseph II to join the project had impeded the empress's plans. French foreign minister Charles Gravier de Vergennes (1719–87) was conscious that participating in the dismemberment of the sultan's dominions could help maintain the balance of power with Russia. However, he feared that if the three powers engaged in aggression, it would ultimately subvert European stability, as other powers would also seek greater gains.[72] A former ambassador to the Porte, Vergennes was worried that partitioning the Ottoman Empire could harm French commercial interests and the economic advantages that France enjoyed in the Levant. He consequently opposed the Greek project.

Even then, Empress Catherine II's minting of coins containing the image of Hagia Sophia and Russian interference in Wallachia and Moldavia heightened anxiety in Istanbul. The real blow came soon after Vergennes died in February 1787, with the visit of Catherine II to the Crimea, together with Joseph II and his ministers. This visit was received in Istanbul as a provocation. Consequently, the fourth and final eighteenth-century Russo-Ottoman War broke out on 14 August 1787. The next year the Ottomans found themselves at war also with Austria, while Sweden declared war on Russia.[73]

After four years of conflict, Ottoman armies were once again humiliated by Russian and Austrian forces. The dreadful news of the fortress of Ochakov's capture by the Russians caused such deep sorrow to Sultan Abulhamid I that it

---

[70] *Düvel-i Ecnebiye*, no. 85, 632–3.
[71] 'Traduction du memoire au nom de la Sublime Porte remis par S.A. Reis Effendi a Mr L'Envoye de Russie, dans la Conference tenue a Giokssou ce 25 Juin 1794', NLS MS 5572, f. 17. To obviate all disputes that could arise between merchants and customs officers with regard to the estimated value of goods, it had been deemed necessary to 'establish a tariff which will serve for all time as a rule for Russian merchants and custom officers in the Ottoman dominions.' For this reason, the Sublime Porte had authorized Haci Mehmed Aga, director of the customs of Istanbul, the envoy of Russia and Nicolas Pisani, the first dragoman of the imperial council, to carry out this arrangement of the tariff in September 1782.
[72] Robert Salomon, *La Politique orientale de Vergennes* (Crimea: Les Presses Modernes, 1935), 194–5.
[73] Aksan, *The Ottomans*, 78–81.

hastened his death on 7 April 1789.[74] While the war was celebrated as the end of fanaticism and pride on the Russian side, Ottoman poet and imam Halil Efendi's lament over the loss of the fortress of Ochakov (in Turkish, Özi) signifies the importance of the defeat for the Ottoman rulers:

> The foundations of the Ottomans have been compromised
> The gate to Istanbul has been conquered by the enemies of faith[75]

The quagmire resulting from the Russian occupation of Ochakov not only drew the world's diplomatic attention to the affairs of the East again. While Liston was in Sweden, it also prompted a governmental crisis in London in the early 1790s. The question of whether to intervene in the Russo-Ottoman War on the side of the latter became a critical question for certain British statesmen.

Foreign Secretary Francis Godolphin Osborne, fifth duke of Leeds, (1751-99), argued in favour of pressuring Russia by invoking the Triple Alliance and securing the balance of power in Eastern Europe. After the conclusion of the Russo-Swedish peace, Britain issued an ultimatum to Russia in March 1791, and demanded the return of Ochakov to the Ottoman Empire as part of the peace terms. Empress Catherine II refused the British demand, after which the Tory prime minister William Pitt the Younger (1759–1806) put forward a pro-Ottoman motion to parliament, requesting extra funds for British naval forces to undertake an attack upon Russia.[76] Pitt found himself having to withdraw his motion, however, in the face of Russophile opposition and concerns an aggressive posture might harm the interests of the Muscovy Company.[77]

While it was not clear to many in Britain what the strategic gains of supporting the Ottoman cause against Russia would be, the situation in the northern shores of the Black Sea raised eyebrows also in Germany, where the physiocrat Johan August Schleitweinn (1731–1802) wrote that the situation in the east was 'the most important matter for Europe' and its resolution was central for 'a system of permanent peace' among the European states.[78]

---

[74] Baycar, *Osmanlı-Rus İlişkileri*, 613; Enver Ziya Karal, *Osmanlı Tarihi: Nizam-ı Cedid ve Tanzimat Devirleri, 1789–1856* (Ankara: Türk Tarih Kurumu, 1983), 13.

[75] Baron d'Estat, *La prise d'Otchakoff: dédiée aux Russes* (Saint Petersburg: L'Imprimerie Impériale, 1789), 2; Halil Efendi's lament was published in German and French the following year. Chalil Efendi, *Klagelied über den Verlust Okzakow's* (Vienna: Bey Gräffer dem jüngern, 1789), 6.

[76] Eric J. Evans, *William Pitt the Younger* (London and New York: Routledge, 1999), 30.

[77] Evans, *William Pitt the Younger*, 30; Cunningham, *Anglo-Ottoman*, 1–31; David S. Katz, *The Shaping of Turkey in the British Imagination, 1776–1923* (London: Palgrave Macmillan, 2016), 20–1.

[78] Johann August Schlettwein, *Die wichtigste Angelegenheit für Europa, oder, System eines festen Friedens unter den europäischen Staaten:nebst einem Anhang über einen besondern Frieden zwischen Russland und der Pforte* (Leipzig: ey Friedrich Gotthold Jacobäer, 1791).

Despite Sultan Selim III's determined efforts – such as forging an alliance with Sweden to prolong her war with Russia and subsequently seeking an alliance with Prussia – the Ottoman Empire suffered repeated defeats in the battlefields. The Russo-Swedish peace concluded at Värälä in 1790 further weakened the Ottoman position. On the advice of his ministers, Selim III decided neither to prolong nor restart war with Russia, at least until his empire could match the military power of his Romanov rivals. He, therefore, agreed to sign the Treaty of Jassy with Russia on 9 January 1792.

Under this treaty, Selim III acknowledged Russia's control over the Crimea, surrendered Ottoman claims to Georgia and accepted the new borders: the Balkans defined by the Dniester River and the Caucasus by the Kuban River. The sultan also pledged to prevent raids from the tribes on the left bank of the Kuban into Russian territory (Article VI).[79]

The recognition of the Crimea as Russian territory was a bitter concession for Selim III. From that moment forward, reclaiming the Crimea and the surrounding regions became his paramount ambition.[80] The challenge, however, lay in his drastically weakened army and navy, internal opposition to reforms, financial weakness and the backdrop of the tumultuous Revolutionary Wars. In such conditions, the question arose: how could Selim III hope to achieve his ultimate goal? In Istanbul, Liston became a direct observer of the sultan's ongoing struggle to overcome these forbidding obstacles.

---

[79] 'Abstract of Articles of Treaties, between Russia and Turkey, 1774–1849', TNA FO 881/280.
[80] Ozavci, *Dangerous Gifts*, 45–6.

3

Forbidding obstacles

'Barbarians of the Bosphorus'

After his appointment to Istanbul in the autumn of 1793, Liston's journey from London to the Ottoman capital was delayed for several months due to illness.[1] During this period, he spent some time back in the family farm in Scotland, researched his route and appointed staff, selecting Barthélemy Pisani of the famous Pisani family as his interpreter in Pera.[2] He hoped to clear some of his debts to acquaintances, assuring a certain lender named Edward Abbott that he would make a payment 'before I leave the cultivated part of Europe and entrust myself to the good faith of the Barbarians of the Bosphorus'.[3] In the coming months, as he would observe the sultan's world first-hand, his perception of the Ottomans would change dramatically.

Liston departed from London in March 1794.[4] As he made his way to Istanbul, the War of the First Coalition (1792–7) in Europe was in its second year. The coalition, initially comprising Austria and Prussia, was seeking to quell the revolutionary fervour spreading from France. Early on, the French armies had suffered defeats, such as at the Battle of Verdun on 2 September 1792, when Prussian forces captured the fortress town and marched towards Paris.[5] However, in September 1792, the French secured a crucial victory at the Battle of Valmy, halting the Prussian advance and emboldening the revolutionaries. Shortly after, the French general Dumouriez triumphed at the Battle of Jemappes, leading to the occupation of the Austrian Netherlands (modern-day Belgium).

---

[1] Robert Liston to [?], 11 January 1794, NLS MS 5579, f. 11.
[2] Robert Liston to Bart. Pisani, 10 January 1794, NLS MS 5579, f. 5.
[3] Robert Liston to Mr Edward Abbott, 28 February 1794, NLS MS 5579, f. 13.
[4] Robert Liston to [?], 23 March 1794, NLS MS 5579, f. 8.
[5] Mikaberidze, *Napoleonic Wars*, 44–67.

These victories enabled France to expand its influence, despite the ongoing threat from coalition forces. The war escalated with the execution of King Louis XVI on 21 January 1793, prompting Britain, Spain and others to formally join the coalition. Thus, the conflict expanded into a broader European war between the revolutionary aspirations of France and the monarchical interests of its opponents.

Traversing a Europe in turmoil at the time, Liston noted down his observations: in France, the Royalists in the Vendée were still in force 'and in spirits'. In Flanders, the coalition's progress was minimal, as they awaited the arrival of Prussian reinforcements. King Frederick William II of Prussia was preoccupied in Poland, leading 25,000 men and around 9,000 Russians to quell nearly 30,000 Polish 'insurgents'.[6]

After a 'tedious' journey of two months, Liston arrived in Istanbul on 19 May 1794.[7] Initially planning to travel via Bucharest, instead he went through Wallachia, crossed the Danube, and stayed close to the Black Sea to avoid the bandits and Bulgarian insurgents around Edirne (Adrianople). His route led him over *Haemus Mons* (the Balkan range) by 'a shortened and less rocky passage', allowing him to bring three carriages to Istanbul, 'one of which an English coach (not lightly loaded) without the smallest accident or delay'.[8]

Prior to his arrival in Ottoman lands, Sultan Selim III had sent out a *firman* to 'all *kadıs*,[9] deputy *kadıs*, military officers, aldermen, deputy-governors, voivodes, chief commanders and other officers, seniors of the towns, and representatives upon the roads from the frontiers to Istanbul'. He requested that Liston be lodged in proper *konak*s (kiosks) and houses, ensuring that 'nothing be neglected to preserve him from any inconvenience and risk, that he may safely and freely pass from one jurisdiction to other and thus reach my Imperial residence with all security'.[10] Throughout his journey in Ottoman dominions, Liston encountered '[g]ood offices and kind protections … and every degree of security and attention'. Since he had changed his route unexpectedly and the Ottoman agents sent to accompany him were informed too late, he arrived in Istanbul unescorted. He was pleased to have eluded 'the ceremonies and embarrassments

---

[6] Robert Liston to [unknown], 8 July 1794, NLS MS 5579, f. 28.
[7] Robert Liston to Lord Grenville, 25 May 1794, NLS MS 5572, f. 1.
[8] Ibid.
[9] Muslim judge.
[10] Personal letters to Liston, 24 April 1794, NLS MS 5574, f. 74.

which the formal escort granted by the Sublime Porte [the term to refer to the Ottoman ministries collectively from at least the 1770s onward] unavoidably brings with it'.[11]

In Istanbul, Liston was warmly received by Sir Robert Ainslie, his predecessor, who provided him with all official papers. Under normal circumstances, a British ambassador would have audiences with senior Ottoman ministers and the sultan soon after his arrival. In Ottoman diplomatic culture, a foreign ambassador was expected to present the sultan and his viziers (ministers) with gifts in exchange for ceremonial robes at these first formal audiences.[12] As historian Michael Talbot explains, 'gifts were a key link in the cycle of friendship' and bonds of peace between Britain and the Ottoman Empire. They were essential for protecting British merchants and representing their interests.[13] However, Liston's cargo from London was delayed. The ship *Canada*, which carried the gifts, ran the risk of being captured by French ships of war and had to divert its route. This delay meant that Liston's audience with the Ottoman imperial court had to be postponed.

Amid all these hitches, Liston took consolation in the sights of Istanbul. Though he could see 'little but the outside of things' from his residence, he had 'only to say that the natural situation of Constantinople is a city certainly the noblest ... thing that human eyes ever beheld'.[14] A few weeks after his arrival, he wrote to his old friend Dalzel to inform him that he was now settling 'in this great and famous city'. He promised to write more about 'the most beautiful of all portions on the globe' shortly.[15]

This was a critical diplomatic post. As historian Pascal Firges tells us, first the 1787–92 Russo-Ottoman War and now the War of the First Coalition (1792–97) had brought Istanbul to centre stage in European diplomacy. The sultan's empire was 'strategically the most important and militarily the most powerful neutral state that hosted diplomats from both the revolutionary and counter-revolutionary side'.[16]

For the new French regime – Britain's principal rival – Istanbul remained as one of the last bastions of French diplomatic presence, alongside the United States

---

[11] Liston to Granville, 24 May 1794, NLS MS 5572, f. 1.
[12] Talbot, *British-Ottoman*, 16.
[13] Ibid., 106.
[14] Robert Liston to [unknown], 28 June 1794, NLS MS 5579, f. 91.
[15] Robert Liston to Andrew Dalzel, 10 June 1794, NLS MS 5579, f. 66.
[16] Pascal Firges, *French Revolutionaries in the Ottoman Empire: Diplomacy, Political Culture, and the Limiting of Universal Revolution, 1792–1798* (Oxford: Oxford University Press, 2017), 44.

Figure 1 Robert Liston by Gilbert Stuart, 1800, National Gallery of Art, Washington DC, Public Domain.

and Switzerland. It was now of paramount importance for Paris to formalize an alliance with the Ottoman Empire.[17] The French agents sent to Istanbul, such as Charles-Louis Huguet de Sémonville (1759–1839), were tasked with this very goal as well as with encouraging an Ottoman assault on Austria and Russia, though the latter aim was concealed during negotiations for an alliance.[18] One of Liston's main duties in Istanbul was to keep Franco-Ottoman relations in check and to prevent the recurrence of Russo-Ottoman antagonisms.

For her part, Empress Catherine II was eager to end hostilities as tensions with France had rapidly escalated in Europe. From then on, she sought a

[17] Ibid., 45.
[18] Ibid., 47–8.

rapprochement with the Ottoman Empire, instructing her new ambassador to Istanbul, Mikhail Illarionovich Golenishev-Kutuzov (1745–1813), that her genuine desire was 'to maintain peace and good understanding with the Porte'. This was deemed essential 'for the revival of trade and the flourishing of our various regions and industries'.[19] She also mandated the prevention of 'any possibility of Ottoman entrance into any anti-Russian alliance' and sought 'to counter the influence of any foreign courts in swaying the Ottomans against Russia'.[20]

As historian Alexander Mikaberidze rightly argues, the outbreak of a new Russo-Ottoman War was hardly a question of 'if' at this stage, but 'when'.[21] The timing of that conflict depended greatly on the unfolding inter-imperial war in Europe and the diplomatic choices made by the Ottoman and Russian rulers.

The relative military weakness of the Ottoman Empire was alarming for Selim III as well as contemporary observers such as the British artist, soldier and engineer George Frederick Koehler (1758–1800), who was hired by the new sultan to survey the fortresses of the Russo-Ottoman frontier between late 1791 and 1794. In a report he wrote for the embassy, one of the first reports Liston read at Istanbul, Koehler noted that the sultan's capital was in a 'defenceless state'.

While the Dardanelles and the Bosphorus would be relatively secure if attack came from the Mediterranean, the situation would be very different if aggression came from the north. There was 'little to oppose' the Russians' taking possession of Istanbul with a small army and a few ships of the line 'before any Power can give the Turks effectual assistance'.[22] As a security precaution, Ottoman imperial elites did not permit any ship to pass through the Anatolia and Rumelia fortresses (*Anadolu ve Rumeli hisarı*) situated at the entrance of the Bosphorus from the north. They were cautious not to admit anyone to these fortresses. Both lacked bastions. They were 'not tenable … against an enemy of

---

[19] Alexander Mikaberidze, *Kutuzov: A Life in War and Peace* (Oxford: Oxford University Press, 2022), 577, fn. 44.
[20] Mikaberidze, *Kutuzov*, 121.
[21] Ibid.
[22] 'Report by Captain George Frederick Koehler, 1793', Robert Ainslie Papers, NLS MS. 5570, ff. 5–42. Koehler returned to Istanbul four years later during the French invasion of Egypt. Caroline Finkel, '"The Clever Engineer Koehler": The Clandestine Activities of George Frederick Koehler (1758–1800) in the Ottoman Lands, 1791–93', in *Ottoman War and Peace Studies in Honor of Virginia H. Aksan*, Frank Castiglione, Ethan Menchinger, and Veysel Şimşek (eds.) (Leiden: Brill, 2019), 327–42, there at 327–9. Just after his departure, the 'French engineer Kauffer took upon the task of improving defence capacity of the sultan's empire. Frédérick Hitzel, 'Un ingénieur français au service de la Sublime Porte: François Kauffer (1751?–1801)', *Observatoire urbain d'Istanbul, Lettre d'information* no. 6 (June, 1994), 17–24.

any force'. The Russians had constructed a harbour for their navy at Aktiar. As the Ottomans were 'deficient in nautical knowledge and experience', a Russian attack could quickly approach the imperial capital. It would allow troops to disembark before Ottoman soldiers could even leave the walls of Istanbul.

The condition of the Ottoman imperial army was hardly promising. Koehler estimated there were 200,000 Janissaries, the backbone of the Ottoman military at the time. However, it would require 'a very great exertion' to deploy even 50,000 of them in the field, as they had 'dwindled into peaceable citizens, and it is with the utmost difficulty that can be obliged to quit their habitations'. Those that could buy exemption from service were doing so, while 'those that are poor, old and infirm, perform their Duty at all times with a bad grace' and were 'much attracted to drunkenness'.

According to Koehler, the Ottoman navy, despite fielding around twenty-one two-decked ships and an equal number of frigates and sloops, was notably weak in 1793. Their vessels, often carrying between twenty and forty guns, suffered from poor construction, with timber that was 'never enough seasoned, except those which have been purchased from Great Britain, or been presented to them, by the Court of France'.[23]

In stark contrast, the Russian fleet in the Black Sea was far more formidable. According to the British captain Monro, it boasted nine powerful ships of the line, including two with eighty guns, five with seventy-four guns and two with sixty guns. Additionally, the Russians had twenty-seven frigates, with three carrying forty guns, nine with thirty-two guns, eight with twenty-eight guns, five with twenty-four guns and one with twenty guns. They also deployed forty-six smaller vessels such as brigs, sloops and schooners, each armed with ten to eighteen guns, as well as seventy gunboats, which carried one thirty-two pounder alongside smaller guns ranging from four to six pounds.[24] Russia's fleet was better built, heavily armed and more versatile, outclassing the Ottomans both in number and strength.

All these apprehensive facts would lead Selim III to embark upon a new and radical reform programme with a view to improving his army, navy, bureaucracy and defence capacities all at once, despite the dire financial situation of his empire. However, as Liston's observations confirm, the Ottoman reform process was complex and further hindered by both internal conflicts and the challenging inter-imperial relations in which the Ottomans were entangled.

---

[23] 'Report by Captain George Frederick Koehler, 1793', Robert Ainslie Papers, NLS MS. 5570, ff. 5–42.
[24] George Monro to Ainslie, 22 April 1793, NLS MS 5570, f. 47.

Diplomacy and reform

Soon after his cargo arrived (September 1794), Liston was granted an audience with Sultan Selim III on 14 October 1794, submitting King George III's letter of credence.[25] He also met with Ottoman ministers to gather further 'authentic' information. His first reports to London regarding the situation of the Ottoman Empire dovetailed with those of the two Russian ambassadors, Kutuzov and Victor Kochubei.

During his brief tenure in Istanbul, Kutuzov had achieved considerable success, preventing a new conflict with the Ottoman Empire and undermining the Sublime Porte's attempts to intervene in the resolution of the Polish 'crisis'.[26] The crisis had resulted from Russia's intervention to overturn Poland's progressive 1791 Constitution, leading to the Second Partition of Poland in 1793 and the weakening of the Polish state.

After Kutuzov, the responsibilities of the Russian mission were carried by an ambitious young diplomat, the twenty-five-year-old Victor Kochubei (1768–1834) who was known to be '[a]lways affable and amiable, with soft manners, polite in address, [and] well versed in the history of political relations in Europe'.[27] He adhered to the same policy as Kutuzov, which was to preserve the Russo-Ottoman peace, especially from French insinuations, as well as to compel the Porte to observe the 1792 Treaty of Jassy.[28]

In a similar vein to Kutuzov and Kochubei, Liston observed that after the removal of Yusuf Paşa as Grand Vizier, the Ottoman ministry was divided into 'two rival parties'. One of these was headed by Yusuf Agha, *kahya* or steward to the mother of Sultan Selim III, Mihrişah Sultan or Valide Sultan (1745–1805, née Agnes). Yusuf Agha was known as 'a man of moderate abilities, hypocritically smooth in his intercourse with his superiors, and overbearing towards those that are below him'. Before his ascent to the throne in 1789, while Selim was living a life of seclusion in the Seraglio as a prince, Yusuf Agha had attended to him. This was considered the foundation of his favour with the sultan, alongside

---

[25] BOA A.DVN.NMH, 45/4.
[26] P.D. Nikolayenko, 'V. P. Kočubei – polnomočnyj ministr Rossii v Turcii', *Vestnik Leningradskogo gosudarstvennogo universiteta im. A. S. Puškina*, 4, no. 4 (2011), 7–18, at 9.
[27] Nikolayenko, 'Kočubei', 11–2; V.I. Kochubei to S.R. Vorontsov, 14 April 1796, *Arkhiv kniazia Vorontsova*, ed. P.I. Bartenev (Moscow: Mamontov, 1880), 18:108, cf. Viktor Taki, *Tsar and Sultan: Russian Encounters with the Ottoman Empire* (London, New York: I.B. Tauris, 2016), 49.
[28] Nikolayenko, 'Kočubei', 11.

his closeness to the Valide Sultan 'to whom the reigning prince looks up with a deference and respect that has no bounds'.[29]

The leader of the opponent party was Küçük Hüseyin Paşa, the grand admiral or the Kapudan Paşa. Originally a slave from the Caucasus, he had risen to prominence at the accession of Selim III, as his favourite valet to the chamber. The two had been friends since childhood, and were now brothers-in-law, as Selim's sister Esma Sultan was married to Hüseyin.[30] According to Liston, Hüseyin's continuance in power was secured primarily by the influence of this marriage and his 'violent and revengeful' character. Hüseyin otherwise possessed little knowledge or experience and relied heavily on the advice of his Vice-Admiral Seyyid Ali, a native of Algiers, 'a man of some abilities in the profession'.[31]

Liston noted that the two factions in the Ottoman ministry were in unison on one point only: the effort 'to curtail the hitherto unlimited powers of the [grand vizier]' and to concentrate the efficient government of the empire in a select council, composed of themselves and their adherents.[32] The newly appointed Grand Vizier Melek Mehmed Paşa (1712–1802) suited the interests of rival parties perfectly. At eighty-two years old, his neutrality 'bended his name to every measure that was adopted by the majority of the council'. For Liston, the most striking figure in the cabinet was Raşid Efendi, the Reis Efendi, or the Ottoman equivalent of foreign secretary. Liston was fond of him: 'Raised himself by merit and length of services', he wrote, Raşid Efendi's knowledge and abilities were so essential that 'it is not imagined any Ottoman ministry could at the present period subsist without his assistance and support'. According to Liston, Raşid steered a 'neutral course between the two parties', prudently avoiding 'to render himself obnoxious to either'.

In his conduct of Ottoman foreign policy, Raşid Efendi received considerable support from George Muruzi (also spelt in foreign correspondence as Murusy, Mourousi, Murusi or Mourouzis), the interpreter of the Sublime Porte. Muruzi was the son of the late prince of Moldavia and the present prince of Wallachia, and was distinguished by his education. He became 'a man of polished manners', great prudence, proficiency in several foreign languages, 'a preserving ambition' and an extensive knowledge of the politics of Europe. 'It is natural,' Liston concluded, 'that he should have much weight and credit with the Ottoman ministry.'[33]

---

[29] Robert Liston to Lord Grenville, 3 July 1794, NLS MS 5572, f. 37.
[30] Liston incorrectly reported that Esma was a cousin of the sultan.
[31] Robert Liston to Lord Grenville, 3 July 1794, NLS MS 5572, f. 37.
[32] Ibid.
[33] Ibid.

According to Liston, neither of these persons was 'so favourable as could be wished to the views of Great Britain'. Raşid had a partiality to the French, which the British ambassador attributed to the Reis Efendi's 'early habits and prejudices', notably his upbringing in the office of his father, a chancery clerk charged with French affairs. The French had paid particular attention to Raşid, recognizing his importance to their interests and showering him with presents.

These connections were carefully maintained by successive French agents in Istanbul, including Marie Louis Henri d'Escorches (1749–1830), also known as Descorches, who had been secretly dispatched to Istanbul in late 1793. Descorches's instructions were to negotiate an alliance (both defensive and offensive) with the Ottoman ministers, along with Sweden and Poland, and secure their 'promise not to conclude a separate peace until the Russians withdrew from the Crimea'.[34]

To repeat, frustrating the Russo-Ottoman peace was of the utmost importance for France. To this end, Descorches pledged to the Porte French support to push Russian forces out of the Crimea. He offered assurances that the French had no desire to revolutionize the sultan's empire.[35] The immediate Ottoman response was not favourable, as the Porte saw the French government as 'not yet sufficiently consolidated'. However, the sultan and his ministers continued to show 'sympathy and generosity' towards Paris. They granted the French regime two loans in late 1793 and early 1794, amounting to a total of 78,000 piasters, which increased to 324,000 piasters through new loans until 1797.[36]

According to Descorches, by January 1794, the 'recognition of the Republic' was in the 'hearts' of the Ottomans: 'It exists de facto, because [the Porte] communicates with me; it is business as usual, as if I had an official character'.[37] He believed that the Ottoman ministers were now in favour of an alliance with France, but were wary that declaring war against Russia and Austria before completing their military preparations would only frustrate their reform programme.

Even though he was ordered to 'focus on an Ottoman attack on Austrian territory only', Descorches explained to Paris the degree of Ottoman indifference towards Austria – 'only Russia is of interest here; this is where all Turkish desires and fears lie'.[38] But the Ottoman ministers were initially uneasy about rushing

---

[34] Firges, *French Revolutionaries*, 48.
[35] Ibid., 49–50.
[36] Ibid., 58.
[37] Ibid., 71.
[38] Ibid., 71.

into an alliance with France before another Great Power did so, ending the Republic's isolation. News of the Terror also gave pause.[39]

In February 1794, Raşid Efendi remarked that Descorches 'should please consider that the Porte is an elephant, which one cannot be forced to run like a hare'.[40] The Porte was looking to postpone any serious talk of an alliance with French agents to first see how the dust would settle in Europe.[41] Even then Descorches made attempts to win over Ottoman ministers to the French cause. For instance, he expended great sums to gain George Muruzi. 'I am mortified to remark', Liston reported, that the partiality of the family of Muruzi appears to be

> founded on a more solid basis than the temporary effect of corruption. They seem to have adopted a system which lead[s] them to consider France as the natural ally and support of this country; and their friendly ideas have been fostered by the perpetual protestations of friendship and the constant marks of deference and facility in the transaction of public business given by the French ministers.[42]

In his conversation with family members in Istanbul and Bucharest, Liston observed that the Muruzis regarded the issue of war in Europe as uncertain. They believed that despite the great victories of the Allied Powers at the onset of the war, these had been counterbalanced by the French in the autumn. They considered it 'wise ... to avoid breaking with [the French] who may possibly in the end establish their power, and who must be accounted sincere in their proffered friendship to this country'.[43]

§   §   §

Liston knew that it was difficult to turn French dominance in Istanbul to his advantage. To this end, he studied the sultan, his character, manners and preferences carefully, hoping to devise a strategy to subdue the French influence. The British ambassador found Selim III to be 'as gracious and attentive' as he could have 'expected from any other sovereign in Europe'. During his first audience, it struck Liston that 'the Sultan did not himself make a return to the compliment I delivered in the Majesty's name, but commanded the answer to

---

[39] Ahmed Cevdet Paşa, *Tarih-i Cevdet III* (Istanbul: Üçdal Neşriyat, 1994), 1564–7.
[40] Firges, *French Revolutionaries*, 72.
[41] Cevdet Paşa, *Tarih-i Cevdet* III, 1566.
[42] Robert Liston to Lord Grenville, 3 July 1794, NLS MS 5572, f. 37.
[43] Ibid.

be pronounced by the Grand Vizier'.[44] To Liston, both the composition of the Ottoman viziers and the general complexion of their measures were highly dependent on the personal inclination and character of the sultan.[45]

Born on 24 December 1761, Selim III had been put into a life of seclusion at the age of thirteen, following the death of his father, according to the 'suspicious policy' of the Ottoman Empire to prevent any palace intrigues to overthrow the sultan. Liston observed that 'some of the chief failures' of the sultan's character could be ascribed to this way of life. Selim had grown up largely in the company of women, male slaves and physicians. The connections and attachments he had formed then had lasting effects. His anxiety to have a perpetual change of scene likely resulted from his frequent removal from one palace to another. His fondness for demolishing, altering and rebuilding, along with his daily pleasure parties on water or horseback were 'carried to a pitch' that met criticism from observers concerned by the economic condition of the Ottoman Empire.[46]

In Liston's interpretation, the amusements and company of the imperial palace had softened the manners of Selim, 'turning his attention to objects of refinement, which had seldom occupied the minds of his predecessors'. Selim developed a taste for European pastimes such as theatrical entertainments and Italian comic performers 'of slender merit'. It was considered an informal duty of the Ottoman sultans to master some handicraft, and Selim chose painting Muslim handkerchiefs, in which he attained a considerable talent. But he showed upon a greater partiality for the fine arts than was considered appropriate by more conservative Muslims. The sultan employed an Italian painter of miniatures, and a number of British paintings adorned the walls of his apartment.

Considered a private man, the sultan was endowed with many good qualities, Liston noted. The British ambassador, who had once referred to the sultan and his family as 'barbarians of the Bosphorus', appeared to have developed a fondness for them. To Liston, the sultan was 'gentle and affable in his manners, dispassionate, generous and possessed of good sense, a clear perception and no despicable share of judgement'. His mother Mihrişah Sultan, originally a Circassian slave, was a woman of fair character and extraordinary talents. Notwithstanding her ostensible adoption of Islam, Liston suspected (and speculated) that she retained a secret attachment to the Christian faith, the religion of her fathers. This had a significant effect in 'liberating the mind of

---

[44] Robert Liston to Lord Grenville, 25 October 1794, NLS MS 5572, f. 86.
[45] Robert Liston to Lord Grenville, 25 November 1794, NLS MS 5572, f. 102.
[46] Ibid.

Selim from ... the common prejudices entertained by the Orthodox Muslims'. Mihrişah's advice respecting the domestic issues of the empire was 'always taken and generally followed' by the sultan.

According to Liston, the male slaves who had been the companions of Selim's youth were not forgotten. They were elevated to the most prominent stations, and maintained in their status until public odium made their removal a matter of prudence. When this happened, their enemies, who had been inciting public demonstrations of discontent, were generally punished with banishment or disgrace. Grand Admiral Hüseyin Paşa could stand his ground against all opposition in part due to 'his liberality, which proves him many friends among the lower classes of the people', and in part due to the 'awful privileges of his office, which empower him in many instances to cut off the heads of those that may happen to displease him without the consent of the sovereign or the forms of law'.

Liston was of the opinion that the sultan's physicians, such as the Italian Lorenzo Noccrola, impressed Selim III's mind 'with an idea of the superiority of the Christian nations in arts, in arms, in finance and of the necessity of improvements and reformation in Turkey, which has given rise to various establishments and attempts at amelioration, that may be attended with important consequences'.[47] These educated men were 'much superior in point of information to the class of Turks' with whom Selim had an opportunity to converse.

This was the order of things in the Ottoman court, in the eyes of the British ambassador: here was an impulsive sultan who had experienced a difficult youth and now admired Western practices, thanks to the influence of his crypto-Christian mother and Christian physicians. As a result, Liston interpreted the Ottoman diplomatic, bureaucratic and military reforms of the time within the (Orientalist) perimeters of Ottoman adoption of European practices, largely as a consequence of the sultan's preferences.

To Liston, Selim III aimed 'to assimilate the Turkish empire to the more polished kingdoms of Europe, particularly in regard to politics'.[48] The sultan sought to have the Sublime Porte assume a rank among 'the polished nations', or to raise the Ottomans 'to a footing of equality' with their rivals in arts and arms.[49] With a few exceptions, Ottoman elites were 'ignorant of the state

---

[47] Ibid.
[48] Robert Liston to Lord Grenville, 10 December 1794, NLS MS 5572, f. 106.
[49] Robert Liston to Sir W. Hamilton, 17 November 1794, NLS MS 5579, f. 45.

of general politics in Europe', but they had become 'sensible of their want of information'. For this reason, they were eager to gather intelligence concerning their comparative strength and reciprocal interests. The sultan began opening permanent diplomatic posts in European capitals.[50]

European engineers, such as the aforementioned Captain Koehler as well as the French François Kauffer, among others, had been employed to repair and improve Ottoman fortifications. European officers had been placed in the service of the sultan to discipline his soldiers and introduce improvements in his navy. Even though some essential steps were made, Liston believed, progress was unequal, with 'innovations in certain cases ill-timed, and the projects injudiciously chosen'.[51] These observations align with those of Kochubei and Kutuzov, who believed that Ottoman reforms would not take root because 'the national prejudices of the Turks, even if weakened, will not tolerate all innovations'.[52]

Liston added that 'it happens unfortunately that those who are most ready to give assistance in Ottoman reforms' were the French. 'Their zeal and activity is [sic] beyond belief and I am sorry to add that their success is too much in proportion.'[53] For the moment he understood that he had little chance of curbing French influence. Despite his efforts to maintain stability in Anglo-Ottoman relations and his careful diplomacy to avoid offending the Ottoman ministers, his success in this regard was limited.

Liston's observations of reform within the Ottoman court were not entirely accurate either. Recent historical scholarship has shown that Selim III's reform programme, widely known as *Nizâm-ı Cedid* or the New Order, was in fact an amalgam of European (especially French) and Islamic (particularly Naqshbandi) networks. It aimed to revive the 'circle of justice' as the underlying political philosophy of the empire.[54] Liston was seemingly unaware of these more complex and diverse dynamics, as well as the religious undertones of reform within the Ottoman Empire. Instead, he believed that 'the diminution of many inveterate prejudices' was linked to the implementation of 'radical reform'.[55] This became a

---

[50] Ibid.
[51] Robert Liston to Lord Grenville, 24 December 1794, NLS MS 5572, f. 113.
[52] Nikolayenko, 'Kočubei', 11–12.
[53] Robert Liston to Sir W. Hamilton, 17 November 1794, NLS MS 5579, f. 45.
[54] Ali Yaycıoğlu, 'Guarding Traditions and Laws – Disciplining Bodies and Souls: Tradition, Religion and Science in the Age of Ottoman Reform', *Modern Asian Studies*, 52, no. 5 (2018), 1542–603. Also see his *Partners of the Empire: The Crisis of the Ottoman Order in the Age of Revolutions* (Stanford, CA: Stanford University Press, 2016).
[55] Robert Liston to Lord Grenville, 24 December 1794, NLS MS 5572, f. 113.

mainstream narrative for historians of the Ottoman Empire for decades, whose analysis remained within the dialectical confines of Ottoman reformists and their opponents.[56]

Liston's assessment of the urgent need for increased revenues was nonetheless accurate, recognizing it as a crucial issue in the unfolding Eastern Question – how to deal with the perceived and relative weakness of the Ottoman Empire and how to address its existential insecurity. To this end, new taxes were levied on several highly productive articles such as brandy, wine, olives, wool, cotton and cattle. There was also an attempt to extend custom tariffs on exports and imports, which had previously been no more than 2 per cent ad valorem. This sparked a quarrel with Russian agents who 'resisted the innovation on the strength of the perpetual tariff' established by previous commercial treaties. As a result, the sultan was forced to put a halt to increasing this important source of income for the time being.[57] Almost immediately, this situation became the recipe for new conflict between the courts of Saint Petersburg and Istanbul.

---

[56] Olivier Bouquet, 'Is It Time to Stop Speaking about Ottoman Modernisation?', in Marc Aymes, Benjamin Gourisse, and Elise Masicard (eds), *Order and Compromise: Government Practices in Turkey from the Late Ottoman Empire to the Early 21st Century* (Leiden: Brill, 2015), 62–3.

[57] Robert Liston to Sir W. Hamilton, 17 November 1794, NLS MS 5579, f. 45.

4

The spirit of treaties

The capitulations

The capitulations – commercial, fiscal and legal privileges granted by Ottoman rulers to European subjects – were a central pillar of the Eastern Question.[1] Initially tools of Ottoman imperial policy, by the mid-eighteenth century, the capitulations had evolved into channels through which European powers exerted dominance over the sultan's empire.[2] This shift is evident in Liston's experiences in Istanbul as well as in the weakening of Ottoman reform efforts due to Russian resistance in the 1790s.

The genesis of the Ottoman capitulations dates back to the fourteenth century, when in 1352 Ottoman elites granted commercial privileges to the Genoese as a means of guaranteeing their support while they were engaged in an epic rivalry with the Venetians in the Mediterranean.[3] From the outset, they were used by Ottoman elites as a leverage to garner support, prevent foreign aggression or pit rival powers against one another. In 1403, during the Ottoman interregnum, privileges were given to Venetian, Byzantine and Rhodian knights to ensure they did not threaten the security of Ottoman dominions. These were followed by new treaties in 1419 and 1446.[4] Mehmed II (the Conqueror) granted capitulations to the Genoese community of Galata immediately after the conquest of Istanbul in 1453.[5]

---

[1] Ozavci, *Dangerous Gifts*, 330–1.
[2] Maurits van den Boogert, *The Capitulations and the Ottoman Legal System: Qadis, Consuls and Beratlis in the Eighteenth Century* (Leiden: Brill, 2005), 7; Kate Fleet, *European and Islamic Trade in the Early Ottoman State: The Merchants of Genoa and Turkey* (Cambridge: Cambridge University Press, 1999).
[3] Halil İnalcık, 'İmtiyazat: Osmanlı Dönemi. Kapitülasyonların Karakter ve Mahiyeti', *Türkiye Diyanet Vakfı İslam Ansiklopedisi* 2000, 245–52, 247, online access, 24 January 2023.
[4] Ibid., 247.
[5] Boogert, *Capitulations*, 7.

In 1569, the Ottomans signed their first capitulatory agreement with a major European power, France. Ottoman historian Halil İnalcık describes this as the first 'real Ottoman capitulatory treaty' due to its bilateral nature. The Franco-Ottoman agreement was followed by a treaty with England (1580), which was renewed twice in the seventeenth century (1601, 1675) so as to recognize England as 'most favoured nation'.[6] English merchants paid 3 per cent tariffs in Ottoman customs while other nations' merchants were paying 5 per cent, sparking jealousy among the powers as well as fierce competition between their merchants and diplomats to obtain greater privileges from the sultan.[7]

In the seventeenth century, the major European powers developed their interpretation of consular status under the capitulatory agreements to include (partial) immunity from Ottoman law.[8] The capitulatory agreement with France was renewed (1673) to give France the right to protect under its flag subjects of other Europeans powers who did not enjoy capitulatory privileges.[9] England received the same right in 1675. Five years later the Dutch joined the Ottoman capitulatory system.[10]

İnalcık argues that a new era in the history of the capitulations began with the advent of the Great Turkish War in 1683. The threat posed by European alliances after 1683 led Ottoman elites to introduce new privileges to European subjects in return for political support. For example, a 1690 *hatt-ı şerif*[11] reduced Egyptian customs tariffs from 10 per cent to 3 per cent for French merchants.[12] When France made peace with the Habsburgs in 1697, new privileges were granted, this time to the English subjects. These included priority in sea trade between Egypt and Istanbul, and the opening of an English consulate in Alexandria.

The eighteenth century saw a brisk increase in the number of European powers – the Habsburgs (1718), Sweden (1737), Denmark (1746), Tuscany (1747), Prussia (1761), Russia (1774) and Spain (1782) – that acquired capitulatory privileges for their subjects.[13] The Ottoman rapprochement with

---

[6] V.L. Ménage, 'The English Capitulation of 1580: A Review Article', *International Journal of Middle East Studies* 12, no. 2 (1980), 373–83.
[7] İnalcık, 'İmtiyazat', 249.
[8] Ibid., 246.
[9] James B. Angell, 'The Turkish Capitulations', *The American Historical Review*, 6, no. 2 (January, 1901), 254–59, there at 256.
[10] Salahi R. Sonyel, 'Protégé System in the Ottoman Empire and Its Abuses', *Belleten*, 55, no. 214, (December 1991), 675–86, there at 675.
[11] An imperial edict or decree issued by the Ottoman sultan.
[12] İnalcık, 'İmtiyazat', 249.
[13] Boogert, *Capitulations*, 7; Reşad Ekrem, *Osmanlı muahedeleri ve kapitülasyonlar 1300-1920* (Istanbul: Muallim Ahmet Halit Kitaphanesi, 1934).

France between 1716 and 1740 and the role the French agents played as mediator during the 1739 Russo-Ottoman peace negotiations gained France the status of 'most favoured nation' the following year.[14] These coincided with the shifting of the balance of military, economic, technological and political powers in favour of the western and northern neighbours of the Ottoman Empire.

A major yet often overlooked moment in the history of the capitulations was the aforementioned 1783 Russo-Ottoman commercial treaty. This agreement, following the precedents set by the 1774 Küçük Kaynarca Treaty and the 1779 Aynalıkavak Convention, represented a significant concession by the Sublime Porte. The Ottomans granted Russia extensive privileges, including the reduction and stabilization of customs tariffs, the freedom to establish consulates in Ottoman territories 'wherever she may desire', and 'perfect freedom of navigation and commerce' in 'all the Ottoman territories and waters without restriction'. Moreover, Russia was granted 'perfect freedom of ... passage up and down the Bosphorus and Dardanelles', effectively elevating her to the status of a 'most favoured nation' within the Ottoman Empire – a status that ignited protests from Britain and France.[15] This development signalled a fierce legal-commercial rivalry within Ottoman dominions that had reached a critical juncture by the late eighteenth century, setting the stage for the strategic competition that would shortly unfold with the Russian occupation of the Crimea and the French invasion of Egypt.

§ § §

Eleven years after the 1783 treaty, differences arising from clashing interpretations became central to Russo-Ottoman diplomatic disputes. On 25 June 1794, Robert Liston reported that the discord between Russia and the Ottoman Empire would 'likely soon lead to a crisis'.[16] Despite the 1774, 1779 and 1783 settlements, their incomplete or flawed implementation, along with their detrimental effects on the Ottoman economy, had engendered new apprehensions.

According to the 1783 Treaty of Commerce, Russian subjects in the Ottoman Empire were to pay no more than 3 per cent on imported or exported merchandise.

---

[14] İnalcık, 'İmtiyazat', 249.
[15] 'Abstract of Articles of Treaties, between Russia and Turkey, 1774–1849', TNA FO 881/280, 5–6; Faruk Bilici, *La politique française en mer noire, 1747–1789* (Istanbul: Les Éditions, 1992), 99, 106–7.
[16] Robert Liston to Lord Grenville, 25 June 1794, NLS MS 5572, f. 12; Robert Liston to Lord Grenville, 29 June 1794, NLS MS 5572, f. 15.

This tariff had been designed to prevent disputes over the value of goods and would 'forever serve as a rule for the Russian merchants and the Turkish officers of the Customs'. However, after 1783, the prices of the merchandise specified in the treaty had rapidly increased. Since the prices on the treaty were fixed, Russian merchants were effectively paying less than 2 per cent, 'in many cases not one, and in some not above 1.5% for the different articles of their trade'. This was why the Ottoman government, in urgent need of funds for their ongoing reform programme, proposed a new tariff they believed to be more adapted to the times.

In fact, this demand was not unique to Russia. Frequent difficulties also arose between Ottoman customs officers and merchants of other nationalities, including the British.[17] Unlike the 1783 Russo-Ottoman treaty, in the case of Anglo-Ottoman trade only five articles of importation (cloth, kersey, coney skins, tin and lead) and half a dozen articles of exportation (cotton, yarn, silk, galls and certain species of Ottoman manufactures) formed the catalogue. It became necessary to expand the tariff due to the growth of trade and the implementation of a 3 per cent tariff in kind.

As with the Russians, price increases made the terms of trade more favourable to the British. 'None of the articles specified pay 3%, many not 2 and some not even 1% on a fair evaluation,' Liston noted.[18] Various additions to the existing agreements had been made between Ottoman revenue officers and merchants on an individual basis for up to 400 articles. However, these agreements, largely favourable to the traders, were never formally confirmed by the Ottoman sultans. In other words, no formal addition had been made to British 'privileges since the year 1645 nor have the tariffs acquired stability by any formal act of the Ottoman government'.[19] The tariffs had been set at a local level by customs officers, 'sometimes for the continuance of their lease ..., sometimes for the share of a year, sometimes for a season, or for the entry of the foods to be brought by the next expected ships'.[20] The officers did not consider themselves obligated to renew or formalize the agreements, and new customers did not feel bound by the commitments of their predecessors.

In early 1793, the Ottoman ministry proposed a plan to improve public revenue through a comprehensive reform in the customhouse duties. The Dutch, Venetians, French, and conditionally the British (represented by Robert

---

[17] Robert Liston to Lord Grenville, 25 October 1794, NLS MS 5572, f. 82.
[18] Ibid.
[19] Ibid.
[20] Ibid.

Ainslie) consented to increase tariffs up to 3 per cent ad valorem. However, it took just one nation to oppose it for the entire scheme to derail. In 1793–4, that opposition came from Saint Petersburg.

Empress Catherine II considered the changes in the proposed tariff 'contrary to the [1783] treaty'. She requested a formal written declaration from the Porte to desist from any tariff reforms, described as 'incompatible with the continuance of friendship and harmony between the two courts'. When a conference was held on 26 June 1794 between Russian envoy Kochubei and Ottoman Reis Efendi, the latter offered reassurance that 'though the Porte regarded the proposed change of the Tariff as perfectly founded in justice', it would not proceed without 'mutual consent'. Without Russia's full consent, the only path forward was 'that of persuasion' and 'friendly negotiation'. The Porte expressed 'such confidence in the justice and equity of Her Imperial Majesty that they would refer the whole to her own decision'. Raşid concluded by noting that until a unanimous agreement was reached 'the old tariff shall remain instructed'.

Kochubei insisted that the Porte declare unconditionally and explicitly that 'the Tariff should be observed as long as the Treaty [of 1783] itself subsisted'.[21] He reminded Raşid of the second and twenty-first articles of the treaty, stressing that the empress's reply was 'decisive'. According to Article 2, the contracting parties were to maintain the treaty 'as religiously as inviolably and to execute it with good faith and exactness'. Article 21 stipulated that the tariff would 'serve forever as a rule for Russian merchants and customs officers in the Ottoman dominions'. The word 'forever' endowed the tariff a perpetual term, he underscored, 'as long as peace and good harmony' between Russia and the Ottoman Empire existed.

Raşid acknowledged that the customs duties to which respective merchants were subject by virtue of commercial treaties always had as their sole object 'not the collection of a duty lower than the established customs duty, but the estimation of the merchants with the mutual consent of the Parties'. For this reason, it was natural to conclude that the article of the 1783 treaty on the formation of the tariff and 3 per cent customs duty, 'as in several articles of the imperial capitulations', could have 'no other purpose, as far as their execution is concerned, than that of reel and 3% duty'.[22]

The 1783 tariff had been drawn up with the consent of the parties, not with the assumption that Russian merchants could eventually pay only 1 per cent

---

[21] Robert Liston to Lord Grenville, 29 June 1794, NLS MS 5572, f. 15.
[22] 'Traduction d'une lettre amicale & confidentielle de S.E. Rashid Effendi', 3 Janvier 1794[?], NLS MS 5572, f. 24.

or less customs duty. This was why the stipulations of the treaty needed to be repaired to ensure that the tariffs were fixed at 3 per cent 'and no more or no less' in accordance with 'the text and the spirit of the treaties'.[23] It would ensure that Russian merchants were treated on the same footing as merchants from other nations, especially Britain and France. Treating the words 'forever' and 'perpetual' as unquestionable terms would undermine equity and transparency, deviating from the treaty's original intent. Raşid continued:

> [I]f on both sides ... they were to become entangled in ways of [misinterpretations], it would happen that in several of the articles, either the imperial capitulations or the treaty of commerce, attention would be paid only to the terms, that in the apparent absence of [explanatory] phrases, they would stray from the spirit of the treaties and without having the appearance of drawing attention to the true meaning of the words, they would allow themselves less praiseworthy steps which would do infinite harm to commerce.[24]

When it became clear to Kochubei that he would not be able to prevail with the Ottoman minister at the meeting, he decided to refer the issue to St Petersburg.[25]

In the meanwhile, Raşid Efendi sought to secure British support for the Ottoman cause and, in a private audience, asked Liston his 'honest opinion'. Raşid was concerned that the question of the tariff was only 'a pretext to pick a quarrel with a view to war'.[26] He noted that the Porte was not ready for war, but warned that if concessions were made on this issue, another matter could soon be used to provoke conflict.

Liston's advice was possibly contrary to what Raşid had hoped. This was a typical example of how the British ambassador sought to pacify and allay tensions, acknowledging the grievances of both parties, while prioritizing Britain's best interests. He had received instruction from British foreign secretary Lord Grenville (William Wyndham Grenville, 1759–1834) to act in Istanbul in accordance with 'the general state of affairs in Europe' where Grenville felt Russia and Britain ought to join forces against France. Liston feared that in the event of an Ottoman refusal, Catherine II might order her troops immediately to enter Moldavia and Wallachia, and control the north of the Danube within weeks.[27]

---

[23] Ibid.
[24] Ibid.
[25] Robert Liston to Lord Grenville, 1 July 1794, NLS MS 5572, f. 20.
[26] Robert Liston to Lord Grenville, 2 July 1794, NLS MS 5572, f. 34.
[27] Ibid.

Although the empress planned no such action at the time, his fears had left Liston 'no room to hesitate'. He made it clear to Raşid that 'the Porte ought to return an affirmative answer to the question put by the Empress'. It had to have 'the appearance of yielding without reluctance, and as much as possible with good grace'.[28] What Ottoman ministers were asking 'might be founded in equity' but it could not be demanded 'as a right' because it was 'contrary to the express terms of [the 1783 Treaty]'. This was merely 'a matter of favour'.[29]

Liston granted that this issue could be used by Russia as a pretext for war and 'if removed it would be succeeded by another and another still'. Nonetheless, he urged the Porte to exercise moderation, because, unprepared for hostilities, it would 'at all events be a gainer by putting off the evil day'.[30] He stressed that 'it was even of importance that, if [the Ottomans] were to be attacked, it should be upon a pretence, which in the eyes of all Europe should be totally ill-founded, and unjust', which was not the case in the current Russo-Ottoman dispute. Raşid Efendi thanked Liston for his 'frankness' and assured him that he would take Liston's advice 'into deep consideration'.[31]

Soon after, an Ottoman imperial council gathered and resolved to accept Russian demands. Kochubei reported in early July 1794 that the Ottomans were still 'not ready for war', and that 'affairs with the Ottoman Porte [were settled] with the desired success and encouraging continuation of peace with it'.[32] The court of Saint Petersburg never sent any explicit reply on the subject. In the next two years, the trade volume between Russia and Turkey dramatically increased from 1,344,376 rubles (1794) to 2,168,126 rubles (1796).[33]

Since the Porte had withdrawn its proposal in Russia's case, Liston aimed to obtain a similar exemption for British merchants, in conformity to the capitulatory agreements that stipulated 'we shall enjoy all the privileges granted to the most favoured nations'. To avoid hostility, the Ottoman ministers complied with this request, granting the Anglo-Ottoman tariffs 'a degree of stability', Liston wrote. However, as we shall see, the poor implementation of these tariffs by Ottoman customs officers led to new difficulties in the following years.[34]

---

[28] Ibid.
[29] Ibid.
[30] Ibid.
[31] Ibid.
[32] Nikolayenko, 'Kočubei', 12.
[33] Ibid., 14.
[34] Robert Liston to Lord Grenville, 25 October 1794, NLS MS 5572, f. 82.

Selling security

The increasingly unequal nature of the capitulatory and commercial treaties was also exposed by the degeneration of the *berat* system, a long-standing but perilous component of Ottoman legal pluralism, increasingly abused by the European powers.[35] The licences, warrants, charters and patents known as *berats* (occasionally spelled *barat* in English) – originally introduced with the establishment of foreign missions in Istanbul – were meant to authorize non-Muslim native subjects of the Ottoman Empire (mainly Armenian, Greek and Jewish) to serve friendly Christian powers as interpreters.[36] However, over time, the *berat* system devolved into an exploitative scheme that severely undermined Ottoman economy, finances, security and even sovereignty.

Berats conferred upon the interpreters, known also by the title of dragoman (from the Arabic word *tarjuman*), a range of legal and fiscal privileges. These included immunities such as exemptions from Ottoman poll (*haraç*), extraordinary (*avarız*), butchery (*kassabiye*) and non-canonical (*tekalif-i örfiyye*) taxes, as well as the payment of a customs tariff of just 3 per cent (often even less in practice), while other natives were paying 10 per cent in 1794. Holders of *berats* were not subject to Ottoman jurisdiction. Their legal affairs fell under the consular jurisdiction of foreign authorities in a similar manner to European subjects with extraterritorial rights.[37] Ottoman legal officers had no authority in family affairs, even after death. Furthermore, unlike other non-Muslim subjects of the empire, *berat*-holders faced no restrictions in their dress, whereas tributary imperial subjects were confined to plain clothes in darker colours.[38]

Berats were granted by the Ottoman government to ambassadors of foreign powers and renewed with each new ambassador.[39] These were offered on the basis of good faith through *ahdnames*, in return for ambassadorial pledges to maintain peaceful relations with the empire. If this pledge was violated, it could result in a unilateral annulment of the *berats*.[40] Otherwise, the *berats* were conferred for life, and unless the holder was guilty of forfeiture or serious misconduct, he could not be stripped of it.

---

[35] Cihan Artunç, 'The Price of Legal Institutions: The Beratlı Merchants in the Eighteenth-Century Ottoman Empire', *The Journal of Economic History*, 75, no. 3 (September, 2015), 720–48, at 722.
[36] Boogert, *Capitulations*, 8.
[37] Artunç, 'Beratlı', 725.
[38] Liston to the R.W. Levant Company, 25 February 1795, MS 5581, f. 28.
[39] Sonyel, 'Protégé System', 675.
[40] Boogert, *Capitulations*, 7; Feroz Ahmad, 'Ottoman Perceptions of the Capitulations, 1800–1914', *Journal of Islamic Studies*, 11, no. 1 (January, 2000), 1–20, there at 2.

Over time, the *berat*s became a mechanism for economic benefit and security for their holders, a great majority of whom did not actually serve as dragomans and, in fact, could not even read their patent. Although these patents were originally granted by the sultan for a limited number of dragomans and their two servants (thirty to forty per state, with certain exceptions such as France, which was granted fifty *berat*s in the early eighteenth century[41]), they eventually came to be sold to thousands of Armenian, Greek and Jewish subjects of the empire.

The corruption of the *berat* system coincided with the evolving nature of the relationship between Ottoman Empire and her European neighbours in the eighteenth century, and especially during the reign of Mustafa III (r. 1757–71). As the *berat*-holders were unable to fulfil the numerous duties of their office, each *berat* came to be accompanied by two *ferman*s for two servants (*nefer*s) assigned to each interpreter.[42] These servants quickly sold their *ferman*s, with all their associated privileges, to wealthy companies and affluent non-Muslim subjects who benefitted from foreign protection in expanding their business. The *berat*-holders themselves became increasingly disinterested in diplomatic affairs and turned to commercial activity, evading taxes and enjoying low customs tariffs. They quickly amassed fortunes. Upon the death of a *berat*-holder, the *berat*s and *ferman*s reverted to the ambassador, who freely disposed of them in the interests of their nation, if not their own.[43]

At the time of Liston's arrival, British *berat*s were sold at the usual price of 2,000 to 6,000 piasters, and *firman*s ranged from 400 to 800 piasters, although Russian *berat*s could cost as much as 10,000 piasters.[44] British embassy profits from the sale of *berat*s vacated by death now stood at around 12,000 piasters annually, compared to between 2,000 and 3,000 piasters at the start of the century. The selling of *berat*s and *firman*s thus became a lucrative business for foreign ambassadors and their subalterns, generating significant revenue, amounting to a £3,000 annual income for the British embassy in the late eighteenth century, which equalled the combined sum received from the Levant Company and the British government.[45] Aside from receiving £3 a day from the British

---

[41] Francis Rey, *La Protection diplomatique et consulaire dans les échelles du levant et de barbarie, avec des documents inédits tires des archives du ministère des affaires étrangeres* (Paris: L. Larose, 1899), 259.
[42] 'Report on Barats', 24 April 1806, NLS MS 5626, f. 81.
[43] Rey, *La Protection*, 260–2.
[44] Robert Liston to A. Hayes, 21 May 1794, NLS MS 5579, f. 39.
[45] At the death of a sultan, the patents had to be renewed for a cost of 500 piasters. The Levant Company was an English chartered trading company established in 1581 to regulate trade with the Ottoman Empire and the Eastern Mediterranean. It played a key role in fostering diplomatic and commercial relations between England and the Ottoman territories until it was abolished in 1825.

government, Liston embassy's entire income had consisted of what he was paid by the company, which amounted to £2,000 per annum.

It was widely agreed among the historical actors that the *berat* system was corrupted. But it was seen not simply a matter of voracious appetites for fiscal and economic gain. It also reflected the lingering security gap in the Ottoman Empire, where non-Muslim subjects of the sultan lacked equal security in their daily lives due to the limitations imposed on those of other faiths. Liston argued that it was natural for 'a patent, which raised a tributary subject from a state of degradation and procured respect to his person, security to his property and the patronage of an Ambassador should soon become an object of ambition'.[46]

Thanks to new capitulatory agreements and to the arrival at the Porte of new ambassadors the unlimited sale of *berats* became both an economic and a major security problem for the empire. The Ottoman administration had 'not only experienced the inconvenience, but felt the danger of the extension of foreign influence among the opulent and native part of the Christian subjects'.[47]

Here the rivalry with Russia and the fear that the Russians could excite the Greek subjects of the Porte to insurrection, as had occurred during the 1768–74 war, were pivotal concerns. In the 1780s, Russian and Austrian consuls distributed patents of protection to anyone who requested them in the Danubian Principalities without charging any fees.[48] Most of their new protégés were people of little income, but they took advantage of their privileged position to avoid taxes and the application of Ottoman law, thus undermining the authority of the local princes (*hospodars*). By the end of the eighteenth century, Austria had more than 200,000 protégés in Moldavia alone, while in Wallachia there were 60,000 patent holders.[49] At the turn of the nineteenth century, more than a 100,000 Greeks possessed Russian *berats*. The system created informal ties of subjecthood, prompting a vicious cycle of inequalities, jealousy, antagonisms, revolutionary sentiments and imperial violence.

At the same time, Ottoman finances suffered a substantial drop in tax revenues. To prevent such irregularities, following the 1774 Küçük Kaynarca Treaty, Ottoman authorities sent circulars to all foreign ministers, explaining the specific purpose of the *berats* and objecting to their being granted to

---

[46] Robert Liston to Levant Company, 25 February 1795, NLS MS 5581, f. 28.
[47] Robert Liston to Chamaud, 18 October 1794, NLS MS 5580, f. 11.
[48] Rey, *La Protection*, 264.
[49] Ibid.

tradesmen and shopkeepers. In a 1784 petition, they set out the grievances of the Principalities, arguing that the consuls of Russia and Austria, 'taking under their protection all those who seek to evade the obedience of the princes, cause the latter to lose all authority in the country'.[50] Ottoman representatives reminded that *berat* holders were meant to serve only as dragomans and reside at the embassy or consulate. However, these protests failed to change behaviour. For their part, Ottoman rulers, caught in a violent stream of fighting with Russia and Austria and frail reform attempts, barely enforced these restrictions. *Berat*-holders and foreign missions easily dodged their demands.

The one exception was the post-revolutionary French. In contrast to the embassies of Vergennes and M. de Choiseul-Gouffier, in 1792 the provisional Executive Council in Paris banned Sémonville and Descorches from engaging in this 'sordid traffic', maintaining that it could not be 'reconciled with the delicacy and noble disinterestedness of a republican minister'.[51] This stance was one of many reasons for Ottoman authorities to show sympathy towards the republican agents, despite it being no secret that Sultan Selim III and his ministers condemned the revolutionary violence and the execution of Louis XVI.

In late 1793, the sultan resolved to end the abuses of the *berat* system. He ordered all foreign ambassadors who sold *berats* not to appoint more interpreters and servants than were actually needed, and retroactively cancelled the *berats* of individuals not serving the embassies and consulates.[52] *Berats* were to be granted only to those actively exercising the office and residing in the location where the consulate or embassy was established.

This development had occurred only months before Liston's arrival in Istanbul, placing the new British ambassador in a moral and fiscal dilemma. On one hand, he believed that the *berat* system was a 'system of abuse'. '[W]e must be candid enough to acknowledge that the Porte is justified in their attempt to introduce a radical reform,' he wrote, '[which] would have been adopted much earlier by any of the great powers in Europe.'[53] However, on the other hand, he felt that 'the manner in which the [Ottoman] reform has been undertaken' lacked 'moderation'. He viewed the reform's retroactive nature as 'improper and unjust' for those who were already in possession of the privileges in question.

---

[50] Ibid., 265.
[51] Ibid., 272–3.
[52] Stanford Shaw, *Between Old and New: The Ottoman Empire under Sultan Selim III, 1789–1807* (Cambridge: MA: Harvard University Press, 1971), 178.
[53] Robert Liston to Wilkinson, 7 October 1794, NLS MS 5580, f. 1.

Liston therefore joined the other ambassadors in resisting the new regulations by sending remonstrances to the Porte.[54] He wrote to 'the merchants of England trading into the Levant Seas' that '[it] is with great regret … that I have arrived in the Levant at a moment … when the Ottoman government appears to have adopted and to have made considerable progress in a system tending to abrogate or abridge the privileges of the European nations'.[55] He assured them that he would strive 'to preserve the rights of those persons whose Barats or Firmans contain no abuses of a restrictive nature'.[56]

To Liston, the matter was as much about ensuring the security of those 'to whom the patronage of the British Embassy might still be of advantage' as it was about protecting the rights of British subjects and protégés. He maintained that the current protégés might be individuals with no interest in the privileges of trade but who felt it necessary 'to secure the enjoyment of property already in their possession'. They might wish to shield themselves and their families 'from insults, avoid the extortion of an overbearing neighbour, elude the jurisdiction of an oppressive magistrate, and prevent interference from Turkish officers of justice in matters of their succession'.[57]

Yet, Liston's dilemma lingered. In a private letter, he confessed that the whole *berat* system was 'hardly compatible with the independence and dignity of character which ought to be maintained by an Ambassador'. He considered the entire system 'a subterfuge', and selling *berat*s nonetheless meant 'the support of falsehood'. He felt 'an invincible repugnance to condescend to have recourse to these expedients', wishing that 'the British protection should be sought after, not offered' and that, 'if at any time the British protection is to be stretched out, to shelter virtue or innocence from oppression, surely regard ought to be had rather to the merit than to the wealth of the solicitors'. With these considerations in view, he did not sell any *berat* after his arrival even though several were vacant.[58] He persisted with this policy until the conclusion of his first posting in Istanbul.

---

[54] Ibid.
[55] Robert Liston to the Merchants of England trading into the Levant Seas, 10 October 1794, NLS MS 5580, f. 3.
[56] Ibid.
[57] Robert Liston to Chamaud, 18 October 1794, NLS MS 5580, f. 11.
[58] Ibid.

Liston did this despite his embassy's urgent need for ready money. He was torn between his conscience and interests. As the embassy's income fell dramatically with the pause in the sale of *berats*, he requested an increase in his salary from the British government and the Levant Company 'to persevere in this conduct'.[59] Liston complained to Andrew Dalzel that he was 'strongly disappointed in this place. I continue to find a great deal of business and very little money.'[60] The Levant Company did agree to a fourth annual payment of £1,000.[61]

However, his request for a salary increase was denied by Lord Grenville 'due to the increased expense brought upon … by the present situation [of war]'.[62] As a matter of fact, during the last months of his first embassy, Liston did not even receive his ordinary wages from the government. He then filed a request to return to Britain and was granted permission.[63]

Despite Liston's insistence on not selling *berats*, the situation ultimately resulted in another debacle for the Ottoman government. The *berat* holders devised methods to undermine Ottoman regulations such as conducting trade in the names of other people.[64] Just as Liston stopped issuing new *berats*, the French reinstated the right to issue them, as the Republic's precarious financial state compelled the Paris government to seek new sources for Les Échelles du Levant.[65] The *berat* system persisted into the following decades.[66] As we will see in the next chapter, it would become one of the causes for the outbreak of the first Russo-Ottoman War in the nineteenth century.

The Mykonos affair

On 17 June 1794, a British Royal Navy squadron led by Captain William Paget's *HMS Romney* engaged in an exchange of broadsides with the French frigate *Sybylle*, then at anchor off the island of Mykonos. The action began at one o'clock

---

[59] Liston to R.W. Levant Company, 25 February 1795, NLS MS 5581, f. 28.
[60] Robert Liston to Andrew Dalzel, 25 September 1794, NLS MS 5579, f. 234.
[61] Christine Laidlaw, *The British in the Levant: Trade and Perception of the Ottoman Empire in the Eighteenth Century* (London, New York: I.B. Tauris, 2020), 37.
[62] Lord Grenville to Robert Liston, 30 June 1795, NLS MS 5572, f. 176.
[63] Lord Grenville to Robert Liston, 4 August 1795, NLS MS 5572, f. 178.
[64] Liston to R.W. Levant Company, 25 February 1795, NLS MS 5581, f. 28.
[65] Rey, *La Protection*, 273.
[66] Ozavci, *Dangerous Gifts*, 293.

in the afternoon and lasted until ten past two, resulting in heavy damage to both ships and significant fatalities. On the British side, at least eight men were killed and twenty-five wounded. The French fared much worse, with more than fifty French sailors died and over a hundred were injured. French survivors attempted to swim to shore, and those who made land fled into the mountains to escape any British landing party.[67]

The British captured the *Sybylle* along with three French merchant ships she was escorting. They detained the fleeing French sailors on the island. According to observers, those under detention were well cared for, with bread, meat, cheese and wine provided by the British commander. The French ships were then sent to Smyrna (Izmir).[68]

What might appear to be merely a minor naval engagement during the War of the First Coalition, known as the Mykonos affair, was yet another example of the clash of empires in the realm of international law. For Liston, it became one of the main issues of British disagreement with the Porte in his first embassy. This was not just because the island of Mykonos was an Ottoman dominion. It was in a neutral zone, and the islanders had suffered damage from the guns of *HMS Romney*. However, the British authorities were unwilling to pay any compensation.

A few weeks after the event, while the Ottoman ambassador to London, Yusuf Agah Efendi, commenced talks with Lord Grenville in Britain, Liston received a letter from Ottoman Reis Efendi Raşid 'couched in forcible terms'.[70] Raşid

Table 1 Greek losses during the Mykonos affair,[69] NLS MS 5579

List containing the particulars of the damage done by the guns of the English (Translated from the Greek – damage estimated by the architects)	
Chapel belonging to Petraki Gatti near the Garden of Conte	260 piasters
Magazine of Nicolo Reisi Solomu near Petraki Gatti's chapel	115 piasters
House of Yorghi Corozuca	3 piasters
House of Mrs Mavroceny	3 piasters
Garden of Marcaki de Suda	6 piasters
Total	387 piasters

[67] 'Literal Translation of a letter written in Greek by the Community of Micone to the Dragoman of the Captain Pasha', NLS MS 5579, f. 97; BOA HAT 193/9541.
[68] BOA HAT 196/9647.
[69] NLS MS 5579, f. 97.
[70] BOA HAT 265/15348.

complained of the breach of the laws of neutrality in the capture of the French frigate and the merchants, requesting punishment for Captain Paget.[71] 'The ships of belligerent Powers', he reminded Liston, 'should not fight or commit hostilities under the cannon of the fortresses of the Ottoman Empire, in the ports, in the roads or within the distance of three miles from the coasts thereof'. 'When ships of the belligerent Powers met in the same port, the weakest should sail the first and the one of greater force not till 24 hours after,' he added. 'The French frigate had found a ship in the port of Miconi [sic], but abstained from molesting her on account of regulations. But the British commander paid no attention to these regulations.' Since many houses, dwellings and churches had been ruined in the island, and many cattle destroyed, the Reis Efendi demanded restitution from the court of Britain for the damage suffered by the islanders 'without fail' and 'speedily'.[72]

At the time Liston received the Reis Efendi's remonstrances he was preoccupied with the everyday repercussions of an ongoing inter-imperial war in a neutral territory. When the *Sybylle* and the captured French merchant vessels arrived in Izmir, their British crews were insulted by French seamen already in port. 'The French republicans, these desperate men', Liston reported to Lord Grenville, had carried matters 'so far as to provide a stack of arms and to amass large quantities of combustible matter'. They were planning to set fire to the street which was occupied by 'the Franks that they may with greater facility plunder the counting houses and murder the families of the British merchants, and the subjects of the other Powers engaged in war with France'. They were holding daily meetings to undertake these measures, binding themselves by 'an oath not to disclose the particular of the atrocious plan'.[73]

As a result, Liston ordered a squadron under the command of Captain Montgomery to anchor at Izmir, 'to keep the bandits in awe and to defend the persons and property of the merchants'.[74] He also appealed to the Porte to ensure peace in the city and requested that a considerable force be sent from the neighbouring districts. Thanks to the arrival of Ottoman forces no major violence occurred in Izmir.[75] Yet the British government remained silent regarding the Ottoman demand for restitution for Mykonos.

---

[71] Robert Liston to Lord Grenville, 1 July 1794, NLS MS 5572, f. 20.
[72] Cypher of the Reis Efendi, 20 July 1794, NLS MS 5572, f. 48.
[73] Robert Liston to Lord Grenville, 10 July 1794, NLS MS 5572, f. 46.
[74] Robert Liston to Lord Grenville, 25 July 1794, NLS MS 5572, f. 47.
[75] BOA HAT 196/9784.

The Sublime Porte dispatched a new protest ten months later when the British captured another French ship near Karaburun.[76] In the meantime, Lord Grenville's response had arrived in Istanbul.[77] The British foreign secretary instructed Liston to assure the Ottoman government that Britain would show proper attention and respect for the neutrality of the Porte. But Grenville refused to pay any restitution:

> It is by no means an established principle or rule in the Law of Nations where vessels or other goods are taken or hostilities committed within the territorial jurisdiction of a neutral power, that Power is obliged to procure to the suffered a restitution of what he has lost if the thing taken is no longer within the neutral jurisdiction.

As France and the Ottoman Empire were negotiating an alliance at the time, there was 'no necessity' for the Porte to demand compensation. The action had caused 'no damage to the subjects of the Porte', and 'a full satisfaction' would be rendered by 'the excuses which [Robert Liston] has been allowed to make in the King's name for what is past'. As precedent, Grenville noted that after an incident off Cape Lagos (a Portuguese territory), in which Admiral Boscawen's fleet had destroyed enemy ships, 'no more was required by the Court of Lisbon than … proper excuses … for the violation of their territory'.[78] Britain dismissed the demands of the Greek islanders in Mykonos.

Was Grenville in the right? Did the law of neutrality as an institution of positive general international law indeed not necessitate restitution because the neutrality of the Porte was in doubt? According to late-eighteenth-century doctrine, in a war in which the identity of the just side was uncertain, neutral powers were expected to maintain 'an attitude of impartiality and treat both belligerents equally'.[79] According to Grenville, the event in Mykonos 'never could have happened if the officers of the Sublime Porte had been vigilant and punctual as their duty required in executing the orders of their government respective the observance of the neutrality', while also claiming that the French had previously broken laws of neutrality.

Grenville was alluding to the fact that, since the outbreak of the war, the French had used Ottoman ports to repair their ships, auctioned off captured vessels and more than once seized neutral vessels. '[W]henever the Porte shall

---

[76] 'Memorial sent by the Ottoman Porte to R. Liston', 5 May 1795, NLS MS 5573, f. 87.
[77] Lord Grenville to Robert Liston, 12 June 1795, NLS MS 5572, f. 171.
[78] Ibid. 171.
[79] Efraim Karsh, *Neutrality and Small States* (London: Routledge, 2011), 15.

cause its neutrality to be respected by the French, His Majesty's Government will according to the uniform tenor of their instructions observe it in the most exact and scrupulous manner.'[80]

The quandary here lay in the fact that, despite the Ottoman support for the French, the Porte had been identified as a neutral power by Britain at the time of the Mykonos affair. According to the legal doctrine of the time, belligerent powers were obliged not to damage in any way the territory or property of a party they considered to be neutral.[81] British historian Allan Cunningham describes Grenville's response to the Ottoman ministers as 'a shameful evasion'.[82] Despite repeated Ottoman protests in the following years, a restitution payment was never made. In 1799, when Britain came to the aid of the Ottoman Empire after the French invasion of the Ottoman Egypt, the two powers became allies, and the subject was permanently dropped from their diplomatic agenda.

§ § §

As early as 1795 Liston had requested his return to Britain after his many frustrations in the Ottoman imperial capital: the success of French agents in gaining the favour of the Porte, his attempts to defend the spurious (in his eyes, at least) rights of the *berat* holders and the financial difficulties his embassy suffered after his refusal to sell *berat*s. He closely monitored the Franco-Ottoman negotiations for an alliance, which ultimately did not materialize.[83] Although Liston contributed to securing Russo-Ottoman peace during his first tenure, it would be an exaggeration to claim he played a central role. As he candidly wrote in July 1795:

> Much pains have been taken by the agents of the new Republic to excite jealousy and ultimately bring on a rupture between the Porte and its powerful neighbour [Russia]. The Ottoman ministers have too much prudence and too strong a sense of present weakness of this country to allow themselves into a departure from their system of neutrality.[84]

By the end of summer, Istanbul was offering 'no public news of importance' for Liston, other than the unresolved *berat* disputes and the Mykonos affair.

---

[80] Cunningham, *Anglo-Ottoman*, 91.
[81] Kentaro Wani, *Neutrality in International Law From the Sixteenth Century to 1945* (Abingdon, Oxon; New York, NY: Routledge, 2017), 55.
[82] Cunningham, *Anglo-Ottoman*, 94.
[83] Ozavci, *Dangerous Gifts*, 36–7.
[84] Robert Liston to S. Foresti, 27 July 1795, NLS MS 5582, f. 80.

In August, King George III granted permission for Liston's return to Britain 'on his private affairs'.[85]

In November 1795, it appeared that 'the Sublime Porte is determined to persevere in her system of peaceful neutrality' and there was no urgent work to be completed by 'this embassy and the Ottoman Ministry'. Liston proposed to set out for England without loss of time.[86] He wanted to avoid the winter and the strict quarantine established by the Austrian government due to the abrupt surge of the plague in the Ottoman Empire. Even though it was not customary for a foreign diplomat to leave Istanbul even on a leave of absence without a public audience with the sultan, he suggested omitting the audience because of the raging epidemic and the danger of infection, opting instead for a friendly visit to the Reis Efendi.

After ten days of hesitation from the Porte, Selim III sent a rescript to Liston, written with his own hand, and granting permission for his departure. On 3 November, the British ambassador visited Reis Efendi Ebubekir Ratib at his house. Ebubekir Ratib presented Liston with the customary snuff box set in diamonds on behalf of the sultan and requested Liston to continue to interpose to ensure peace between Russia and the Ottoman Empire.

Liston departed from Pera a few days later, unaware at the time that he would return to hold the same post seventeen years later. He left his secretary Spencer Smith (1769–1845), the elder brother of Sidney Smith, a close associate of Liston, who obtained him the position, in charge of affairs until a new ambassador arrived, which would occur only three years later.[87] Liston's old friend Dalzel was curious 'what the reason maybe of [Liston's] returning so soon', but did not expect to learn from his letters: 'I know it would have been very improper to write upon that subject.'[88] Liston arrived in London in late January 1796. A few weeks later, he married Henrietta.

---

[85] Lord Grenville to Robert Liston, 4 August 1795, NLS MS 5572, f. 178.
[86] Robert Liston to Lord Grenville, 4 November 1795, NLS MS 5572, f. 167.
[87] Ibid.
[88] A. Dalzel to Robert Liston, 31 January 1796, NLS MS 5589, f. 6.

5

Intermission

Henrietta

It remains a mystery exactly when Robert first crossed paths with Henrietta (née Marchant) (1752–1828) or when they decided to get married.[1] But, on 27 February 1796, just a few weeks after Robert's return to Britain, the two found themselves standing before a minister in the Episcopal Chapel in Glasgow, pledging their vows.[2]

Henrietta, the daughter of Nathaniel Marchant, a plantation owner in Antigua, West Indies, and Sarah Nanton, whose parents were also planters, was baptized on 17 March 1752 at St Paul's Church, Falmouth in Antigua. She grew up amidst the 'jessamine hedge' charm of the Piccadilly plantation, spending her leisure time catching shrimps with her maid in a nearby stream.[3] Her idyllic childhood took a sorrowful turn with the loss of her mother in 1759 and her father in 1761. But Nathaniel Marchant ensured Henrietta was provided for, leaving her a sum of £2,000 (around £516,000 today) at the age of twenty-one and four 'negroes'.[4]

We know little about Henrietta's enslaved people, as Dora Petherbridge perceptively underlines, but it is clear that Henrietta was 'a child of the plantocracy', directly 'profit[ing] from slavery'.[5] Of her eleven siblings, only three were still alive in 1796. She was the only remaining daughter. After their parents' passing, Henrietta moved to Glasgow with her brothers Nathaniel, Benjamin and Ambrose, where they were raised under the guardianship of her aunt, Henrietta Nanton, and her aunt's husband, James Jackson, the postmaster of Glasgow.

---

[1] Petherbridge, 'Henrietta', 11.
[2] McCall, *Some Old Families*, 91.
[3] North, *The Travel Journals*, xiii; Petherbridge, 'Henrietta', 10.
[4] Petherbridge, 'Henrietta', 10.
[5] Ibid., 10–1.

During her time in Glasgow, young Henrietta acquired a fine command of French and some Italian, and she developed considerable botanical knowledge.[6]

She likely knew the Listons as early as 1773, a connection we can trace in the letters of her Edinburgh-based friend, Ann Polson, who was also an old acquaintance of the Listons.[7] Robert Liston's private correspondence suggests that Ann Polson was the person through whom he got to know Henrietta. In one letter, dated March 1782, he asked Ann about Henrietta in the 'NB': 'Remember me in respectful & affectionate terms to your lovely Harriet. Is she married?'[8]

The following year, Henrietta (or Harriet, as Robert often affectionately called her) was already speaking of 'our ambassador' fondly and expressing the hope of 'at least seeing him'. During his journey from Turin to Madrid, passing through Britain for preparation, Robert visited Ann Polson, but from that point onward, for about a decade, there was no further mention of Henrietta in his letters or of Liston in hers. It appears that a brief romantic possibility had flickered, only to fade away just as quickly.

In 1784, at age thirty-two, Henrietta wrote to Ann Polson that 'love & marriage are excluded from my plan of happiness'. Her preference was 'a comfortable house in a retired country, a fortune sufficient to keep free from debt, and assist in the immediate needs of my neighbours, a good library, dry and pleasant walks, and a friend now and then'.[9] In a will she drew up two years later in 1786, she left instructions for Robert to be given 'a ring with her hair', expressing her hope that 'Robert Liston will be pleased to accept ... as a small memorial of Friendship'.[10]

As noted in Chapter 1, Robert was swiftly advancing in his diplomatic career at the time, with postings in Turin, Madrid and Stockholm. Yet he had also lost hopes of, and perhaps even any desire for, getting married. After his mother passed away in 1790, he wrote to her aunt Peggy Liston, expressing that retirement in his homeland with a pension was still a distant prospect. He gently pushed back on his aunt's suggestions for his future, writing:

> I cannot ... avoid wishing that no more schemes may be formed for me than that of a neat cottage in which I may sink to rest when this bustle is over. And if you should by any chance know any young woman who may have other ideas of my

---

[6] North, *Travel Journals*, xiv; Petherbridge, 'Henrietta Liston', 10–1.
[7] Ann Polson to Henrietta Liston, n.d., 1773, NLS MS 5514, f. 227.
[8] Robert Liston to Ann Polson, 16 March 1782, NLS MS 5523, f. 82.
[9] Henrietta Liston to Ann Polson, 11 December 1784, NLS MS 5542, f. 147, cited also in Petherbridge, 'Henrietta Liston', 11.
[10] Will of Henrietta Liston can be found in NLS CH 5791. I should like to thank Dora Petherbridge for drawing my attention to this source.

intentions and who may consequently be foolish enough to wait for me, I beg you will be charitable to warn her of her danger and assure her that I have given up all ideas of marriage.[11]

After Robert's departure from Stockholm in the autumn of 1793 and during his brief stay in Scotland in the winter of 1794, it seems that the connection between him and Henrietta rekindled and took on a more romantic tone, at least from Henrietta's perspective. In a letter to Ann, Henrietta admitted that, despite being 'so long convinced of [Robert's] indifference', their last meeting at Damhead during breakfast had stirred a 'very different feeling'.[12]

The breakfast itself had not been prearranged, as Henrietta had already planned her visit to Damhead before learning that Robert was in Scotland. Nevertheless, his behaviour on the morning of the breakfast left an impression on her. It was 'more different from what it used to be – was I a very vain woman I certainly would have thought that there was something of affection in the subject and spirit of our conversation … This has naturally enlivened my feelings'.[13] Henrietta admitted that she had never met a man like Robert who was 'so interesting or so much to my taste' and that her attachment to him would likely last for life. She continued: 'His Marriage or mine are perhaps the only circumstances that could weaken it'.[14]

However, Henrietta was troubled by 'the silence of Mr. L.' since their meeting, confiding to Ann that 'I shall be unhappy till I hear that he has written to you … [T]o me it is almost impossible he can write'. She cautiously held back from expecting anything more, remarking that she entertained 'not the most distant idea of our being ever more to each other than the very best friends'.[15]

Henrietta and Robert likely continued their correspondence while he was in Istanbul, but, as far as I could determine, there are no surviving letters in their private papers from 1794 to 1796 concerning their relationship or marriage plans. The only record is a marriage contract dated 26 February 1796, a day before their religious ceremony. This contract allowed Henrietta 'full disposal [of] … her property, estate [the house on Charlotte Street in Glasgow] and effects of every mind, in any manner she shall think proper, without consent' of

---

[11] Robert Liston to Peggy Liston, 14 September 1791, NLS MS 5566, f. 79.
[12] [Henrietta] Marchant to Miss Polson, 2 March 1794, NLS MS 5572, f. 43.
[13] Ibid.
[14] Ibid.
[15] Ibid.

her husband.[16] Whether this arrangement was progressive for the time or merely reflective of Robert's lesser financial standing (or both) is open to interpretation.

At the ages of fifty-four and forty-four respectively, which was considered late for marriage at the time, Robert and Henrietta's decision to marry seemed sudden and came as a surprise to many of their family and acquaintances – including Robert's long-time friend Andrew Dalzel, who was eager to meet Henrietta, now Mrs Liston.[17] The day after their wedding, the couple embarked on a journey to the United States, where Robert was to take up his new role as envoy extraordinary in Philadelphia, the capital at that time. Dalzel wrote to Robert: 'America must be a very new and unknown scene for you, a transition from a despotic to a free government.'[18]

§ § §

The Listons' six-week voyage across the Atlantic was eventful and rather unpleasant, especially for Henrietta, who endured 'embarrassments' and 'fatigue' due to heavy storms.[19] For his part, Robert was 'perfectly happy'. 'Henrietta has arrived here in good spirits,' he wrote to her uncle James Jackson, 'in improved health and rejoicing in the exertion of all those good qualities for which she has so long been remarkable. My expectations have been fully answered … Accept of my repeated thanks for the share you have had in preparing the felicity I now enjoy.'[20]

When it comes to his new role in Philadelphia, Robert was far from content. His posting to the United States as minister plenipotentiary may seem like a step back in the diplomatic ladder of the time. However, since the outbreak of the War of the First Coalition, the French advances had led to the closing of several British legations, and limited the number of possibilities. Even then, upon his appointment, Robert Liston confessed to a friend '*entre nous*' that 'I would much rather go anywhere else'. He fretted about the 'severe climate, hard work and being surrounded with ill-disposed Yankee doctrinaires', which might 'at my time of life, probably finish me off in a year or two'.[21] But Lord Grenville had told Robert that he was 'the only man suitable; the French are making infinite

---

[16] NLS CH 5787, cited also in Petherbridge, 'Henrietta Liston', 12. I should like to thank Dora Petherbridge for drawing my attention to this source.
[17] A. Dalzel to Robert Liston, 2 March 1796, NLS MS 5583, f. 29.
[18] Ibid.
[19] James Jackson to Henrietta Liston, 11 March 1796, NLS MS 5583, f. 45.
[20] Robert Liston to James Jackson, 8 May 1796, NLS MS 5593, f. 6.
[21] Cited in Esmond Wright, 'Robert Liston: Second British Minister to the United States', *History Today*, 11, no. 2, 2 February 1961, accessed 20 October 2023.

trouble in that quarter and must be thwarted'. The previous ambassador George Hammond (1763–1853) had engaged in acid controversies with American statesmen, unreasonably severing diplomatic ties, and needed replacement.[22]

Soon after they disembarked in New York harbour and began their new life in the New World, Henrietta began keeping detailed diaries of her travels as an ambassadress.[23] Her journals and letters to her uncle James offer vivid accounts of their American sojourn and have been analysed by James C. Nicholls and Louise V. North, among others.[24]

Unlike Robert's predecessor, the couple was well received in America. They travelled extensively along the East Coast and as far as Canada, forming 'formal'

Figure 2 Henrietta Liston by Gilbert Stuart, 1800, National Gallery of Art, Washington DC, Public Domain.

---

[22] Perkins, 'A Diplomat's Wife', 592–632, at 592.
[23] North, *Travel Journals*, xviii.
[24] Ibid.

friendships with key figures, including President George Washington during their three-and-a-half-year stay.[25] It was then that the only known painting of Henrietta was painted by American painter Gilbert Stuart in Philadelphia, shortly before their departure in 1800.

In North America, Robert was tasked with the delicate mission of mending strained Anglo-American relations. He offered a liberal interpretation to the Jay Treaty of 1794, which had eased some of the immediate tensions between the two nations after the liberation of the United States from the British Empire. It had addressed issues such as British military posts in the Northwest Territory and American debts owed to British creditors. The treaty was highly unpopular among many Americans, particularly those aligned with the Democratic-Republican Party, who saw it as overly conciliatory towards the British and a betrayal of the Franco-American alliance.[26]

Liston strove to avoid the mistakes Hammond had made and particularly to stay aloof from American political strife – even though he found himself on the receiving end of Democratic-Republican assaults – and endeavoured to cultivate amicable relations with all factions.[27] Henrietta, meanwhile, was thrust for the first time into the whirlwind of diplomatic life. '[T]ho' I do not find it easy', she confessed to her uncle about the life of an ambassadress, 'I am reconciled to dine abroad, have Company at home, or attend a publick amusement in the Evening.'[28] The Listons returned back to Europe in 1800, having achieved relative success, as Robert effectively prevented the United States and Britain from drifting into hostile camps.[29]

On their way back, the couple also visited Antigua, where Henrietta was born. As soon as they arrived there on 25 December 1800, Henrietta felt

> the painful pleasure of finding myself near the ashes of my parents. The affectionate reception of some old relations who remembered me in infancy, the visits of those remaining Negroes, that belonged to my Father & Mother, & whom I recollected in my childhood. All inspired an agitating pleasure which no future circumstance, or situation, can ever erase.[30]

---

[25] Nicholls, 'Lady Henrietta', 512.
[26] Stanley Elkins and Eric McKitrick, *The Age of Federalism* (Oxford: Oxford University Press, 1995).
[27] Perkins, 'A Diplomat's Wife', 593–4.
[28] Henrietta Liston to James Jackson, 15 January 1797, cited in Perkins, 'A Diplomat's Wife', 607.
[29] George W. Kyte, 'Robert Liston and Anglo-American Cooperation, 1796–1800', *Proceedings of the American Philosophical Society*, 93, no. 3 (June, 1949), 259–66, there at 266.
[30] Henrietta Liston's Journal to Copenhagen and Sweden, April 1804, NLS MS 5706, f. 83–4.

In September 1802, Robert assumed a new position as envoy extraordinary and minister plenipotentiary in the Batavian Republic.[31] His mission was 'to cultivate and improve the good understanding' that had been 're-established' between the UK and the Dutch after the War of the Second Coalition.[32] The next year (1803), he was dispatched to Copenhagen on a special mission aimed at securing Danish neutrality and monitoring French influence, much like his previous efforts in Istanbul during the 1790s.[33]

However, in early 1804, the Listons were suddenly summoned back to Britain. As Robert noted in February, 'The Secretary of State [Lord Hawkesbury (Robert Jenkinson, second earl of Liverpool, 1770–1828)], without giving me any hint with regard to my future state, has desired me to return to England as soon as I can make it convenient.'[34] His 'sudden recall' had given the couple some *inquiétude*, Henrietta wrote in her diaries. She speculated that the reason might be related to the potential threat of French aggression, noting, 'Should Bonaparte put his threats against Denmark in execution it may prove to have been an unfortunate measure.'[35]

Rumours were rife that Liston was called back because he would soon be appointed as the British ambassador to Istanbul again.[36] Instead of a new posting, the sixty-two-year-old Robert was retired with a pension of £1,786, due, possibly, to his old age and limited possibilities for a new posting at the time. Their family was relieved that the couple could now enjoy the safety of their home rather than remain in the midst of continental Europe's turmoil. But Robert was displeased with how the situation unfolded. Shortly after their return to Britain, he wrote: 'I find myself unexpectedly laid on the shelf.'[37]

For the next six years, the Listons observed developments in Europe from the serene environs of Edinburgh, first from Damhead Farm and then from Milburn Tower, their new residence, whose construction the couple oversaw.[38] Henrietta committed herself to cultivating her garden and conservatory.[39] After the passing of Andrew Dalzel in 1806, shocked and distressed by the news, Robert

---

[31] *Star*, 4 August 1802.
[32] George III to the Government of the State of the Batavian Republic, 16 September 1802, HETNA 2.01.08/344.
[33] *The Sun*, 10 May 1804.
[34] Robert Liston to Coul (?), 25 February 1804, NLS MS 5621, f. 23.
[35] Henrietta Liston's Journal to Copenhagen and Sweden, March 1804, NLS MS 5706, f. 61.
[36] *The Aberdeen Journal*, 29 February 1804.
[37] Robert Liston to [unknown], 21 May 1804, NLS MS 5621, f. 31.
[38] Robert Liston to Balfour, 10 May 1810, NLS MS 5621, f. 56.
[39] Robert Liston to Balfour, 10 May 1810, NLS MS 5623, f. 56.

sought consolation in writing a memorial of his friend's life, collecting materials and preparing notes from his own recollections. However, when he himself experienced health issues, including 'a loss of memory', he abandoned the project.[40]

Instead, Robert immersed himself in building a mill, spending much of his time in the company of his cats and horses. He also gave counsel to young diplomats on how to master the art of diplomacy and negotiation. One of his letters to a certain L.H.S., possibly Lord Henry Stuart (1777–1809), the fifth son of the politician and diplomat the first marquess of Bute, John Stuart and secretary to Liston during his tenure in Philadelphia, is especially noteworthy here.[41]

According to Liston, the cornerstone of diplomatic knowledge began with a thorough grasp of 'Modern History', yet he found existing works lacking in effectively bridging the gap between ancient and contemporary accounts. Nevertheless, he advocated for Edward Gibbon's *The History of the Decline and Fall of the Roman Empire* as a must-read, and recommended Abbe Millot's *Elements of General History* as a work with 'merit'.[42]

When it came to political summaries, Liston highly praised John Campbell's *Present State of Europe*, which covered events up to 1756. For the years following, he valued the *Annual Register*, started by Lawrance Dundass Campbell and continued by figures like Edmund Burke. He considered these works valuable as they offered a condensed yet insightful overview of European affairs, making them excellent reference points for a diplomat trying to keep abreast of current events.[43]

To complement this foundation, Liston advised delving into histories and memoirs that captured particular periods and influential personalities – Voltaire's historical accounts, and the memoirs of figures like Cardinal de Retz. Such works, he argued, offered context and character to the broader political landscape. For those aspiring to understand the complexities of treaties and international agreements, he placed Père Bougeant's *History of the Treaties of Westphalia* at the top of his list, despite cautioning about the author's Catholic bias.[44]

---

[40] Innes, *Memoir of Andrew Dalzel*, iii.
[41] 'Note for L.H.S.', n.d., NLS MS 5658, f. 64. I should like to thank Dora Petherbridge for drawing my attention to this source.
[42] Ibid.
[43] Ibid.
[44] Ibid.

Liston was wary of prejudices in historical narratives. He pointed out the overt biases in L'abbé de Mably's *Droit Public de l'Europe*, where French perspectives informed interpretations. Even so, he valued the general clarity of Mably's style. Similarly, he appreciated the broad strokes and elegant manner of Henry St. John, First Viscount Bolingbroke's works, though he lamented that they were often overshadowed by political partisanship.[45]

For a more systematic approach, Liston believed in mastering the law of nations. He recommended acquiring Grotius, Pufendorf, Vattel and Martens as foundational texts, as well as Jean Dumont's *Corps Diplomatique*, which he viewed as a valuable, though overly extensive, reference. He also suggested works like Pecquet's *Art de Negocier avec les Souverains*, praising its brevity and practical wisdom, and Abraham de Wicquefort's *Parfait Ambassadeur*, although he admitted its focus on ceremonial matters made it a tedious read.[46]

In addition, Liston found a unique educational value in Lord Chesterfield's *Letters to His Son*. While the work was not specifically diplomatic, he believed Chesterfield's keen observations on conduct, manners and the subtleties of human nature offered useful lessons for any diplomat. Ultimately, Liston's reading list at the time underscored his philosophy that a diplomat needed historical knowledge; but also more than that: they needed a nuanced understanding of people, politics and the law.[47]

The Ottoman Napoleonic Wars

During the Listons' time in North America and Western Europe, and following their retirement, the international diplomatic landscape deteriorated significantly, leading to two new episodes of the Eastern Question. The War of the First Coalition concluded in 1797. But peace in Europe was brief. The French invasion of Egypt in 1798 sparked a new conflict, further destabilizing the continent.

Even though, as we have seen in the previous chapters, Sultan Selim III sought to maintain neutrality in the revolutionary wars and viewed France as a long-term ally in his ambition to recapture the Crimea, French aggression unexpectedly drew the Ottoman Empire into European turmoil. General Napoleon Bonaparte

[45] Ibid.
[46] Ibid.
[47] Ibid.

and Foreign Minister Charles Talleyrand aimed to strike at the jugular vein of their main rival, the British Empire, by severing its communication routes to India, as well as by capturing the grain-rich, strategically significant dominion of the sultan.[48] France invaded Egypt under the guise of ending the unruly dominance of the Mamluk beys there. Two years into the occupation, it forged an alliance with some of the beys.[49]

Bonaparte and Talleyrand did so because, against all odds, the beleaguered Selim III had signed alliances with Russia and Britain in December 1798 and January 1799, respectively.[50] The sultan's declaration of war on France and his alliances ignited the War of the Second Coalition. British troops landed in Egypt, while Russia launched a campaign in the Ionian Islands.[51] The war terminated with the French evacuation from Egypt, facilitated by British ships, and peace was sealed by the treaties of Paris (1801) and Amiens (1802). However, shortly after, British and Ottoman forces in Egypt found themselves in 'a position of war' against each other due to their differing ambitions for the post-occupation political order.[52] The British refusal to evacuate Alexandria until their demands were met only exacerbated the tensions. The situation was finally resolved in 1803, but by then a civil war had begun to ravage Egypt, a turmoil that would last until 1811.[53]

The War of the Second Coalition led to significant diplomatic and economic developments. During this period, the Anglo-Ottoman customs tariffs that had been set during Liston's first embassy were renegotiated at the request of the Porte. The primary reasons for this renegotiation included the depreciation of the Ottoman currency, rising prices, and the fact that, despite a commercial agreement setting import and export tariffs at 3 per cent, the actual tariffs averaged only 1.5 per cent. Even though a new agreement was signed on 1 July 1800, its implementation was suspended after complaints from British merchants who felt disadvantaged compared to those of other nations. Despite the Porte's proposal to Britain on 4 January 1801 to restart negotiations, British agents insisted on delaying any new deal until the conclusion of Franco-Ottoman tariff talks that were underway at the time.

---

[48] Ozavci, *Dangerous Gifts*, 39–40.
[49] Ibid., 82.
[50] Ibid., 62.
[51] Jonathan Parry, *Promised Lands: The British and the Ottoman Middle East* (Princeton, NJ: Princeton University Press, 2022), 64–6.
[52] Ozavci, *Dangerous Gifts*, 87.
[53] Ibid., 86–7.

The 1802 Franco-Ottoman peace treaty included significant commercial clauses, ensuring the free navigation of French ships in the Black Sea and renewing the capitulatory privileges that France had enjoyed before the war.[54] Despite this, both Britain and France were reluctant to agree to any increase in customs duties without the other power's consent, resulting in diplomatic deadlock.[55] It was not until 1804, during Charles Arbuthnot's (1767–1850) tenure as British ambassador to Istanbul (1804–7) that the Ottomans reached another agreement with Britain, soon followed by a similar settlement with France.[56] However, as we shall see, the rapid and tragic turn of events over the next few years prevented the implementation of these settlements.

§ § §

In 1805, the War of the Third Coalition, or what now, after Bonaparte's rise to power, had become the Napoleonic Wars, broke out due to fears of French territorial expansion and Napoleon's increasing influence across Europe, especially after his coronation as emperor. The main allies in the Coalition were Britain, Austria, Russia and Sweden. In this episode of the Napoleonic Wars, Selim III found himself under intense pressure from both Napoleon and Russian emperor Alexander I, each vying to win him to their side amidst their ongoing hostilities.

While the sultan was eager to maintain his neutrality, he faced a delicate balancing act, struggling under the demands of the two powerful adversaries. Playing the European powers against one another was a survival tactic for the Ottoman Porte during the Napoleonic Wars, though it was a precarious and costly strategy. In 1806, Selim III agreed to sign an alliance treaty with Russia primarily due to the imminent Russian threat, with troops stationed ominously on the Ottoman border. But soon, he had a change of heart and this had to do with the fact that the *berat* system emerged as a battlefield in its own right for France and Russia at the time.

On 14 January 1806, Reis Efendi Ahmed Vasıf issued a circular to foreign missions, reiterating the directives of 1793–4. The edict required *berat*-holders to perform their functions as dragomans, don the appropriate interpreters' attire

---

[54] (London) to Arbuthnot, 1804, NLS MS 5625, f. 29.
[55] Ibid.
[56] 'A statement serving to explain the new Tariff for the British Levant Trade, by which the Ottoman duties of Custom are to be henceforth regulated', n.d., NLS MS 5625, f. 41.

and abstain from any form of commerce.[57] The foreign missions in Istanbul, notably the French, Russian and Prussian, balked at this measure, branding it as arbitrary. On 23 March 1806, a follow-up note was circulated, declaring that 'all the Sublime Porte asks for on this occasion is that each Baratli and Firmanli shall go to the place for his patent is made out, and shall confine himself purely and simply to the function of a Dragoman or Servant of a Dragoman'.[58] Even though at war, French and Russian envoys dug their heels, invoking the stipulations of their capitulatory agreements to resist the Porte's demands.

However, at about the same time, Napoleon recognized that the Porte's regulation to halt the sale of the *berats* was a calculated move, specifically designed to curtail Russian influence. He instructed his representative in Istanbul, Colonel Horace François Bastien Sébastiani de La Porta (1771–1851) to highlight the abuses of the *berat* system perpetrated by the Russians. The latter had placed thousands of Greeks under their protection, whereas France had engaged in a less harmful policy. Sébastiani told the Reis Efendi that 'the one hundred and fifty [*berat* holders] [France] protected could not constitute a danger to the rest of Turkey'.[59] As noted in the previous chapter, by the mid-1800s, nearly 110,000 Greeks were under Russian protection – something the Porte viewed as a serious security threat.

Therefore, in a bold move to corner the Russians, in July 1806, Napoleon Bonaparte renounced the right to issue *berats* on condition that 'no other power would henceforth grant them'. Furthermore, it was stipulated that 'no Greek, Armenian or Turk could ever sail under any foreign flag', especially under the Russian flag. Bonaparte's decree asserted that 'no Greek or Armenian could ever obtain Russian nationality or any other nationality by naturalization', and that naturalizations granted in the past four years would be cancelled.[60]

Bolstered by the news of French victories against the Coalition forces as well as Napoleon's decree, Selim III ultimately made the decisive choice to refuse the renewal of his (1799) treaty of alliance with Britain. In a symbolic gesture, he recognized Napoleon as emperor of France – much to the chagrin of Alexander I. The sultan then took further steps to diminish Russian influence by cancelling all Russian *berat*s, and prohibiting Greek ships to sail under Russian flags. He appointed new *hospodars* (princes) in Moldova and Wallachia, replacing Constantine Ypsilantis and Alexander Muruzi, who were allegedly inclined to Russia.

---

[57] Rey, *La Protection*, 273–4; 'Report on Barats', 24 April 1806, NLS MS 5626, f. 81.
[58] Ibid.
[59] Rey, *La Protection*, 277.
[60] Sebastiani to M. de Talleyrand, 25 August 1806, cf. Rey, *La Protection*, 278.

The Russian envoy to Istanbul Andrey Y. d'Italinsky (1743–1827) sternly warned Ottoman ministers that despite Napoleon's seemingly friendly gestures, promises and gifts to the sultan, the French ruler's ultimate aim was nothing less than the destruction of the Ottoman Empire.[61] When the Porte remained steadfast in its decision, d'Italinsky shifted tactics, keeping the Ottomans 'in fear'. He threatened Reis Efendi Ahmed Vasıf that if the Porte closed the straits, the tsar would command his troops to cross the Dniester and 'pass through Your Highness's dominions in order to meet the French in Dalmatia, while on her part England, Russia's inseparable ally and undivided ruler of the seas, will bring famine and terror everywhere by drawing ships to the Archipelago'.[62]

This threat intimidated Selim III, who reluctantly agreed to re-appoint Muruzi and Ypsilantis as *hospodars* of the Danubian Principalities. However, before the news could reach Saint Petersburg, Alexander I's troops swiftly entered the Danubian Principalities in October 1806, catching Selim III off guard.[63] Bewildered, he asked his ministers, 'Can you make sense how they have decided to declare war on us while they have an enemy like France?'[64]

The sultan retaliated by closing the straits to all foreign naval and commercial ships, continue the prohibition on the sale of *berats* and ceasing the implementation of commercial agreements. His decisions ultimately led to the outbreak of the first nineteenth-century Russo-Ottoman War at the end of 1806. The fighting continued intermittently for six years and concluded with the somewhat inconclusive Treaty of Bucharest, signed just days before Robert Liston's return to Istanbul in June 1812.

Revolutions

Around the time that the Russo-Ottoman War broke out, the Porte had been wrestling with a major revolution in the Balkans. The Serbs had risen two years earlier, not against Sultan Selim III, who was actually looking to execute his 'New Order' reform program in Serbia, but against the janissary leaders, known as *dayıs*, who had returned to the Pashalik of Belgrade (or *Sırp sancağı*, as the

---

[61] V.N. Vinogradov, '"Strannaja" russko-tureckaja vojna (1806–1812) i Buxarestskij mir,' in *Aleksandr I, Napoleon i Balkany*, V.K. Vinogradov (ed.) (Moscow: Nauka, 1997), 169–202.
[62] Ibid., 172.
[63] Arbuthnot to Charles James Fox, 6 June 1806, NLS MS f. 99; Ozavci, *Dangerous Gifts*, 69.
[64] Enver Z. Karal, *Selim III'ün Hat-ti Hümayunları, Nizam-ı Cedit, 1789–1807* (Ankara: Türk Tarih Kurumu Basımevi, 1988).

Ottomans would call it) back in 1799, during the War of the Second Coalition.[65] Their return had led to the severe deterioration of the financial situation of the Serbs because of the privileges (and corruption) that favoured the janissaries in trade, usury, the system of payoffs and in the production of profitable handicrafts such as pottery, while hindering Serbian trade with Austria.[66]

Serbian appeals to Sultan Selim III and later the Austrians (guarantor of peace and order in Belgrade since the 1791 Treaty of Sistovski) engendered mayhem in February 1804 as more than seventy of the most authoritative Serbian elites (oberknez, knezes, merchants and priests) were killed by the janissaries.[67] It resulted in a revolution, the first phase of which lasted until 1813.

Historian Lawrence P. Meriage argues that one can trace the origins of the Eastern Question in the nineteenth century to the Serbian revolution that erupted in the 1800s.[68] This is a bold argument given that the revolution, albeit of immense importance, was only one of the many vectors and episodes that fed into the complex constellation that was the Eastern Question – vectors such as the strategic rivalries among the Great Powers in the Balkans, the Black Sea (especially the Crimea) and the Mediterranean, the unequal nature and the ill-implementation of the capitulations and the *berat* system, the situation of the straits, the (mis)treatment of Ottoman subject peoples, as well as widening imbalances in military, technological and political power. This being said, it is true that the Serbian revolution would become crucial in the invention of the Eastern Question as a semantic category in the following decades.

Led by an illiterate livestock dealer called Djordje Petrovic Cerny (1762–1817), commonly known as Karadjordje, the revolutionaries achieved considerable success at first. In fact, the sultan's *sipahis* joined the Serbs in the fight against the Janissaries. According to the letters they sent to the sultan and from the detailed programmes they presented to the Ottoman authorities, Karadjordje and fellow rebel leader Jakov Nenadović (1765–1836) aimed for Serbian autonomy. They proposed the consolidation of the independence of the Serbian Church in spiritual and temporal matters and the right to testify in the court of the

---

[65] Yusuf Ziya Karabıçak, 'Sultan's Clergy: The Orthodox Patriarchate of Constantinople between Serbian Communities and Ottoman Government, 1797-1813', *Bulletin de correspondance hellénique moderne et contemporain*, (online) 2 (2020), http://journals.openedition.org/bchmc/42.

[66] L.V. Zelenina, 'Pervoe serbskoe vosstanie: načal'nyj ètap',in V.N. Vinogradov, *Aleksandr I, Napoleon i Balkany* (Moscow: Nauka, 1997), 143–59, at 144.

[67] Zelenina, 'Pervoe serbskoe vosstanie', 145; Lawrence P. Meriage, 'The First Serbian Uprising (1804–1813) and the Nineteenth-Century Origins of the Eastern Question', *Slavic Review*, 37, no. 3 (September, 1978), 421–39, at 422.

[68] Meriage, 'The First Serbian Uprising'.

Ottoman judge (*kadı*). They even started to collect their own taxes from the local population and sought the support of Austria.[69]

When Karadjordje and Nenadović failed to obtain permission from the Ottoman authorities for autonomy, and found Vienna was unwilling to help, they turned to Russia. Russian foreign minister Prince Adam Czartoryski (1770–1861) saw important benefits in establishing new chains of influence in the Balkans with the Slavic population. However, since the 1806 Russo-Ottoman War had not broken out yet (it started officially in December) and Russia was still seeking an alliance with the Porte, he advised his agents not to take any direct action to avoid provoking the Porte.[70] Even when the Serbs appealed for the 'immediate protection and patronage of Russia' after establishing 'an independent' Slavic Serbian state, Czartoryski refused to openly support them, because Russia's conflict with France required maintaining peace with the Porte.

This stance changed with the outbreak of the Russo-Ottoman War in December 1806. Especially after the success of Serbian forces, now numbering up to 30,000 men, in capturing Belgrade and Sabac at the same month, the tsar's agents lost no time in informing Karadjordje that Russia was now prepared 'to promote their independence from Ottoman rule'.[71]

The Serbians' mass killing of Muslim men and the enslavement of women during the revolution cemented a decisive break with the Sublime Porte. Russian envoys then provided the Serbians with food, gunpowder, ammunition and lead.[72] In March 1807, Sultan Selim III sent a new agent to Belgrade to negotiate a settlement and ask the Serbians to stand with him in the war against Russia. But the Serbs rejected his proposal and killed his agent, which marked the revolution's point of no return.[73]

§ § §

While the Serbian revolution was underway, the latest Russo-Ottoman War placed Tsar Alexander I's ally, Britain, in a position of enmity with the Ottoman Empire. At the request of Ambassador Arbuthnot, who fled to Bozcaada

---

[69] Zelenina, 'Pervoe serbskoe vosstanie', 148.
[70] Ibid., 149.
[71] Meriage, 'The First Serbian Uprising', 428.
[72] Denis R. Šarafutdinov, 'Andrej Jakovlevič Italinskij – Diplomatičeskij Poslannik V Konstantinopole', *Istoričeskie, filosofskie, političeskie i juridičeskie nauki, kul'turologija I iskusstvovedenie. Voprosy teorii i praktiki*, 1, no. 37 (2013), 204–07, at 206; Zelenina, 'Pervoe serbskoe vosstanie', 157.
[73] Zelenina, 'Pervoe serbskoe vosstanie', 157.

immediately after the outbreak of the war in December 1806, the court of St. James sent a squadron to Istanbul to pressure the sultan to reverse course and end his alliance with Napoleon. On 19 February 1807, six ships of the line, three frigates and one brig under the command of Admiral John Thomas Duckworth (1748–1817) entered the Dardanelles, pressuring the Ottoman navy – whose sailors were ashore on the occasion of the Eid al-Ahda – into the Marmara Sea and training their artilleries. On 20 February, the British squadron anchored in sight of the Topkapı Palace.[74]

This was an unprecedented show of power. Ambassador Arbuthnot was in the flagship *Royal George*. He sent an ultimatum to Sultan Selim III, demanding the discharge of the French agent Sébastiani, a renewed Ottoman alliance with Britain and Russia, permission for the tsar to keep his troops in the Danubian Principalities until peace was concluded, and the right for British ships to remain in the Straits. The sultan was unwilling to yield. Vigorous preparations to defend Istanbul began. Embankments were erected on the coast. Five hundred and thirty guns and 110 mortars were placed under Sébastiani's command.

Since the British squadron was in the open and would be easy prey, Admiral Duckworth could not extend his ill-fated campaign for more than ten days. With the first favourable winds, the British squadron left Istanbul. At the mouth of the Dardanelles they suffered considerable damage from Ottoman shelling. Soon after, the British launched an attack on Egypt to secure it from a potential French invasion and pressure the sultan. But once again, Ottoman forces on the ground drove them out.[75]

Even though British attempts bore no immediate favourable diplomatic results for them, the panic it created in Istanbul mounted pressure on Selim III. Along with domestic opposition to his reforms, high inflation and court intrigues, this tension helped spark another revolution, this time in the imperial capital, in which, historian Kemal Beydilli argues, Russian and British agents also played a role.[76] Led by Janissary leaders, the revolt resulted in the sultan's downfall in May 1807.[77] Selim III was succeeded by his cousin Mustafa IV.

---

[74] Vinogradov, 'Russko-Tureckaja vojna', 175; Fatih Yeşil, 'İstanbul Önlerinde Bir İngiliz Filosu', in *Nizam-ı Kadim'den Nizam-ı Cedid'e III. Selim ve Dönemi*, Seyfi Kenan (ed.) (Istanbul: ISAM, 2010), 404–5.

[75] Parry, *Promised Lands*, 46–7.

[76] Kemal Beydilli, 'III. Selim Aydınlanmış Hükümdar', in *Nizam-ı Kadim'den Nizam-ı Cedid'e III. Selim ve Dönemi*, Seyfi Kenan (ed.) (Istanbul: ISAM, 2010), 27–58.

[77] Ali Yaycıoğlu, 'Révolutions de Constantinople: France and the Ottoman World in the Age of Revolutions', in *French Mediterraneans: Transnational and Imperial Histories*, Patricia M. E. Lorchin and Todd Shephard (ed.) (Lincoln, NE: University of Nebraska Press, 2016), 21–51.

Just weeks later, the new sultan received the jaw-dropping news of the Russo-French peace from Tilsit. Alexander I and Napoleon Bonaparte were no longer enemies. They had even forged an alliance and haggled over the partition of the Ottoman Empire, without, however, reaching an agreement. In March 1808, the French and the Russians gathered again in Saint Petersburg for a second attempt at the partition of the Ottoman Empire. Even though Russia agreed to concede the Pashalik of Belgrade to Austria, the tsar's insistence on Istanbul and the straits occasioned the suspension of the talks.[78]

Peace

The Franco-Russian alliance at Tilsit disrupted Anglo-Russian relations, turning the courts of London and Saint Petersburg from allies into reluctant adversaries. These events also paved the way for the rapprochement of Britain and the Ottoman Empire. The two powers ended their hostilities by signing the 1809 Treaty of Dardanelles. Negotiated by the then British ambassador Robert Adair (in post from 1808 to 1810) and the talented Ottoman statesman Seyyid Mehmed Emin Vahid Efendi, the treaty stipulated that Britain would provide naval and military assistance to the Ottoman Empire in the event that France unjustly declared war on the sultan.[79] Furthermore, if Britain made peace with Russia before the Ottomans, it would also use its 'good offices' to secure a peace between Russia and the Ottoman Empire, a peace that would be 'honourable' and 'beneficial to the Sublime Porte' securing 'independence to [and] complete integrity of the Ottoman dominions'.[80]

Article XI of the treaty affirmed 'the ancient regulations of the Ottoman Empire' with respect to the prohibition of foreign warships passing the Straits (Dardanelles and Bosphorus). Moreover, the *berat* system was placed on a new footing. The number of British dragomans was limited 'as they shall stand in need of'. Britain was not to 'grant the "Barat" of Dragoman in favour of individuals who do not execute that duty'.[81]

With the 1809 treaty, Britain launched a new eastern policy that was bent on protecting the territorial integrity of the Ottoman Empire and supporting her cause

---

[78] Meriage, 'First Serbian Uprising', 429.
[79] Şânî-zâde Mehmed 'Atâ'ullah Efendi, *Şânîzâde Tarihi*, Ziya Yılmazer (ed.) (Istanbul: Çamlıca Yayınları, 2012), 173.
[80] Steven Richmond, *The Voice of England in the East: Stratford Canning and Diplomacy with the Ottoman Empire* (London, New York: I.B. Tauris, 2014), 43.
[81] Richmond, *Voice of England*, 44.

in the Straits. The primary goal was to secure transportation and communication routes to British colonies – most notably India – from foreign control, particularly by France and Russia.[82] This strategic concern became a core element of Britain's approach to the Eastern Question throughout the nineteenth century.

§ § §

The Listons returned to diplomatic service at this moment, just as Anglo-Ottoman relations had been restored. In December 1809, when Richard Colley Wellesley, First Marquess Wellesley (1760–1842), became secretary of state for foreign affairs, Robert sent to him expressing his desire to take up a new diplomatic post following a five-year hiatus:

> After spending many years abroad in the Line of Foreign Affairs, I have for some time past resided on my farm in the Country, enjoying a very handsome provision granted to me by His Majesty's goodness .... I still consider my services as due to the public, if called for. Should therefore any diplomatic commission occur in which you may think it likely that I could render myself essentially useful, you will find me ready to obey your order with alacrity and with zeal.[83]

Robert hoped to be posted to another European court. He confessed to a friend that he was 'disinclined to cross the Atlantic' again. The relations with America were 'of an alarming nature', he observed, and 'sooner or later might lead to a rupture between the two countries'.[84] At the age of sixty-eight, he felt such a situation would be too much to handle. As a matter of fact, less than three years later, in 1812, a new Anglo-American war erupted.

Around the time Robert Liston wrote to Wellesley, the current British ambassador to Istanbul, Adair was asking permission to return home due to poor health.[85] Adair was granted leave even before a replacement had been appointed. He departed Istanbul on 12 July 1810, entrusting the affairs of Britain in the Ottoman imperial capital into the hands of his secretary, the young Stratford Canning, the future viscount Stratford de Redcliffe (1786–1880), until a new appointment was made.[86]

---

[82] G.C.B. Sir Robery Adair, *The Negotiations for the Peace of the Dardanelles in 1808–1809: With Dispatches and Official Documents*, vol. 1 (London: Longman, Brown, Green and Longmans, 1845).
[83] Robert Liston to Marquis Wellesley, 16 January 1810, NLS MS 5623, f. 11.
[84] Robert Liston to Rolleston, 17 January 1810, NLS MS 5623.
[85] Richmond, *Voice of England*, 60–1.
[86] Ibid., 63.

Wellesley initially offered the post in Istanbul to George Hamilton Gordon, the fourth earl of Aberdeen (1784–1860), but he declined, arguing that the sultan's empire was on the brink of collapse.[87] Wellesley then approached John Fane (1759–1841), who was a former aide-de-camp to his brother Arthur Wellesley, the future duke of Wellington (1769–1852), and who had been with Duckworth's fleet during the Dardanelles Operation. But this appointment also fell through.[88] Only then did Wellesley turn to Robert Liston.

Liston's appointment coincided with news of Napoleon Bonaparte's plans for a Russian campaign. Securing the Russo-Ottoman peace had once again become a critical priority for Britain, as the fall of Russia at the hands of Napoleon could spell disaster for Britain also. Therefore, despite being Wellesley's third choice, the selection of Robert – who was reputed for his favourable relations with the Porte and his experience in securing Russo-Ottoman peace – was likely deemed sufficiently advantageous. On 12 March 1811, Wellesley appointed Robert to the position of ambassador extraordinary and plenipotentiary at the Sublime Porte, instructing him to proceed to London at once to prepare himself for departure to Istanbul.[89]

Robert was already en route to London for a dinner when Wellesley's letter arrived at Milburn Tower. It was Henrietta who received the letter and forwarded it 'in haste' to her husband, hoping it would reach Robert on his arrival at the Royal Hotel in Pall Mall.[90] From Henrietta, we understand that the Listons were already expecting this appointment: 'Mon tres cher Marie', she wrote in an accompanying note, 'The longer I can stay here the better for I am not a moment idle even in sleep I am employed.'[91] Though shortly after, the couple was worried that Wellesley might 'recede' if the Regent asked the post to be given to a certain Lady H's son 'Lord Y, who may wish to make money at C[onstantinople] and his wife to make merchandise of shawls'.[92] As soon as she saw the name of Mr Robert Adair, the former ambassador to Istanbul, in the list at Carlston House, 'C[onstantinople] immediately struck me as the most likely', but the prospects of moving to a world so unknown to her left her feeling 'agitated and distressed'.[93] It is unclear whether she was more concerned about leaving Milburn Tower or the idea of living in Istanbul.

[87] Ibid., 61–2.
[88] Ibid., 89.
[89] Marquis Wellesley to Robert Liston, 12 March 1811, NLS MS 5618, f. 53.
[90] Henrietta Liston to Robert Liston, 15 March 1811, NLS MS 5618, f. 59.
[91] Henrietta Liston to Robert Liston, 16 March 1811, NLS MS 5618, f. 67.
[92] Henrietta Liston to Robert Liston, 21 March 1811, NLS MS 5618, f. 75.
[93] Henrietta Liston to Robert Liston, 17 May 1811, NLS MS 5618, f. 69.

On 21 March, Henrietta received a letter signed by a 'Wellesley' that was not Marques Wellesley, who was mentioned in the text, and it is unlikely that it was Arthur Wellesley, the future duke of the Wellington, who was in Spain at the time. The letter was sent most likely by Henry Wellesley, his younger brother. Its contents made Henrietta feel more uncomfortable, though slightly less unwilling about their impending move. Wellesley had spent the previous night with Robert, and after consulting him, took the liberty to write to Henrietta the next day. 'I take up the pen with joy, my dear madam', the letter began, to convey the significance of the appointment, which 'will be good to thousands, both in Turkey and Russia' thanks to Robert's 'benevolence', 'intelligence and mildness'. Robert 'is the very man for such important missions'.[94] He continued with a patronizing tone: 'I think I see you at Constantinople taking care of Mr Liston's health and your own health is the grand point … He is afraid of the climate on you but I trust he will be made happy and will be seeing you so and having the comfort of your sanity which in happy married life affords true pleasure.'[95]

Henrietta found Wellesley's letter 'abominable'. Still, after a day of reflection, she wrote to Robert: 'I certainly cannot object to your acceptance of what [will] raise you to the head of your profession, gives money as well as consequence and perhaps the Regent may be more ready than the King might have been to make you a Privy Counsellor – the only rank I wish you to accept.'[96] On the same day, Robert sent to Henrietta, informing her that he had just returned from the office of the secretary of state: 'The transaction is complete … [M]y appointment will appear in the Gazette of next Saturday.'[97]

Five days later, he sent another letter to Milburn Tower: 'Ma chère femme, my dearest Harriet! … [W]hat with reading the Constantinople correspondence, what with paying and receiving visits, and with attendance at the Secretary of State's office, it is astonishing how very much I am occupied.' He agreed that Wellesley's letter was 'very loathsome certainly', but he still hoped that Henrietta would 'find the frolick [sic] agreeable. There are many things to be seen as we sail along, and I think with a large house, and a garden, we shall do very well' in Istanbul.[98] Henrietta replied in kind: 'I have now made up my … mind and will willingly attend your footsteps anywhere.'[99]

---

[94] H.W. to Henrietta Liston, 21 March 1811, NLS MS 5618, f. 79.
[95] Ibid.
[96] Henrietta Liston to Robert Liston, 22 March 1811, NLS MS 5618, f. 81.
[97] Robert Liston to Henrietta Liston, 21 March 1811, NLS MS 5624, f. 27.
[98] Robert Liston to Henrietta Liston, 26 March 1811, NLS MS 5624, f. 33.
[99] Henrietta Liston to Robert Liston, 17 May 1811, NLS MS 5618, f. 69.

The Listons continued their preparations. Robert preferred to take only one footman and suggested to Henrietta that 'if you could do without any other maid than Peggy, so much the better. Servants from home, at that distance, are a great plague, and expense and incumbrance'.[100] In March, Robert was appointed a privy counsellor to the king.[101] By May 1811, Henrietta was also addressing her letters from the Royal Hotel in Pall Mall, eagerly anticipating their departure for Istanbul. However, their plans were hampered by an 'unaccountable delay'.

The government was waiting 'to see whether the reports of peace between Turkey and Russia are finally confirmed or found to be false', Robert wrote to a friend. He was not certain of the situation but was not making himself 'miserable about it'.[102] He was taking the delay 'very quietly' and saw 'no reason why a man ... who is paid (handsomely), eats good dinners, go to Ambassadors and Princes' Fetes, and as many public and private audiences as he likes in the evenings has any great reason to fret or to complain'. Though Henrietta did 'evince a little', he admitted, 'when she receives a letter from Milburn, describing the beauty of [her] conservatory ... she often repeats: why, we might have been there now, for any good we are doing here'.[103]

A few weeks later, in July 1811, Robert, now growing more impatient, complained that they were still in London: 'here we are and here for ought I know we may be for some days, or weeks, or months, longer, if as some politicians wish to persuade me, we are to wait till the present discussions between France and Russia are brought to a conclusion'.[104] Robert's credentials were ready. Almost the whole of their baggage was on board the ship *Argo*. They were prepared to depart at two days' notice. But the Listons were only able to leave Britain on 8 April 1812, almost a year after their arrival in London.[105]

The reason for their delay was a 'secret', Robert thought, into which he had not been let, likely because he 'could not contribute to the removal of the difficulties – whatever they are – that stand in the way'.[106] Whether this was entirely true is uncertain. One wonders if the delay was related to Marquess Wellesley's approach to foreign policy vis-à-vis France, 'framed on principles of

---

[100] Robert Liston to Henrietta Liston, 26 March 1811, NLS MS 5624, f. 33.
[101] 'The Oath of a Privy Counsellor taken by the Right Honourable Robert Liston', 26 March 1812, NLS MS 5637, f. 219.
[102] Robert Liston to W.A. Miles, 22 June 1811, NLS MS 5624, f. 107.
[103] Ibid.
[104] Robert Liston to M. de Bezerra, 16 July 1811, NLS MS 5624, f. 135.
[105] Liston to Castlereagh, 11 July 1812, NLS MS 5627, f. 1.
[106] Robert Liston to M. de Bezerra, 10 October 1811, NLS MS 5624, f. 184.

slow operation' and expected to 'produce remote results'. The object was not to 'destroy the power of France or to overthrow its present form of government for the purpose of introducing another of our election'. Instead 'the fair and rational object of the system' was to enable Britain in the first instance and ultimately the European concert to 'restrain France within such limits as might be necessary to the safety, liberty and tranquillity of Europe and to check the design of universal dominion, which, of late years, has been so successful pursued by the present ruler of France'. Wellesley sought to create 'a power diversion in the Spanish peninsula' while gaining time for Russia to prepare for Bonaparte's invasion.[107]

After Napoleon acquired the Hanse towns and the Duchy of Oldenburg to his cause, Alexander I's preparations intensified. Marquess Wellesley was anxious that Russia's conflicts with the Ottoman Empire and Persia were 'unfavourable to the prosecution of any great and vigorous effort against France'. The Russian emperor was carrying on a 'war of ambition and aggrandizement with his southern neighbours and he had to come to terms with both'. Britain was not in a position to supply Russia with financial support, and it might not be 'in our power to give her any military assistance'.[108] Assistance could be provided through maritime operations, and by supplying arms and stores, but for the moment, the court of London preferred to wait and see.

According to historian Stephane Richmond, there was another, more practical reason for the delay in Robert's departure. He infers this from the fact that the young Stratford Canning, the British representative in Istanbul, had been kept completely in the dark for months. He had received no instructions from Marquess Wellesley, nor had Wellesley responded to any of Stratford's despatches.[109] Richmond contends that Wellesley's apathy and 'poor professional conduct as foreign secretary', as well as the distractions of 'his harem', could be the real cause of the delay.[110] Indeed, in time, Robert Liston began to question whether Wellesley could 'with impunity apply his attention to more important or interesting objects'.[111] However, the presence of mistresses during this era was not altogether unusual and may not have been the principal factor behind

---

[107] 'Notes of the General State of Europe by the Marquess Wellesley,' London, 15 May 1811, *The Wellesley Papers. The Life and Correspondence Of Richard Colley Wellesley Marquess Wellesley 1760-1842*, vol. 2 (London: Herbert Jenkins, 1914), 44.
[108] Ibid., 50-1.
[109] Richmond, *Voice of England*, 82.
[110] Ibid., 82-3.
[111] Robert Liston to W.A. Miles, 22 June 1811, NLS MS 5624, f. 107.

Wellesley's lack of initiative. It is true, however, that the British aristocracy increasingly endeavoured to moderate such conduct in the nineteenth century.[112]

Whatever (or whomever?) may have captured Wellesley's attention more, it was not he but Robert Stewart, Viscount Castlereagh (1769–1822), that granted Liston permission to leave, after Marquess Wellesley resigned on 18 February 1812 and Castlereagh assumed the role of foreign secretary on 4 March 1812. After an eight-year hiatus, during which new wars had erupted, revolutions unfolded and the last Anglo-Ottoman peace been signed, Robert returned to diplomatic service, now accompanied by Henrietta.

---

[112] For more on the subject, see, Linda Colley, *Britons: Forging the Nation* (New Haven: Yale University Press, 1992). I should like to thank Jonathan Conlin for bringing this source to my attention.

6

A peace worse than war?

The sultan's fears

'Where in the name of heaven is the dear Mr. Liston about all this time?', wondered Stratford Canning in September 1811. He was continually on 'the look-out for the new ambassador, but alas', there was still no news about Liston's departure time.[1] Stratford was barely twenty-four years old and had been an undergraduate at Cambridge only a few years prior to finding himself as the British chargé d'affaires at the sultan's court. He had participated in the Anglo-Ottoman peace negotiations as Adair's aid in 1809. Now, alone in Istanbul, his patience was growing thin.[2] He was without any instructions from London as the Russo-Ottoman conflict recommenced.

Robert's appointment as ambassador to Istanbul in March 1811 coincided with a critical moment for the unfolding Eastern Question – how to deal with the perceived weakness of the Ottoman Empire. For the new sultan Mahmud II, the war with Russia, ongoing since 1806, had laid bare many of the persistent problems plaguing his empire: its lingering financial difficulties, the further fragmentation of governance with the rise of aspiring local leaders (*ayan*s), the degeneration of the janissary units and the challenges of mobilization.[3]

The imbalance between the two empires' military power had made it clear to him that recapturing the Crimea, Selim III's dream, was now a pipe dream. The tsar's armies had scored considerable victories on the battlefield.[4] By 1808, Russian commander Peter I. Bagration (1765–1812) had occupied the fortresses of Ismail, Breila and Machin, besieging Silistria and repulsing an Ottoman

---

[1] Richmond, *Voice of England*, 90.
[2] Ibid., 89–90.
[3] Mehmet Mert Sunar, '1806-1812 Osmanlı-Rus Harbi'ni Çalışmaya Bir Girizgâh: Sefer İçin Asker Toplanması', *History Studies / International Journal of History*, 10, no. 2 (April, 2018), 239–56, there at 250–1, 254.
[4] Zelenina, 'Pervoe serbskoe vosstanie', 217.

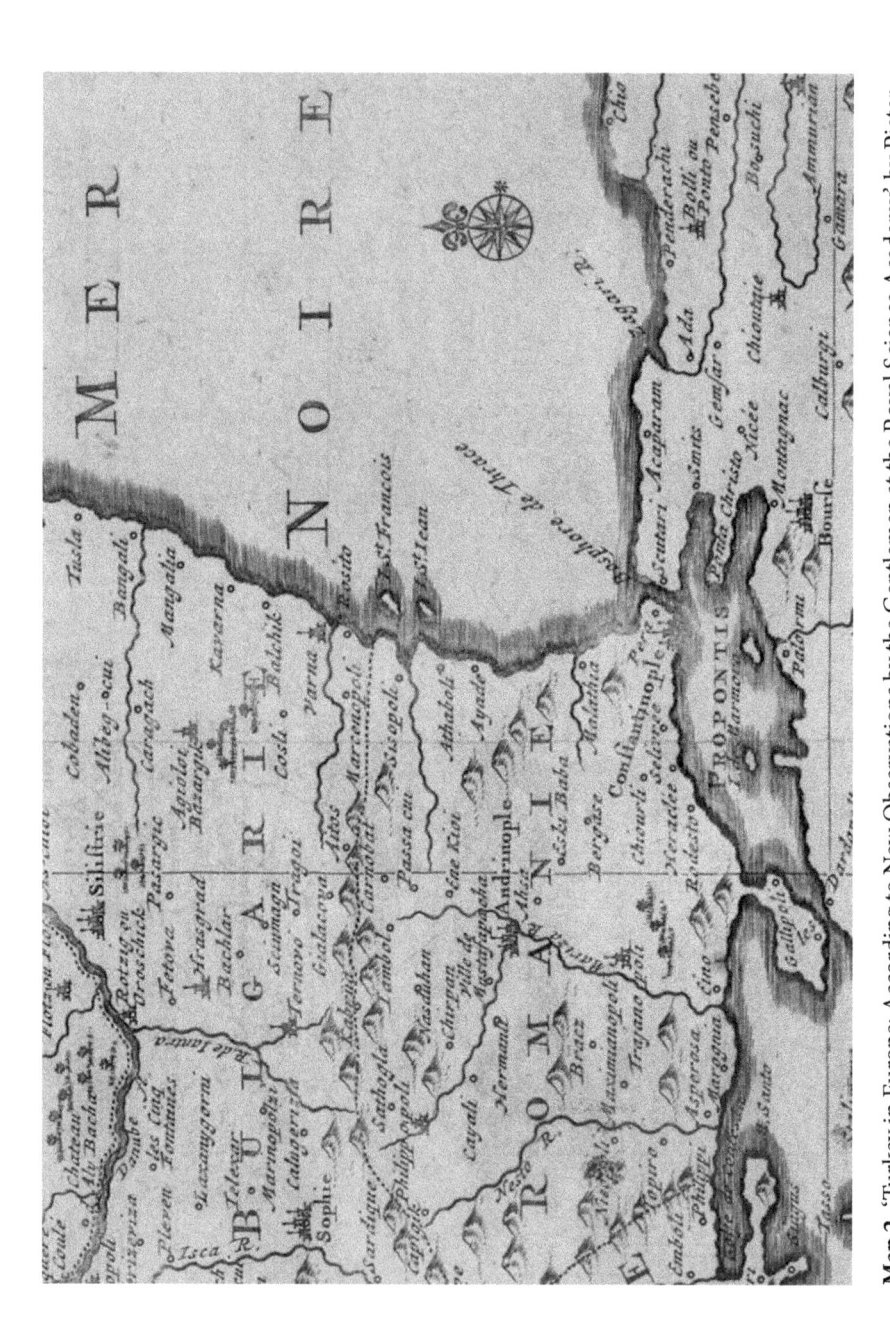

Map 2 'Turkey in Europe: According to New Observations by the Gentlemen at the Royal Science Academy', by Pieter van der Aa, 1729, Source: Library of Congress.

assault on Bucharest. The next year, General Nikolai M. Kamensky (1776–1811) made significant advances, capturing Ruschuk, the last stronghold before Edirne (Adrianople). But neither Russian commander had the troops to march further.

Even then, peace seemed unlikely. Alexander I's terms were too harsh for Mahmud II to accept. The tsar sought amnesty for those involved in the Serbian revolution, alongside Serbs' complete freedom to form their own autonomous government 'according to the common wish of the [Serbian] people'. Alexander I also insisted on the withdrawal of Ottoman troops from Serbian territory. The Porte was to steer clear of Serbia's internal affairs, with Serbian obligations towards the sultan reduced to an annual tribute. Furthermore, the straits were to be opened to Russian merchant vessels and warships. Dominion over the principalities of Moldavia and Wallachia, along with Bessarabia in the Balkans (where the Danube would serve as the new border) and Georgia in the Caucasus, was to be handed over to Russia.[5] Unwilling to entertain such demands, the sultan chose to continue the fight, refusing even to enter into negotiations under these terms.

In March 1811, just as the Listons were informed of their new post, Tsar Alexander I appointed General Kutuzov, his former ambassador to Istanbul, as the new commander of the Army of Moldavia. The tsar was determined to bring a swift end to the war, on his own terms. Kutuzov was the perfect man for such a task, yet he recognized that the tsar's demands were unattainable. Upon assuming his new role, he immediately set about tempering the tsar's expectations. In July he reported that the sultan could not possibly accede to Alexander I's terms, particularly concerning the Danube border.[6] The hardline chancellor Nikolai Rumyantsev (1754–1826) shared this belief. But, unlike Kutuzov, Rumyantsev was convinced that the path to resolution laid solely in securing a conclusive victory on the battlefield.

Kutuzov had only four divisions (27,000 soldiers, more than 13,000 cavalrymen and 4,500 artillerymen) at his disposal, while Grand Vizier Laz Ahmed Paşa had about 60,000 men at Shumen (Shumla) alone.[7] Even a highly capable commander like Kutuzov would struggle to obtain the decisive military victory Rumyantsev wanted. But the Russian general was known as a slow and cautious strategist, who preferred manoeuvre to confrontation. He adopted this very line in the autumn and winter of 1811.

[5] Vinogradov, 'Russko-Tureckaja vojna', 188.
[6] Ibid., 189.
[7] Ibid., 190.

Instead of attacking Ahmed Paşa, he lured the Ottoman grand vizier out of the fortress of Shumen, using disinformation to exaggerate the plight of his army and evacuating his forces from the right bank of the Danube, except for Ruschuk and its environs. When the grand vizier attacked the Russian forces, he was repulsed. Kutuzov then demolished the fortifications around Ruschuk and ferried his troops across the Danube in order to entice the grand vizier further into Moldavia. Ahmed Paşa took the bait and fell prey at Slobozia, where he was surrounded by Russian forces.[8]

As the Ottoman imperial army was trapped, the Porte immediately asked for a truce and ceasefire negotiations. Several meetings took place between Kutuzov and d'Italinksy and an Ottoman delegation led by Mehmed Said Galib Efendi (1763–1829), that included Müftüzade Selim Efendi, Hamid Efendi, a secretary of the janissaries, and Dimitris Mourouzis, the dragoman of the Porte.[9] Forced to make greater concessions, Grand Vizier Ahmed Paşa instructed his agents to accept a border on the Siret River.[10] Russian insistence on keeping Asian territories they had occupied during the war vexed the Porte, as it would mean Russian control over the Georgian, Abaza and Circassian populations. Sultan Mahmud II feared that this would pave the way for 'Russian domination over the entire Black Sea'.[11] He was convinced that the more 'the enemy' saw of 'our frail complacency', the more 'arrogant' they would become. Under these circumstances such a peace was 'a hundred times worse than war'.[12]

The course of the negotiations shifted, first with the Ottoman recapture of Ruschuk and then due to a major international development which redirected the attention of both Russia and the Ottoman Empire westward. The movement of French forces towards Poland, coupled with Napoleon's behaviour towards the Russian ambassador in Paris suggested that a rupture between France and Russia was imminent.[13]

This was potentially a colossal threat to both the Porte and Russia, because French forces could first defeat the tsar and then imperil the territorial integrity of the sultan's dominions. At first, Ottoman ministers opted for a wait-and-see policy.[14] Russian plenipotentiary d'Italinsky denied that any coldness existed

---

[8] *VPR* I/VI, 406–17.
[9] Şânî-zâde Mehmed 'Atâ'ullah Efendi, *Şânî-zâde Tarihi* I, 526; Cevdet Paşa, *Tarih-i Cevdet* IV, 2442; Fehmi Ismail, 'The Making of the Treaty of Bucharest, 1811–1812', *Middle Eastern Studies*, 15, no. 2 (May, 1979), 163–92, there at 165.
[10] Şânî-zâde Mehmed 'Atâ'ullah Efendi, *Şânî-zâde Tarihi* I, 526.
[11] Ibid. 527.
[12] Ibid.
[13] Vinogradov, 'Russko-Tureckaja vojna', 189; Cevdet Paşa, *Tarih-i Cevdet* IV, 2438.
[14] Şânî-zâde Mehmed 'Atâ'ullah Efendi, *Şânî-zâde Tarihi* I, 528.

between the courts of Paris and Saint Petersburg. General Kutuzov echoed this line in private correspondence with the grand vizier, Laz Ahmed Paşa.[15] By the end of 1811, however, the Porte had received multiple reports from Vienna detailing Napoleon's concrete plans for the annihilation of the Russian Empire.[16] As a result, Galib Efendi was ordered to insist on the Prut River as the new Russo-Ottoman border.[17]

The change in Ottoman terms incensed Tsar Alexander I. Despite the pacific advice of his plenipotentiaries, the tsar insisted that only by severely intimidating the Ottomans could he strong-arm them into a favourable peace. Rather than damage 'Russian honour' he commanded Kutuzov to resume hostilities.[18] Negotiations broke down on 12 January 1812.[19] The following month Kutuzov scored new victories on the ground and pushed beyond the Danube. But this was not enough to coerce the Ottomans.[20]

§ § §

Another factor contributing to the persistent Ottoman diplomatic resistance was the support the Porte received from France and Austria, which were allies at the time. The French chargé d'affaires in Istanbul, Just-Pons-Florimond de Fay de La Tour-Maubourg (1781–1837) and the Austrian plenipotentiary Baron Ignaz Lorenz Freiherr van Stürmer (1750–1829) were working together to persuade the sultan to continue hostilities with Russia.[21] Napoleon proposed an alliance and promised Mahmud II the recovery of both Wallachia and Moldavia, as well as the whole of the Crimean Peninsula.[22] The sultan's ministers reminded La Tour-Maubourg that the emperor had made the same promises to Selim III in 1806 and not fulfilled them. Instead, Napoleon had entered an alliance with Russia in 1807.[23] The memory of this 'trickery' was still fresh in the sultan's mind, prompting him to adopt a more defensive stance on the international stage.

The same fears also elicited Ottoman reluctance to extend hostilities with Russia. It was too big a risk for the Porte to take. Their armies scattered,

---

[15] AVPRI, f. 321. 1809, d. 8. l. 15., cf. Vinogradov, 'Russko-Tureckaja vojna', 189.
[16] BOA HAT 1200/47205; BOA TS.MA.e 439/31; BOA HAT 250/14197; BOA HAT 956/40987.
[17] Cevdet Paşa, *Tarih-i Cevdet* IV, 2445.
[18] Mikaberidze, *Kutuzov*, 333–4.
[19] Cevdet Paşa, *Tarih-i Cevdet* IV, 2446–7.
[20] Ibid.
[21] Ismail, 'Treaty of Bucharest', 174.
[22] Mikaberdize, *Kutuzov*, 335.
[23] Cevdet Paşa, *Tarih-i Cevdet* IV, 2449; Ismail, 'Treaty of Bucharest', 175.

their economy and finances in dire straits, and with the political instability suffered due to local notables' and ethno-religious (Serbian) uprisings, Ottoman ministers could not avoid negotiations with the tsar as it could run the risk of having to face a dual Russo-French threat.[24]

Kutuzov played on these fears. He told the sultan's plenipotentiaries that a French victory in Russia and the wider European continent would be against the best interests of the sultan's empire, because Napoleon had long been toying with the idea of partitioning it.[25] News of an Anglo-Russian rapprochement, which the Ottoman ministers interpreted as 'the unveiling [of the two powers'] hypocrisy', led the Porte to err on the side of caution.[26]

Grand Vizier Laz Ahmed Paşa insisted on remaining neutral, isolating the Ottoman Empire from the mayhem as much as possible. '[N]one of the infidels, apart from the Englishman are reliable', he wrote to the sultan, '[e]ach is seeking to further their own interests. This being the case, we must not be deceived by them.'[27] In a private conversation, the first Ottoman plenipotentiary Galib Efendi, who was eager for peace with Russia, cautiously informed Kutuzov that for the sultan the acceptable terms would be a border on the Prut River, with the fortresses of Ismail and Kilia to remain within the Ottoman Empire.[28]

The knot of the Russo-Ottoman disagreements was cut only after Alexander I stepped back. The pacts France concluded with Prussia and Austria in March and April 1812 respectively had secured Napoleon free passage for his second *Grande Armée* in his Russian campaign. On 3 April 1812, the tsar himself drafted an 'extremely secret' rescript for Kutuzov, instructing him that, if it proved impossible to induce the Ottoman plenipotentiaries to agree to Russian peace terms, Kutuzov was to make concessions on the border in Asia, and '[i]n the most extreme case' to conclude peace by making the Prut River the border.[29] 'International circumstances assume greater importance with each passing hour,' the tsar confessed.[30] Russia had to free up troops for its fight against France.

---

[24] Cevdet Paşa, *Tarih-i Cevdet IV*, 2455.
[25] Mikaberidze, *Kutuzov*, 337.
[26] Şânî-zâde Mehmed 'Atâ'ullah Efendi, *Şânî-zâde Tarihi* I, 531.
[27] Grand Vizier to the Kaymakam, 15 April 1812, BOA HH 41832, cf. Ismail, 'Treaty of Bucharest', 176.
[28] Vinogradov, 'Russko-Tureckaja vojna', 195.
[29] *M. I. Kutuzov: sbornik dokumentov. 1808–1812*, vol. 3 (Moscow: Voennoe Izdatelístvo Ministerstva Oborony SSSR, 1952), l. 893, 979, cf. Vinogradov, 'Russko-Tureckaja vojna', 196.
[30] Mikaberidze, *Kutuzov*, 336.

The Treaty of Bucharest

Even though the tsar yielded to Ottoman demands in the spring of 1812, it was subject to conditions. He ordered Kutuzov to conclude a treaty that would also stipulate an offensive and defensive alliance with the sultan against France. Alexander I's strategy here was inspired in part by Czartoryski's aforementioned ambitions[31] and partly by two memoranda written by Ioannis Kapodistrias (1776–1831) in 1810 and 1811. Originally from Corfu, Kapodistrias was a Greek liberationist who had risen to the rank of state councillor. His memoranda detailed how Russia could terminate the war with the Ottomans and create a diversion in the case of a Russo-French war.[32]

In the first memorandum, Kapodistrias proposed offering the Phanariots (Ottoman Greek elites) 'consolidated political and cultural dominance in the [Danubian] principalities, which would be detached from the Ottoman Empire and placed under Russian protection'.[33] In the second, he maintained that Napoleon's territorial expansionism was as much a threat to the Ottomans as it was to Russia, because after the Russian campaign, the French emperor would turn on the sultan's empire.

Kapodistrias proposed the formation of an alliance with the Ottomans against France. If this was accepted, the tsar would send the Army of Moldavia to Dalmatia, i.e. the Illyrian Provinces, to attack the French satellite kingdom there, across lands populated by the Slavs, creating a diversion to pressure Austria into abandoning its alliance with France. If the Ottomans refused an alliance with the tsar, Russian forces would be sent to the Straits and organize an uprising in the European territories of the Ottoman Empire. Rumours would be spread among the Greeks and Armenians, creating panic in Istanbul which would pressure the sultan to agree to an alliance with Russia.[34]

---

[31] See Chapter 4.
[32] Ioannis Kapodistrias, 'Mémoire sur les moyens qui peuvent concourir à terminer la guerre actuelle entre la Russie et la Porte', 31 January 1810, AVPRI, f. 133, op. 468, d. 13377, ll. 237–240v, cf. Viktor Taki, Russian Danube, 68; I. Kapodistrias, 'Mémoire sur une diversion à opérer dans le Midi de l'Europe en cas de guerre entre la Russie et la France, 1811', AVPRI, f. 133. op. 468. d. 11607, ll. 301, cf. Viktor Taki, *Russia on the Danube: Empire, Elites, and Reform in Moldavia and Wallachia, 1812–1834* (Budapest: Central European University Press, 2021), 70.
[33] Ibid., 68.
[34] Ibid., 69–70.

Kapodistrias's plan was communicated to Tsar Alexander I in mid-1812 by Admiral Pavel Vassilievitch Chichagov (1767–1849), a liberal-minded officer and confidant of the tsar.[35] As Prussia and Austria had settled defensive and offensive alliances with France, Chichagov proposed that the enraged tsar 'make a strong diversion', as detailed in Kapodistrias's memoranda, by employing the Army of Moldavia in Wallachia and taking advantage of all resources the Slavic populations could offer to Russia.

The tsar approved the proposal and entrusted the mission to Chichagov himself, who was ordered to lead the Army of Moldavia (renamed the Army of the Danube) in place of Kutuzov, as 'time is short, and the loss of correspondence and indecision would cause the campaign to fail'.[36] In his instructions to Chichagov dated 19 April 1812, the tsar widened the scope of Czartoryski and Kapodistrias's plan.[37] The new object was set as the occupation of Bosnia, Dalmatia and Croatia, after which their militias would be directed to the most important points on the Adriatic shore. By this means, Chichagov would make contact with the British fleet there and stir up discontent in Tyrol and Switzerland to the detriment of France.

The admiral was also ordered to get the Slavic population behind the Russian campaign. For this, Alexander I wrote, 'you must promise them independence, the erection of a Slavic kingdom, pecuniary rewards for the most influential men among them, decorations and suitable titles for leaders and troops'. Should a peace have already been signed with the Ottoman Empire before Chichagov arrived, he was empowered to expand that peace into an offensive and defensive alliance. To persuade the Porte, he would insinuate that the republics of Ragusa and the Ionian Islands would be returned to the sultan.[38] Chichagov would send d'Italinsky to Istanbul for the negotiations. If after all this, however, peace with the Ottomans was still not reached, Chichagov would have to 'incite the Greeks to shake of the yoke of the Turks ... We should enter into negotiations with Ali Pasha [of Janina], and make him hope for independence and the title of King of Epirus.' The admiral would form an Albanian militia. If Ali Paşa could not be won over in this way, Chichagov would employ every means to overthrow

---

[35] Konstantin Adamovich, *Iz zapisok P. V. Chichagova* (Saint Petersburg: Tipo-litografiya T-va 'Svet', 1909).
[36] *Mémoires de l'amiral Tchichagov (1767–1849). Avec une notice biographique D'après des documents authentiques* (Gollion: Infolio, 2012), 54–5.
[37] Ibid., 57.
[38] Ibid., 58–9.

him and establish a power more favourable to Russia.[39] Chichagov left Saint Petersburg on 2 May 1812, the very day peace negotiations between Russia and the Ottoman Empire restarted in Bucharest.

Meanwhile, Austrian, Swedish and especially British representatives in Istanbul were attempting to influence the Russo-Ottoman negotiations in opposite directions – Austria apprising the Porte of the formation of an Austro-French alliance that guaranteed the integrity of the Ottoman Empire, the latter two urging the sultan to make peace with Russia without delay.[40] As the observations of Grand Vizier Ahmed Paşa cited above indicate, the British were possibly the only European power that Sultan Mahmud II was willing to trust after relations between the British and Ottoman Empires had been mended in 1809. Though he had not received any instructions from London, the young Canning looked to hasten the conclusion of the Russo-Ottoman peace and – in line with the British policy towards the territorial integrity of the Ottoman Empire – strove to prevent the sultan's ministers from making risky decisions by prolonging the war.

Conversely, the Russian plenipotentiaries suspected that it was Canning who encouraged the Ottoman plenipotentiaries to include a clause in the peace treaty on Persia and reject the incorporation of Georgia into Russia. Kutuzov wrote that '[t]his new difficulty I consider to be solely the consequence of Mr Canning's suggestions, born of the mercantile self-interest of his government'.[41] The truth was that Ottoman ministers tended to look down on Canning, on account of his youth. More importantly, Canning had offended the Porte more than once – making veiled threats to the Ottoman Reis Efendi and sending an agent (without the Reis Efendi's authorization) to the Russian camp to establish direct contact and inform Kutuzov and d'Italinsky about Ottoman expectations. These 'essentially altered' the Porte's confidence in him, he was told. He had 'nothing to add about the Russian business', the inexperienced diplomat reported back to London. 'The conduct of the Porte has made me indifferent to it' at the most crucial hour of the Russo-Ottoman peace negotiations.[42]

---

[39] Ibid., 59–60.
[40] Ismail, 'Treaty of Bucharest', 177.
[41] Vinogradov, 'Russko-Tureckaja vojna', 195.
[42] Richmond, *Voice of England*, 116.

§ § §

On 28 May 1812, just as Napoleon's armies were marching eastward, a peace treaty was finally signed by the Russian and Ottoman delegates.[43] Neither party was fully satisfied with it. But both felt compelled to put pen to paper and sign – Russia to strengthen itself against the French campaign, and the Ottomans to extricate themselves from the Napoleonic Wars, and the uncertainty and difficulties that they had befallen their empire in the last half decade.[44]

The treaty included sixteen patent and two secret articles. With Article III, all past treaties and conventions between Russia and the Ottoman Empire were 'completely confirmed in all respects', and both parties committed 'to observe them sacredly and inviolably'.[45] Russian plenipotentiaries had inserted this article to restore free passage from the straits for their commercial ships, which had been banned since the outbreak of the war, and to restore capitulatory and commercial agreements which the Porte had suspended since 1806.

Article IV set the inter-imperial borders at the Prut River 'from its entrance into Moldova to its connection with the Danube and the left bank of the Danube from this connection to the mouth of the Chilia and to the sea'. With this, Russia gained control of Bessarabia. Article VI determined the borders on the Asian side, restoring them 'exactly as they were *before the war*'.[46] Russia agreed to return the fortresses and castles that it had 'conquered' during the fighting. The second secret article also pertained to this border. It reserved Russia an area in Mingrelia for passage through the Phasis (Rioni) Valley, which would allow them to speedily move munitions in the event of a war with Persia or the Ottoman Empire.

The tsar's plenipotentiaries did manage to include an article (Article VIII) on the future of the Serbs. It stipulated that the Sublime Porte would 'use leniency and generosity against the Serbian people', granting a general amnesty to them for past deeds, including the capture of Belgrade and the mass killings that had ensued. The fortresses that had been built during the war in the lands the Serbians occupied would be destroyed and the Porte would take possession of all other fortresses and establish garrisons at its discretion, as long as they did 'not do any oppression to the Serbs' for whose security the Porte was responsible.[47]

---

[43] Şânî-zâde Mehmed 'Atâ'ullah Efendi, *Şânî-zâde Tarihi* I, 546.
[44] Cevdet Paşa, *Tarih-i Cevdet IV*, 2450–3.
[45] Şânî-zâde Mehmed 'Atâ'ullah Efendi, *Şânî-zâde Tarihi* I, 552.
[46] Emphasis mine.
[47] VPR I/VI, 406–17.

Map 3 Mingrelia and the Phasis River, Source: NLS MS 5579.

The treaty was so hastily prepared that objections to some of its clauses arrived from Istanbul after it was signed. The sultan and his ministers suspected that the secret article on the Caucasus showed ulterior motives on the Russians' part. They feared that Russian 'interest in the Anatolian question lies in the conveyance of munitions. Their aim hereafter is to conquer Georgia, Iran, Abkhazia and Circassia totally, and to execute the designs they have long harboured against the Ottoman Empire.'[48]

When a copy of the treaty was brought to Istanbul on 10 June 1812, therefore, Sultan Mahmud I was reluctant to ratify it. An imperial council gathered at

---

[48] The Kaymakam to the Grand Vizier, 20 May 1812, BOA HH 41286A, cf. Ismail, 'Treaty of Bucharest', 181.

the house of Sheikh-ul Islam the next day. They demanded the renunciation of the second secret article and modification of Article VIII. Furthermore, they were anxious that local notables to the north of the Prut River, whose lands would now remain in Russian dominions, would object to the territorial changes.[49]

Despite his earlier frustration, Canning urged the Russian delegation, now presided by Chichagov and d'Italinsky, to drop the second secret article. But Chichagov refused, stating that the Ottomans had 'acknowledged Russia's need for communications along the Phasis' and that the munitions conveyed to Georgia would not be used against Persia. The tsar was impatient; the sultan adamant. Canning's last intervention prior to the Listons' arrival did not have the intended effect.[50] Robert Liston would continue his predecessor's work that aimed at settling the differences between Russia and the Ottoman Empire and ensuring the ratification of the treaty at the 'turning point' of the Napoleonic Wars.[51]

Voyage to Istanbul

After a delay of nearly a year, Henrietta and Robert Liston left London late in the evening of Tuesday, 31 March 1812.[52] They set out for Portsmouth, in a coach-and-four. Their four servants followed in a post-chaise. On 8 April 1812, their party set sail in the frigate *Argo*. The Listons were accompanied by Sir Robert Thomas Wilson (1777–1849), a brigadier-general in the British army, who was to assist Liston 'in the conduct of the negotiation for peace between Turkey and Russia', as well as, Bartholomew Frere (1776–1851), secretary of embassy, William Turner (1792–1867) of the secretary of state's office, and Robert Liston Elliot (1797–1862), whom Robert described as 'a very young man, a godson and protégé of my own whom I wish to breed as a Turkish [*sic.*, Oriental] secretary', besides five soldiers.[53] They arrived at the Dardanelles on 12 June, after a two-month journey. Foreign Secretary Castlereagh gave permission for them to break their journey for a week at Cadiz, a week at Palermo and six

---

[49] Cevdet Paşa, *Tarih-i Cevdet IV*, 2457; Ismail, 'Treaty of Bucharest', 183–4.
[50] Ismail, 'Treaty of Bucharest', 184–5.
[51] Mikaberidze, *Napoleonic Wars*, 525–51.
[52] 'Description of Constantinople', NLS MS 5709, f. 1.
[53] General Sir Robert Wilson, C.M.T., *Private Diary of Travels, Personal Services, and Public Events, during Mission and Employment with the European Armies in the Campaigns of 1812, 1813, 1814. From the Invasion of Russia to the Capture of Paris* (London: John Murray, 1861), 113; Genera l K.M.T. Sir Robert Wilson, *Narrative of Events during the Invasion of Russia by Napoleon Bonaparte and the Retreat of the French Army*, Second Edition (London: John Murray, 1860), 98.

days in Malta, so that Robert Liston could carry with him 'the latest and most important information'.⁵⁴

The Listons were detained at the Dardanelles for four days because the *Argo*, as a foreign warship, was prohibited under the 1809 treaty from advancing to Istanbul. During their wait for an Ottoman escort (*mihmandar*), a customary practice for incoming foreign ambassadors, Robert read the latest intelligence from Stratford Canning:⁵⁵ The Russo-Ottoman peace preliminaries had been signed at Bucharest; the Russian envoy Chevalier d'Italinsky was en route to Istanbul; Canning urged Liston to 'strongly hasten his journey'.⁵⁶ The incoming British ambassador also read a worrisome dispatch from Edward Cooke, Castlereagh's undersecretary at the Foreign Office:

> By best intelligence received from Paris, there is every reason to believe that the ultimate Object of Bonaparte's is the taking of Constantinople and placing himself on the throne of Constantinople … His intention is to make a strong and sudden attack on Russia, + then to offer her advantageous terms of peace, on Her consenting to assist Him in the taking of Constantinople. She is to have the three Greek Provinces – Austria, the Delta of the Danube + Silesia – + he is to be crowned at Constantinople.⁵⁷

A few days later, the Ottoman mihmandar Çavuş Ağa and Teşrifati Efendi arrived in Vezir Port, where the Listons were stationed. They attended the British ambassador and his wife amidst the crowds that had gathered to see them, as well as during the ceremonial visits of various district governors and other formal meals, which Robert described as 'a long continuance of irksome restraint'.⁵⁸ In accordance with custom, the Ottoman imperial government presented sable pelisses to the Listons.⁵⁹

The couple reached Silivri, on the shores of the Sea of Marmara, on the very day the Russian envoy extraordinary d'Italinsky was passing through.⁶⁰ The latter paid a visit to Robert to make the acquaintance of someone he knew 'well from reputation'.⁶¹ He had been sent by Admiral Chichagov to induce the Porte

---

54 Robert Liston to Lord Castlereagh, 11 July 1812, NLS MS 5627, f. 1.
55 *Câbî Târihi* II, 853; Robert Liston to Lord Castlereagh, 11 July 1812, NSL MS 5627, f. 1.
56 'Description of Constantinople', NLS MS 5709, f. 26–7, 33.
57 TNA FO 78/79, f. 88–9, cf. Richmond, *Voice of England*, 117.
58 *Câbî Târihi* II, 870; Robert Liston to Lord Castlereagh, 11 July 1812, NLS MS 5627, f. 1.
59 *Câbî Târihi (Târîh-i Sultân Selîm-i Sâlis ve Mahmûd-ı Sânî) Tahlîl ve Tenkidli Metin*, I-II, Mehmet Ali Beyhan (ed.) (Ankara: Türk Tarih Kurumu, 2003), 870.
60 A. Y. Italinsky to P. V. Chichagov, 17 July 1812, *VPR* I/VI, 477–82.
61 'Description of Constantinople', NLS MS 5709, f. 34.

to ratify the peace treaty and to enter a defensive and offensive alliance with Russia, as part of the aforementioned 'diversion plan'.

Robert's junior by a year, d'Italinsky was also from a humble background, born to a poor noble family from the Prilutsky district. Like Liston, he had initially studied theology before studying medicine in Moscow, Saint Petersburg, Edinburgh, London and Leiden. He had also joined the diplomatic service relatively late and unexpectedly, at age thirty-eight, and would remain in that service to the end of his days.[62] D'Italinsky had previous diplomatic experience in Istanbul, having served there between 1802 and 1806, admired for his analytical mind, eloquence and profound knowledge, especially of the Ottoman Empire and Italy.[63]

As noted above, Liston and d'Italinsky's governments had officially been at war since the 1807 Tilsit agreement, albeit without much direct armed conflict.[64] Even though Russian participation in Napoleon's Continental System resulted in the occasional seizure of the tsar's ships by Britain, the courts of London and Saint Petersburg remained reluctant enemies. British foreign secretary George Canning (o. 1807–1809) felt Britain and Russia to have many interests in common. Though British ministers had reminded Alexander I of this as often as they could, only after clouds began to form over his alliance with Napoleon did the tsar begin to lend an ear.[65]

The fact was that, especially in the Balkans and the Levant, the policies of Russia and Britain were antithetical. The closure of the straits to foreign war ships by the 1809 Anglo-Ottoman Treaty of Dardanelles was a huge blow to Russian ambitions. Historian V. N. Vinogradov notes that, for Russia, peace with Britain would mean war with Bonaparte, which Alexander I had long wished to avoid. Russian aspirations in the Balkans and the Caucasus were incompatible with the British goal of supporting the territorial integrity of the sultan's dominions since 1809.[66] As Napoleon's *Grande Armée* marched on Russia in 1812, however, the two empires found themselves having to set aside their differences.

As Henrietta wrote in her diary, 'It was a singular occurrence of circumstances that the Russian and English ambassadors should meet at the last stage before

---

[62] Sharafutdinov, 'Andrej Jakovlevič Italinskij – Diplomatičeskij Poslannik V Konstantinopole', *Istoričeskie, filosofskie, političeskie i juridičeskie nauki, kul'turologija I iskusstvovedenie. Voprosy teorii i praktiki*, 1, no. 37 (2013), 204–07, there at 205.
[63] Ibid. 205.
[64] Vinogradov, 'Russko-Tureckaja vojna', 192.
[65] Ibid., 193.
[66] Ibid.

entering Constantinople at a moment so critical for their respective countries.'[67] D'Italinsky and Liston talked about how to persuade the sultan and his ministers to ratify the Treaty of Bucharest. On 15 June, d'Italinsky had informed the Grand Vizier Ahmed Paşa of Napoleon's plans for dismembering the Ottoman Empire, inviting the Porte into an alliance, but to no avail.[68] Now he was in need of Liston's support in persuading the Porte to enter an offensive and defensive alliance with Russia in the war against France.

Liston was uncomfortable with the 'diversion plan' – and that without knowing Chichagov's alternative plot to invade Istanbul should the sultan refuse the Russian proposal. To Liston, the key was to secure peace between Russian and Ottoman Empires and 'inspire the Porte with full confidence' of Anglo-Russian intentions to prepare it for the proposal of an alliance.[69] There was 'no need to rush' the proposal. He told d'Italinsky that 'diversions might be more readily carried out' once Russia and Britain prevailed over the French.[70] Since d'Italinsky was very tired after his journey in great heat and on bad roads, he decided to stay in Silivri for a few days. By contrast, after reading Cooke's letter and at Stratford Canning's request, the Listons made haste, and arrived in Istanbul the next day, on 28 June 1812.

§ § §

As the Listons approached Istanbul by water, Henrietta recorded her impressions: 'The first striking object that presented itself was the Seven Towers – their form differs from that of other public buildings and would render them very remarkable did they all exist, but so little use seems to have been lately made of them.' As they advanced the city opened itself up to them

> regularly ascending a range of high grounds or hills with a number of fine Mosques and elegant minarets overtopping the tall cypresses with which they are delightfully mixed ... [T]o these buildings, with great quantity of trees, particularly cypresses, Constantinople and its adjoining suburbs chiefly owe their beauty; for otherwise the houses, notwithstanding their fine situation would appear poor. In its present state, however, it presents a *coup d'oeil* altogether unique.[71]

---

[67] 'Description of Constantinople', NLS MS 5709, f. 34.
[68] A. Y. Italinsky to P. V. Chichagov, 15 June 1812, *VPR* I/VI, 431.
[69] A. Y. Italinsky to P. V. Chichagov, 17 July 1812, *VPR* I/VI, 477–82.
[70] Ibid.
[71] 'Description of Constantinople', NLS MS 5709, f. 34. Also in, *Turkish Journals*, 121–2.

They landed at Tophane, where a great crowd gathered on the shore. Horses were waiting for Robert and the other men, and a sedan chair for Henrietta, which was carried by four men 'through a number of narrow streets up a very steep hill, and set down at a large handsome house belonging to the Embassy, and termed the British Palace', whose construction had been completed in 1803 during the term of Thomas Bruce, earl of Elgin (1766–1841).[72]

The Listons were very well received by Stratford Canning. Robert was impressed with the 'state of order and correctness' of the embassy's papers and official correspondence. Canning's interference in the negotiations between the Ottoman Empire and Russia 'seems to have been managed with equal skill, energy and discretion', he reported to Castlereagh, though in reality, the young diplomat had had limited influence, as Robert would soon discover.[73]

In their first days in Istanbul, Henrietta familiarized herself with her surroundings and her neighbours in Pera, taking tea with the other ambassadresses, while Robert had his first public audiences with Ottoman ministers: Grand Admiral Mehmed Hüsrev Paşa (1769–1855), Grand Vizier Ahmed Paşa, Reis Efendi Küçük Ârif Mehmed (1740–1826) and most importantly, Sultan Mahmud II.[74] Robert Wilson noted in his diary that Liston's presence caused 'great satisfaction' on the part of the Ottoman ministers, after the near rupture created by Stratford Canning.[75] Indeed, Liston's influence in Istanbul – especially in comparison to his French counterparts – was immediately felt, thanks to his prior experience in the 1790s, particularly with respect to the *berat* system.[76]

Before his departure from London, Castlereagh had given Liston two main instructions: 'the speedy termination of the war between Turkey and Russia and the frustration of any plans that might be laid for the formation of an intimate connection between [Turkey] and France'.[77] Liston immediately realized that peace between Russia and the Ottoman Empire was far from done and dusted. Despite d'Italinsky's demands for a meeting, Liston postponed until after he met with the Reis Efendi, so as not to 'arouse the distrust of the Ottoman ministry'.[78]

---

[72] Hart, *Turkish Journals*, 123.
[73] Robert Liston to Lord Castlereagh, 11 July 1812, NLS MS 5627, f. 1.
[74] Wilson, *Diary*, 113; Robert Liston to Lord Castlereagh, 13 July 1812, NLS MS 5627, f. 9.
[75] Wilson, *Diary* I, 124.
[76] Cevdet Paşa, *Tarih-i Cevdet*, IV, 2459.
[77] Robert Liston to Lord Castlereagh, 27 August 1812, NLS MS 5627, f. 25.
[78] A. Y. Italinsky to P. V. Chichagov, 17 July 1812, VPR I/VI, 477–82.

At his audience with Reis Efendi Ârif Mehmed in early July 1812, Liston observed that the Porte was still hesitating over treaty ratification.[79] The Reis Efendi reiterated the sultan's concerns with Article VIII (Serbian exemptions and rights), which he believed amounted 'nearly to independence'. He lamented that the Serbians felt 'entitled to negotiate with their masters'. In the event of any disagreement, 'they would complain to whom?', he asked rhetorically. 'To Russia, their protectress, united to them by the ties of a similar religion who would thus usurp a right of interfering in the internal affairs of the [Ottoman] Empire.'[80]

Since a great majority of the inhabitants of the European dominions of the sultan were Christians, if the Porte conceded to Russian demands, other districts could be seduced by the example of Serbia and ask for 'equal privileges: so that the country would ultimately be formed into independent republics, ready at the instigation of the Court of Petersburg to unite for the purpose of shaking off their allegiance to their Turkish sovereign'.[81] To the Reis Efendi, the Russian demand of a settlement in Mingrelia near the mouth of the Phasis (Rioni) River and of free passage through the valley were equally alarming. 'It was evident', he told Liston, 'that such pretension gave reason to suspect plans of future attack and conquest'. This was inconsistent with the 'sort of peace to which the sultan could wish to give his sanction'.

Liston sought to ease tensions by responding that if Russia were 'unreasonable enough' to resist on its demands, he hoped that the Porte would not hazard the peace 'for the sake of what was after all an inferior object', while 'a rupture ... might prove fatal to both'. However, the British ambassador's words left the Reis Efendi unsatisfied. For the Ottoman ministers, the differences were hardly 'inferior' and posed significant risks, potentially escalating into existential threats for their empire.[82]

§ § §

The day before Napoleon's army crossed the Nieman River and commenced his Russian campaign on 24 June, Tsar Alexander I ratified the Treaty of Bucharest.[83] He immediately wrote to Admiral Chichagov, informing him of the onset of the hostilities with France, adding that '[t]he delay in your news and in the ratification

---

[79] Robert Liston to Lord Castlereagh, 13 July 1812, NLS MS 5627, f. 9.
[80] Ibid.
[81] Ibid.
[82] BOA HAT 1105/44599.
[83] Mikaberidze, *Kutuzov*, 342.

of the [treaty by the sultan] gives me some cause for concern'. The tsar feared that the arrival of the new French ambassador, General Antoine-François Andréossi (1761–1828), would undermine Russian efforts to secure ratification.[84]

Yet there was still no word from the sultan. The Porte bought time by not recognizing d'Italinsky as Russian envoy extraordinary. Chichagov believed that Ottoman ministers were swayed by Canning's earlier suggestions to exclude the secret article on the Caucasus. He, too, accused the young British chargé d'affaires of being preoccupied with improbable threats to British India should Russia advance beyond the Caucasus. 'Such is the policy of England: the shadow of a danger to her colonies is enough to make her change her foreign policy and sacrifice the interests of her allies,' Chichagov complained.[85] Anglo-Russian rivalry in West and Central Asia, later dubbed the 'Great Game', was simmering alongside the Eastern Question, even as Britain and Russia officially ended their state of war.[86]

In his subsequent meetings with Liston in Istanbul, d'Italinsky's efforts to obtain the British ambassador's support for the Russian cause proved futile. The Russian envoy found Liston 'extremely reserved' in his comments on the disputes over the Phasis River. Liston advised that Russia should allay the fears of both the Porte and the shah of Persia. The shah had expressed his alarm to the British agents at his court following the news of the Treaty of Bucharest, and even warned the Porte not to sacrifice the interests of Persia in her negotiations with Russia. As for the alliance and diversion plan, Liston stood by what he had said at Silivri: 'the first thing to be done was to secure peace' between Russia and the Ottoman Empire, and to draw the Porte's attention to Napoleon's plans against it and 'the necessity of taking care to preserve its independence'. Britain, he noted, 'had not the forces at her disposal' to act with Russia on the Adriatic coast.[87]

The diversion plan

Despite Liston's reluctance to cooperate with Russia on the 'diversion plan', the Russians continued to implement it. After the signing of the Treaty of Bucharest, Chichagov had reported back to Alexander I that the Porte was not in favour of an alliance with Russia, while the Illyrians, the Croats and Dalmatians were

---

[84] *Mémoires de l'amiral Tchichagov*, 76–7.
[85] Ibid., 78.
[86] 'Russo-English Peace Treaty', 18 July 1812, *VPR* I/VI, 495.
[87] A.Y. Italinsky to P. V. Chichagov, 17 July 1812, *VPR* I/VI, 477–82.

favourably disposed.⁸⁸ The admiral had even ordered his Lieutenant-Colonel A. Polevu to proceed to Belgrade with haste and inform Karadjordje that 'as soon as the war breaks out between Russia and France, our armies may enter Serbia, and together with the Serbs act for the liberation of the Slavic peoples and the subjugation of our opponents'.⁸⁹

By early July 1812, with no news of ratification by the Porte, Tsar Alexander I anxiously ordered Chichagov that the exchange of ratifications of the non-secret articles of the Russo-Ottoman treaty should proceed, leaving the secret articles to be ratified separately, as 'the rejection of the latter will not bring great harm to Russia'.⁹⁰ But Chichagov had a different idea. He proposed that the tsar renew the war with the Porte and 'to undertake a campaign against Constantinople, which … will lead to the cession by Turkey of the European part of its possession to Russia and create favourable conditions in the war with France'.⁹¹ As his attention was focused on the western front, the tsar agreed: 'The best thing I can do is to rely on you, on your discernment', he replied, 'and leave you to make the decision which you consider most reasonable.' Alexander I 'prefer[red] the diversion'. He had no leisure to write anything further on the subject to the admiral.⁹²

§   §   §

The much-awaited news from Istanbul arrived just at the same time, in mid-July. Despite fears of public – especially janissary – protests, Sultan Mahmud II agreed to ratify the treaty. The decision was made soon after the news of France's Russian campaign reached Istanbul and following Mehmed Galib's memorandum, which warned that Napoleon might turn towards Istanbul and attempt to conquer the Ottoman imperial capital after his Russian campaign.⁹³ The sultan had hoped his plenipotentiaries would persuade the tsar's representatives regarding the secret articles.⁹⁴ On 13 July, Galib Efendi ratified the treaty without modifying the article on Serbian autonomy, leading to his immediate dismissal by the irate sultan.⁹⁵

---

⁸⁸ Chichagov to Alexander I, 8 June 1812, *VPR* I/VI, 419.
⁸⁹ P.V. Chichagov to A. Polevu, 15 June 1812, *VPR* I/VI, 431.
⁹⁰ Alexander I to P.V. Chichagov, 6 July 1812, *VPR* I/VI, 456.
⁹¹ P.V. Chichagov to Alexander I, 11 July 1812, *VPR* I/VI, 460.
⁹² Alexander I to P.V. Chichagov, 12 July 1812, *VPR* I/VI, 460–1.
⁹³ Mehmed Galib Efendi to the Grand Vizier, 20 June 1812, BOA TS.MA.e 440/11.
⁹⁴ Cevdet Paşa, *Tarih-i Cevdet* IV, 2457.
⁹⁵ Ibid., 2457–8.

Following the Ottoman ratification of the Treaty of Bucharest, Admiral Chichagov, the commander of the Army of Danube, hurried to relay the news to Tsar Alexander I. The admiral anxiously noted that, while the peace was beneficial for Russia for the time being, it should be viewed as 'an ephemeral transaction'. The treaty lacked an alliance clause, and he had 'no time to lose'. Chichagov therefore decided to proceed 'as if the alliance [with the Porte] had been concluded' and planned a surprise attack on French Dalmatia via the Danube. If the sultan persisted in refusing an alliance, Chichagov intended to turn towards Istanbul and assault it by land and sea. 'The Turks may find it bad', he wrote to the tsar, but it was preferable to displease them than to bind Russian hands and paralyse an entire army. 'I can almost guarantee Your Majesty that the break-up would not have an unpleasant influence on people's minds in Russia, because people would not be informed of these events until I was already halfway to Constantinople.'[96]

Chichagov calculated that he could reach the gates of Istanbul before news of his departure reached the courts of Vienna and Paris. He believed that embroiled in a great struggle, enemies would not be able to turn back to aid the sultan with any speed. In the meantime, he planned to assemble 'swarms of soldiers' in the Slavic lands, ready to make a diversion or for any other undertaking. 'Napoleon had wanted the Turkish war to continue in order to get rid of a Russian army,' Chichagov wrote in his memoirs years later. 'Now this war was going to take place, but in a manner most unpleasant to him.'[97]

Besides these strategic considerations, Chichagov justified his plan on the grounds that the Ottoman Empire had already been on 'the verge of collapse'. Previously it had owed 'its moral strength to religion, [and] its political and military strength to despotism', but now religion was 'no more than an incoherent assemblage of bizarre prejudices, incapable of serving as a rallying point for the public spirit'. Ottoman despotism was 'null and void'. He expected little resistance from the sultan's forces during his march and great panic in the Ottoman imperial capital at his forces' approach. It would make 'the foundation of a new empire possible', and 'by striking the spirits of Napoleon's allies, [it] would suspend their attack on Russian territory'.[98]

With these hopes, Chichagov sent a part of his army to Wallachia and Serbia.[99] He raised a corps among the Wallachians, 'dressed and disciplined

---

[96] *Memoires De L'amiral Tchichagov*, 79–80.
[97] Ibid., 84.
[98] Ibid., 83–4.
[99] P.V. Chichagov to Karadjordge, 6 August 1812, VPR VI, 528; Robert Liston to Lord Castlereagh, 27 August 1812, NLS MS 5627, f. 25.

in the Russian manner' and ordered to prepare provisions. He declared to the locals that 'if an alliance was made between Russia and the Porte, they would fight to defend their country against the encroachments of France and if the [Russo-Ottoman] war was renewed they would vindicate their liberties against the Tyranny of the Turks'.[100] Everything was prepared, Chichagov reported. The troops were organized 'in such a way as to have the greatest possible mobility'. The Black Sea fleet was ready to sail with landing troops to attack Istanbul. The Slavic populations were 'ready to welcome us and only waiting for the signal to act with us'.[101] Indeed, the Serbian revolutionary leader Karadjordje had agreed to joint action and fielded up to 42,000 men.[102]

When the news of the march of Russian forces towards Serbia came to the knowledge of the Porte, it occasioned great anger. The release of Russian prisoners from the arsenal was postponed, despite the stipulations of the Treaty of Bucharest. At imperial council meetings Ottoman ministers discussed a proposal for the recommencement of hostilities. But they deferred any decision until the course of events became clear.[103]

For his part, Liston was disappointed with the course of action pursued by Russian agents. He was unaware of Chichagov's alternative plan to march on Istanbul. D'Italinsky may have been ignorant as well. But Liston well knew that Mahmud II would never consent to an alliance with Russia or the presence of Russian forces in his territories. It would lead to the 'immediate vengeance of France and hostility of Austria', outrage public opinion and lead to new difficulties regarding the eventual removal of the Russians from his dominions – much like Britain in Egypt after 1801.[104] The Ottomans were now 'not only fatigued but disgusted'. To Liston, the diversion plan was too 'premature'.[105]

This was why the British ambassador expressed to d'Italinsky his deep regret that the tsar had not endeavoured to calm the Ottoman public mind or to gain confidence in the Ottoman Empire through an 'empathetic policy' and 'by renouncing the system of exterior aggrandizement and by giving up all demand that even wore the appearance of a spirit of encroachments on his neighbours'.[106]

---

[100] Robert Liston to Lord Castlereagh, 14 September 1812, NLS MS 5627, f. 43; BOA C.HR. 70/3492.
[101] *Memoires De L'amiral Tchichagov*, 87.
[102] Zelenina, 'Pervoe serbskoe vosstanie: kul'minacija i tragedija', in V.N. Vinogradov, *Aleksandr I, Napoleon i Balkany* (Moscow: Nauka, 1997), 215–24, at 222; P. V. Chichagov to Alexander I, 12 August 1812, VPR I/VI, 538.
[103] Robert Liston to Lord Castlereagh, 14 September 1812, NLS MS 5627, f. 43.
[104] Cevdet Paşa, *Tarih-i Cevdet* IV, 2458–9.
[105] Robert Liston to Lord Castlereagh, 27 August 1812, NLS MS 5627, f. 25.
[106] Ibid.

D'Italinsky told Liston that, surrounded by hawkish figures like Rumyantsev, such considerations had not been 'sufficiently impressed upon the mind of the Emperor'. He asked Liston to 'state his opinion in writing' and promised to 'have it brought to the knowledge of [the tsar]'. Upon this, Liston wrote to an old friend in Saint Petersburg, Viktor Kochubei, whom he had known from his first embassy in Istanbul in the 1790s. Now serving as the chairman of the Department of Laws of the Council of State, Kochubei was a moderate who could persuade the tsar to take a more pacific stance towards the Porte.[107] In point of fact, he was one of the architects of Russia's so-called weak neighbour policy towards the Ottoman Empire, advocating for its maintenance as a weak entity, serving as a buffer on the borders of the tsar's dominions, rather than its total destruction.

Liston entrusted Sir Robert Wilson with the commission to deliver the letter to Kochubei. He instructed him 'to prevent the threatened renewal of [Russo-Ottoman] hostilities' and supply dependable information from the field about the course of the war.[108] The French embassy in Istanbul was in 'the habit of endeavouring to blind and seduce the people … by fabricated accounts of splendid French victories'.[109] For their part, the Russian mission contradicted and confuted 'these falsehoods', though they sometimes exaggerated their own advantages. The Ottoman ministers were at a loss what to believe and generally discredited both sides.[110] Reliable intelligence from Wilson would help Liston gain the trust of the Porte.

After receiving the sultan's authorization, Wilson set out for Bucharest on 30 July. On his way he met Grand Vizier Ahmed Paşa at Shumen and obtained his assurances that 'he would forbear from all hostile operations'.[111] Wilson then met Admiral Chichagov in Jassy with the hope that he would be able to dissuade him from the 'diversion plan'.[112] During dinner on the evening of 2 August 1812, Chichagov told Wilson that he had been ready to quit Wallachia and Moldavia 'in most perfect accord' with the Ottomans, for 'the immediate evacuation of Servia … and the march of his disposable force, thirty-six thousand men … to act … on the line of the enemy's Polish communications'.[113]

---

[107] See Chapter 2 of this book.
[108] Wilson, *Narrative*, 99.
[109] Robert Liston to Lord Castlereagh, 27 August 1812, NLS MS 5627, f. 25.
[110] BOA HAT 954/40958.
[111] Wilson, *Narrative*, 99.
[112] Wilson, *Diary I*, 135–39.
[113] Ibid., 139.

Though Wilson thought he had persuaded Chichagov, in fact, the 'diversion plan' had already been postponed on the orders of Tsar Alexander I in mid-July, on account of the advanced season and the 'impossibility of cooperation' with the British.[114] Following the sultan's ratification of the Treaty of Bucharest, the tsar had been in a quandary over the 'diversion plan', which he considered 'very vast' and 'very bold'. He sent a warning to Chichagov that the plan could lead to embarrassments by shocking 'our allies, the British and the Swedes'. The admiral could end up trapped in the Balkans between the Ottoman armies and those of Austria and France. A decision wiser 'than all the rest' would be to remain 'content for the moment with this peace without imperiously demanding the alliance' and to move the Army of the Danube to Podolia rather than Dalmatia and the Adriatic coast.[115]

'The story of Constantinople can be repeated later,' the tsar added. '[O]nce our affairs are going well against Napoleon, we can take up your plan against the Turks straight away.'[116] Chichagov was disappointed, but complied with the orders. Shortly after, he commenced his march, not towards Istanbul, but towards Podolia, i.e. to the north of Odessa.

By the autumn of 1812, despite the signing of the Treaty of Bucharest in the face of the French menace, Russo-Ottoman disputes remained unresolved. They lingered due to the Russian forces' continued presence in the Caucasus and the Ottomans' failure to dismantle the fortresses around the Danube, among other factors. Additionally, the ratification of the treaty did little to assuage Ottoman and Serbian discontent with Article VIII. Tsar Alexander I deemed the treaty to be 'God-given', as it allowed him to redeploy more troops to Podolia.[117] But, for the sultan as well as the Serbs, it represented an unfavourable peace – a catalyst for the dreadful violence that would soon erupt.

---

[114] P.V. Chichagov to d'Italinsky, 3 August 1812, *VPR* VI, 524.
[115] *Memoires De L'amiral Tchichagov*, 85; Cevdet Paşa, *Tarih-i Cevdet* VI, 2459–60.
[116] *Memoires De L'amiral Tchichagov*, 86.
[117] Mikaberidze, *Kutuzov*, 342.

7

Either war or plague

A 'very strange' government

The autumn and winter of 1812–13 in Istanbul were filled with violence and hardship. While awaiting news of the Russian defence against Napoleon's *Grande Armée*, the Listons saw Istanbul ravaged by two fires, a deadly epidemic and harsh cold. The first fire began on 26 September 1812 in a guardhouse in Balat, a neighbourhood primarily inhabited by Jews, with a scattering of Greeks and Turks. It raged through the night until noon the next day, consuming more than 20,000 shops and houses, and killing up to 600 people. The 'extreme narrowness of the streets prevented the sufferers (often crouching in opposite directions) from making their escape', Liston reported.[1]

The second fire began on 5 October 1812 in Galata and lasted seven hours, destroying approximately 5,000 shops and houses belonging to local inhabitants, including the hotel of the Austrian internuncio Baron Stürmer.[2] As stockpiles of combustible materials were found in different parts of the city 'with an apparent intention', Liston suspected that the fires could be 'symptoms of public discontent among the Janissaries'. The Janissaries were highly suspicious of Sultan Mahmud II's 'secret plans' to reform the military.[3]

Meanwhile a malignant fever had been spreading in Pera and Galata.[4] Just as the Russo-Ottoman peace was concluded, this fever was acknowledged to be plague.[5] Henrietta Liston observed that it justified the 'remark of the Turks that they "must have either War [with Russians] or Plague"'.[6] By November, the

---

[1] Robert Liston to Lord Castlereagh, 8 October 1812, NLS MS 5627, f. 49.
[2] Ibid.
[3] Ibid.
[4] Robert Liston to Lord Castlereagh, 27 July 1812, NLS MS 5627, f. 21.
[5] Robert Liston to Lord Castlereagh, 4 September 1812, NLS MS 5627, f. 41.
[6] 'Arrival in Constantinople', NLS MS 5707, July 1812, f. 3.

disease was raging in Istanbul and its suburbs, claiming around a thousand victims a day.[7] Only after the weather grew colder was there a considerable diminution of the plague. It disappeared entirely in February when the frost was at its peak, having claimed the lives of 220,000 Turks, 40,800 Armenians, 32,000 Jews, 28,000 Greeks, 50 Aleppins, 80 Islanders and 25 'Franks', that is, a total of 320,955 lives.[8]

The plague 'kept us prisoners for three months', Henrietta complained to Sir Robert Wilson in a letter, 'not even a servant going out of the gates, the one who brought provisions living without it'. 'The dull round of our desolate garden' was their only exercise, she added, before teasing Wilson: '[H]ow glad I was that you were gone, for you would undoubtedly either have hanged yourself or have brought the plague amongst us.'[9]

Discontent among the wider population, especially the lower classes, had also become widespread as the persistent bad weather had prevented the supply of provisions, especially of oil, which was an article used for both light and cooking.[10] Withdrawal of goods from the bazaars to the black market created additional distress.[11]

In the few opportunities she had to interact with the locals, Henrietta observed that the Ottoman imperial government was 'very strange'. 'The most arbitrary act a despotism can be guilty of is here', she wrote in her diary,

> performed with a promptitude and silence quite astonishing. If a Vizier to be dismissed whether from momentary disgust or some very trifling offence, the ceremony is that an officer enters his office, holding in his hand a bit of cotton, with which he wipes the viziers pen. The Vizier upon this walks out and disposes himself as he pleases, provided he quits Constantinople. Most of the guilt merits either banishment or death … He is led by the officer into a small apartment of the Seraglio where he waits in numbing [word missing] his doom.[12]

Henrietta's observations of Sultan Mahmud II were no less flattering. He was 'a bigot or affects it', she wrote in her diary, 'and a man of blood, which [he] spills, if not with pleasure, at least with a [word missing] remorse'.[13] But then, when Henrietta saw the sultan in person for the first time in February 1813, she

---

[7] Robert Liston to Lord Castlereagh, 12 November 1812, NLS MS 5627, f. 55.
[8] Robert Liston to Lord Castlereagh, 22 March 1813, NLS MS 5627, f. 89.
[9] Mrs Liston to Sir Robert Wilson, 12 February 1813, Wilson, *Diary I*, 412.
[10] *Câbî Târihi* II, 937, 942, 944.
[11] Robert Liston to Lord Castlereagh, 22 March 1813, NLS MS 5627, f. 89.
[12] 'Description of Constantinople', NLS MS 5709, f. 48.
[13] Hart, *The Turkish Journals*, 146.

remarked that Mahmud II 'appears older than twenty-eight, and as far as the figure of a Turk (always enveloped in pelisses) can be judged of, is a graceful man'. She found his features 'regular, his complexion pale, almost to lividness, his eyes large and black, his beard and eyebrows so far as to create suspicion that he follows the common practice of the country and dyes them'.[14]

For his part, Robert was of the opinion that an 'essential trait' of the sultan's character was that he appeared to be 'insensible to fear', and ready to confront any obstacle to establish his sovereign authority.[15] D'Italinsky held similar views. But, to him, what distinguished this sultan from previous rulers was that he had read the history of his empire with some care, and drawn ideas of 'grandeur and power' from it. Mahmud II desired to imitate earlier mighty sultans and believed that one way to achieve this would be to enrich his treasury while the first step towards power was 'the consolidation of his sovereign authority'.[16]

Indeed, as historian Şükrü Ilıcak aptly notes, the sultan and his ministers embarked on a domestic campaign of *de-ayanization* in the 1810s. They aimed to subdue local notables (*ayans*) upon whom the sultan's military had become dependent, while also reallocating the tax farms (*mukataas*) and various state revenues from the local notables to imperial viziers.[17]

As for the outside world, both Liston and d'Italinsky rightly observed that the sultan was not indifferent to what was happening in Europe.[18] Maintaining peace with the 'Christian courts' was a feature of his current plans, d'Italinsky wrote, but Mahmud II harboured suspicions about France. Its immense power made him fearful. Russia inspired the same feelings. As a result, the sultan 'delighted' in the present struggle of the two colossi. He did not want either to acquire a superiority over the other. He hoped that they would counterbalance each other, because it would secure his empire from any enterprise on the part of either.[19]

By working their respective contacts (in the case of Liston, Mustafa Mazhar Efendi and his dragomans B. Pisani and A. Fonton), Liston and d'Italinsky reached the same conclusion, that the Ottoman ministry was divided into two parties. The two groups were 'apparently friends but in reality determined

---

[14] Ibid., 152.
[15] Robert Liston to Lord Castlereagh, 25 February 1815, NLS MS 5630, f. 27.
[16] A. Y. Italinsky to Alexander I, 13 February 1813, *VPR* I/VII, 46–50.
[17] Şükrü Ilıcak, 'The Decade prior to the Greek Revolution: A Black Hole in Ottoman History', in *The Greek Revolution in the Age of Revolutions (1776–1848): Reappraisals and Comparisons*, Paschalis M. Kitromilides (ed.) (London, New York: Routledge, 2020), 139–49, there at 140–1.
[18] Kemal Beydilli, 'Mahmud II', *TDV İslam Ansiklopedisi*, https://islamansiklopedisi.org.tr/mahmud-ii-osmanli (last accessed 12 August 2023).
[19] A. Y. Italinsky to Alexander I, 13 February 1813, *VPR* I/VII, 46–50.

enemies', the British ambassador wrote. They carried on 'the business of the government conformably to the opinion of the majority or in obedience to the direct orders of the sovereign'. There was no 'open difference or apparent collision'. They were united 'in the declared wish to avoid all intimate alliance with the nations of Europe'.

One party, led by the former *kahya bey* (steward) and chief Ottoman delegate at Bucharest, Mehmed Galib Efendi, feared the 'gigantic projects of Bonaparte' to capture Istanbul and proclaim an eastern empire once his Russian campaign was over.[20] When the news of the defection of Prussia and the emperor's retreat to Paris arrived in Istanbul, they rejoiced. They sought to remove 'all the stumbling blocks that now lie in the way of a permanent good understanding with Russia'. They were keen for opportunities to present their opinion to the imperial council and especially the sultan. But the sultan dreaded a friendly relationship with Russia as it could lead to negotiation for an offensive and defensive alliance, something he strongly wished to avoid, lest it become an immediate source of tension with France.

The other party, presided by Mehmed Said Halet Efendi (1761–1822), the present *kahya bey* and former ambassador to Paris, and Hacı Halil Efendi, the minister of conferences, was said to have 'great might' with the sultan.[21] Halet was the head of the *de-ayanization* project and known to be a man with considerable influence over the empire thanks to his relationships with formidable governors, such as the paşas of Egypt and Janina, the Janissary aghas and Phanariots and *hospodars* (ruling princes) in the Danubian Principalities.[22]

Liston considered this party to 'still fondly lean towards France'. They were willing to 'foster the causes of present or future quarrels with Russia', expecting that Napoleon would be able to carry on the war against the Allies and might even recover his former domination in Europe.[23] It appears that both Liston and d'Italinsky perceived this group as 'the French party' not because it was devoted to the French cause, but more because its members believed that the existence of France as a major threat to Russia in Europe dovetailed with the interests of the Porte.

---

[20] Robert Liston to Lord Castlereagh, 27 March 1813, NLS MS 5627, f. 99.
[21] Robert Liston to Lord Castlereagh, 12 November 1812, NLS MS 5627, f. 57.
[22] On Halet, see, Süheyla Yenidünya Gürgen, *Devletin Kâhyası, Sultanin Efendisi: Mehmed Said Halet Efendi* (Istanbul: Dergâh Yayınları, 2018).
[23] Robert Liston to Lord Castlereagh, 27 March 1813, NLS MS 5627, f. 99.

Since the beginning of 1812, the so-called French party had been proclaiming 'the invariable success and the irresistible power of Bonaparte'.[24] In February 1813, d'Italinsky warned that the 'French party' in the Porte had acquired 'a decided superiority'. As a result he feared that the war with Russia, 'a war which has scarcely ended', could be restarted by 'the madness of the[se] characters'.[25] This was why Foreign Minister Rumyantsev ordered d'Italinsky to immediately make use of the news of 'the almost complete destruction of the French army' once it reached Istanbul, in order to 'paralyze the efforts of the French party' in the Ottoman imperial council.[26] Indeed, shortly after, the language of the Porte towards Britain and Russia switched from its previously neutral, if not distant, tone to a more friendly one. Even the non-evacuation of the Phasis Valley by Russian forces was rarely mentioned now.[27]

However, this situation did not last long. After the recommencement of hostilities in Europe, the tone of Ottoman communication shifted once again. Complaints were lodged about the non-execution of the Treaty of Bucharest.[28] Reis Efendi Küçük Ârif sent a protest to d'Italinsky, alleging that the Russian agent in Belgrade, F. I. Nedoba, was inciting the Serbs against the Ottoman Empire.[29] D'Italinsky denied these accusations, suggesting that the Porte should instead focus on French and Austrian attempts to win over the Serbs.[30] Amidst this inter-imperial haggling, mayhem ensued. It was the Serbs who suffered the most, while major European empires and Liston remained largely silent.

The Serbian question revisited

During the Russo-Ottoman peace negotiations in the spring and summer of 1812, the Serbs had been never consulted on issues regarding their future.[31] When Chichagov was sent to Bucharest to negotiate an alliance with the Porte and launch the diversion plan, however, he made contact with the Serbian leader

---

[24] Robert Liston to Lord Castlereagh, 10 August 1813, NLS MS 5627, f. 131.
[25] A. Y. Italinsky to Alexander I, 13 February 1813, VPR I/VII, 46–50.
[26] Minister of Foreign Affairs H. P. Rumyantsev to A.Y. Italinsky, 7 January 1813, VPR I/VI, 669–70.
[27] Robert Liston to Lord Castlereagh, 27 March 1813; Robert Liston to Lord Castlereagh, 9 July 1813, NLS MS 5627, f. 101, 125.
[28] Robert Liston to Lord Castlereagh, 22 September 1813, NLS MS 5627, f. 147.
[29] A. Y. Italinsky to N. P. Rumyantsev, 7 January 1813, VPR I/VI, 673.
[30] Ibid.
[31] V.P. Grachev, 'Buxarestskij Mir 1812 G. I Serbskij Vopros', *Slavjane i Rossija*, no. 1 (2013), 437–88, there at 442.

Karadjordje and pledged Russian support for the eventual independence of the Serbs, in exchange for their backing of his diversion plan.

After the ratification of the Treaty of Bucharest, which did not grant the Serbs independence and ensured the return of Ottoman forces to Belgrade, Chichagov was anxious to inform Karadjordje of the inter-imperial settlement, conscious that the Ottomans would lose no time to demand the surrender of Serbian fortresses.[32] Serbian leaders were disappointed that the Russian authorities had not kept their promise for complete independence of Serbia.[33] The cancellation of the diversion plan dealt them yet another blow.

'I myself could not believe that our affairs could have taken such a turn,' Chichagov confessed to Karadjordje.[34] But when the French 'rushed to the ruin of Russia' and Napoleon threatened to penetrate even into 'the heart of the tsar's empire', necessity had compelled the Russians to 'unite all our forces against him and hurry to oppose them'. He high-handedly concluded that 'in such a case, the resentment of the Serbian people, who are committed to us, would be unfounded'.[35] Napoleon's power was great. Now Russia had to 'offer him a great and stubborn resistance'. The tsar's promise of patronage to the Serbians would 'appear [again] at the first opportunity'.[36]

This was why, when Chichagov ordered his officers to leave Serbia by the end of July, he requested that the Serbian leaders not 'annoy' the Ottomans. The plan now was to maintain peace with the latter and avoid an 'untimely rupture', which could 'destroy all the hopes of the Serbians'. The Serbs were instructed to avoid fighting against the Porte, and 'let them turn their hatred to the French'.[37]

As per Chichagov's requests, at first the Serbian leaders stalled, hoping that they would receive renewed support from Russia or Austria eventually. However, in October 1812 their assembly decided to take matters into their own hands and send a deputation to the sultan to revise Article VIII of the Treaty of Bucharest.[38] The Serbian deputies met the governor of Sofia, Çelebi Mustafa Reşid Efendi, and governor of Rumelia, Silahdar Ali Paşa, in Niš on 5 December 1812.[39] The

---

[32] P. V. Chichagov to Alexander I, 12 August 1812, *VPR* I/VI, 538.
[33] Grachev, 'Buxarestskij Mir', 442.
[34] P. V. Chichagov to Karadjordje, 6 August 1812, *VPR* VI, 528.
[35] Ibid.
[36] Instructions of the Commander-in-Chief of the Danube Army P. V. Chichagov to General M. K. Ivelich, 28 July 1812, *VPR* I/VI, 518–19.
[37] Ibid.
[38] Zelenina, 'Kul'minacija i tragedija', 222.
[39] Şânî-zâde Mehmed 'Atâ'ullah Efendi, *Şânî-zâde Tarihi* I, 611.

Serbs proposed that they should pay a fixed annual tribute to the sultan. The sum should be delivered to the Ottoman treasury by Serbian commissioners, with no Ottoman officer entering Serbian territories for the purpose of levying or receiving any impositions. Since Ottoman garrisons would be unnecessary, the Serbian deputies suggested their withdrawal. They also claimed the right to have their own form of government and to choose their chief magistrate in the same way the rulers of Moldavia and Wallachia were, that is under the nominal sovereignty of the sultan.[40]

The Ottoman delegates refused these demands outright. They insisted that their own officers should collect tribute, maintain the fortresses, keep up their garrisons and appoint the governor of Serbia. The meeting ended without any resolution.[41] While I was unable to access Serbian sources due to logistic and linguistic limitations, Ottoman sources suggest that subsequent meetings saw Karadjordje refuse to recognize the Treaty of Bucharest and steadfastly demand Serbian independence.[42] Under various pretexts, he consistently avoided the implementation of the treaty's stipulations.[43]

In February, a new round of talks between Serbian deputies and the Ottoman authorities began in Niš.[44] The Serbs once again demanded autonomy, proposing that only a paşa with fifty men be admitted to the fortress of Belgrade. They wanted control over all the fortified places and entrenched camps, and a prince following the example of Wallachia and Moldavia. D'Italinsky reported that, despite his conciliatory language, the Ottoman delegate Mustafa Çelebi could not persuade the Serbs to withdraw their proposal.[45] When the final round of talks between Serbian and Ottoman representatives took place in May 1813 in Sofia, neither party was willing to make concessions.[46]

Upon this, d'Italinsky offered the Porte Russian mediation to bring the Serbs 'back to obedience and acceptance of the article stipulated in the Treaty of Bucharest'. Even though Ottoman Reis Efendi Küçük Ârif accepted the offer in principle, the so-called French party in the Porte objected to it. According to d'Italinsky, this faction, bolstered by the 'intrigues' of the French, was advocating

---

[40] Robert Liston to Lord Castlereagh, 15 October 1812, NLS MS 5627, f. 52.
[41] Ibid.
[42] Cevdet Paşa, *Tarih-i Cevdet* V, 2520.
[43] Grachev, 'Buxarestskij Mir', 484; Cevdet Paşa, *Tarih-i Cevdet* V, 2520.
[44] Zelenina, 'Kul'minacija i tragedija', 222–3; Şânî-zâde Mehmed 'Atâ'ullah Efendi, *Şânî-zâde Tarihi* I, 616.
[45] A.Y. Italinsky to N. P. Rumyantsev, 14 April 1813, *VPR* I/VII, 162–4.
[46] Zelenina, 'Kul'minacija i tragedija', 223.

for violence against the Serbs, both to subdue them and to provoke a fresh quarrel between Russia and the Ottoman Empire.[47]

Yet according to Şanizâde, the sultan was no less inclined to violence at this point. After receiving the reports from Niš, he wrote that by showing such recklessness and demanding too much, the Serbs were risking their lives.[48] In a similar vein, Grand Vizier Hurşid Ahmed Paşa proposed to meet Serbian 'impugnation' with a show of 'power' and 'determination', mobilizing 2,000 to 3,000 men.[49] The sultan approved this plan. At the end of May 1813, the Porte informed d'Italinsky of its intention to conquer Serbia by force of arms.[50] Although d'Italinsky instructed his agent in Belgrade to advise the Serbian leaders to resume negotiations and 'seek the security promised by the Porte to the Serbian people' to avoid bloodshed, it was too late.[51]

Despite initial Serbian successes against Ottoman troops in June 1813, the surrender of the Vidin left the road to Belgrade open and boded ill for the revolutionaries.[52] The Porte leveraged the Napoleonic Wars to its advantage and secured a promise from the Austrians not to provide ammunition and provisions to the Serbs. Karadjordje was trapped. What ensued was the tragic end of the first Serbian revolution.

As Liston reported, in early August some 120 Serbian heads, said to have been removed from the revolutionaries during the final engagements, were delivered to Istanbul and displayed in the Topkapı Palace.[53] On 23 September, Ottoman forces entered Belgrade and scenes of great bloodshed followed. Those who could escape – tens of thousands of them, including Karadjordje – fled to Austria and Russia.[54]

While the Serbs were being killed and displaced in great numbers, the courts of Vienna and Saint Petersburg remained largely inactive. As the inter-imperial war in Europe was still underway, they were both intent on avoiding any rupture with Sultan Mahmud II. They turned their backs to the Serbians who bore the harsh consequences of inter-imperial rivalry and the brunt of imperial oppression.

---

[47] Ibid.
[48] Şânî-zâde Mehmed 'Atâ'ullah Efendi, *Şânî-zâde Tarihi* I, 616.
[49] Ibid.
[50] A. Y. Italinsky to F. I. Nedobe, 28 May 1813, *VPR* I/VII, 219–20; Cevdet Paşa, *Tarih-i Cevdet* V, 2520.
[51] Süleyman Uygun, 'Sırp İsyanı ve Hurşid Ahmet Paşa', *Uluslararası Sosyal Araştırmalar Dergisi*, 17, no. 4 (2011), 416–36, there at 431–2.
[52] Şânî-zâde Mehmed 'Atâ'ullah Efendi, *Şânî-zâde Tarihi* I, 647–8.
[53] Robert Liston to Lord Castlereagh, 31 August 1813, NLS MS 5627, f. 141.
[54] Zelenina, 'Kul'minacija i tragedija', 223; Grachev, 'Buxarestskij Mir', 484.

The conundrum

The challenging position in which both Russian and Ottoman authorities found themselves created a diplomatic conundrum in 1813. Each side accused the other of failing to implement the 1812 Treaty of Bucharest. Both continued to act in certain matters as if the treaty had never been signed. The Porte did not promulgate the Russo-Ottoman peace even weeks after its ratification. Ottoman authorities neither destroyed the fortresses of Ismail and Kfili on the banks of the Danube nor opened the Straits for commercial ships, despite the treaty's clear stipulations.

Similarly, Russian admiral Chichagov was convinced that he 'certainly had the right to suspend the evacuation of Asia'. He ordered the governor of the Crimea to vacate the interior of Phasis Valley, but instructed the latter to concentrate a small number of troops in the area of the coast, at the mouth of the river, which, Chichagov believed, the Russians were 'assured of by a secret article'. Chichagov was confident that the tsar would also 'find [his decision] convenient'.[55] As we have seen above, the question of the secret article had been postponed by Russian authorities after the sultan refused to ratify it.

At this moment, every subject of complaint, even spurious ones, carried the risk of an open rupture between Russia and the Ottoman Empire, Liston reported. As the success of Russia against France became critical for British interests, Liston came to see the behaviour of the Porte as 'cold, captious … haughty … overbearing and unjust', while commending Russian envoy d'Italinsky for his efforts to avoid anything that could lead to war, meeting 'intemperance' with 'moderation', and 'incivility' with 'distant and dignified politeness'.

Yet even then, as Liston wrote in a cyphered letter to Lord Castlereagh, the British ambassador's 'fixed opinion' was that the Russo-Ottoman conundrum could be resolved by Saint Petersburg: '[T]he only means to produce a cordial good understanding between the Ottoman Empire and Russia, indeed the only means to ensure the permanent tranquillity of the Russian Empire', he remarked, was the 'renunciation on the part of the Emperor of all projects of external acquisition or encroachment, and the restitution of the whole, or at least the greatest part of his late conquests from the Ottoman dominions', whether by force or diplomacy.[56]

---

[55] P. V. Chichagov to A.Y. Italinsky, 3 August 1812, *VPR* VI, 524.
[56] Robert Liston to Lord Castlereagh, 12 November 1812, NLS MS 5627, f. 57.

Liston was well aware that Russian strategists, such as Foreign Minister Count Rumyantsev and their envoy in Istanbul, d'Italinsky, saw the situation in a different light. Rumyantsev's system of politics was decidedly hostile to the Ottoman Empire. In fact, Rumyantsev had instructed d'Italinsky to suspend negotiations over the implementation of the treaty, leaving it to 'the care of the English ambassador as it is much more the interest of England than of Russia that the treaty should take place'.[57]

D'Italinsky defended the Russian policy, arguing that the importance the Porte attached to the lands in the Phasis Valley stemmed from their strategic utility in wartime. The inhabitants of the region, he noted, would raid Russia even during peacetime, offering no other tangible benefits to the Ottoman Empire. Their 'savage population' neither contributed the troops to the Ottoman army nor paid any taxes to the sultan. The coast of Mingrelia, 'almost deserted', boasted an anchorage point crucial for Russia's communication with all its possessions between the Black and Caspian Seas. If the Russians abandoned this coast, they would be forced to rely for communication on a perilous and lengthy route along the highest part of the Caucasus ridge. For these reasons alone, fortifying the Phasis Valley was 'absolutely necessary'.[58]

In the meantime, new border disputes arose concerning Bessarabia, which had been ceded to Russia under the Treaty of Bucharest. The Ottoman commissioner Ahmet Zeki Efendi, who had been sent to the region to advise the sultan on the Porte's policy, demanded the expulsion from Bessarabia of all Ottomans, prisoners or not, who had converted to Christianity at a mature age and did not wish to return to the Ottoman Empire; the expulsion of all persons born in the Ottoman dominions who during the war had remained in Bessarabia or voluntarily moved there; the extradition of several Ottoman women who had converted to Christianity, married Russian officers and had children by these marriages; the transfer of all the islands on the Danube to the Ottoman Empire; the drawing of the frontier line on only an hour's journey from Ismail and Kilik, and the granting to Ottoman vessels of the right of travelling along the left bank of the Prut, using towing crews.[59]

General Harting (Garting), the Russian governor of the province was of the opinion that the first three of these were 'strange demands' and in his talks with

---

[57] Ibid.; P. V. Chichagov to General M. K. Ivelich, 2 July 1812, *VPR* I/V, 518–9; N.P. Rumyantsev to A. Y. Italinsky, 19 September 1812, *VPR* I/V, 563.
[58] A. Y. Italinsky to K. V. Nesselrode, 25 March 1815, *VPR* I/VIII, 245–7.
[59] Note from A. Y. Italinsky to the Ottoman Government, 1 September 1813, *VPR* I/VII, 363–4.

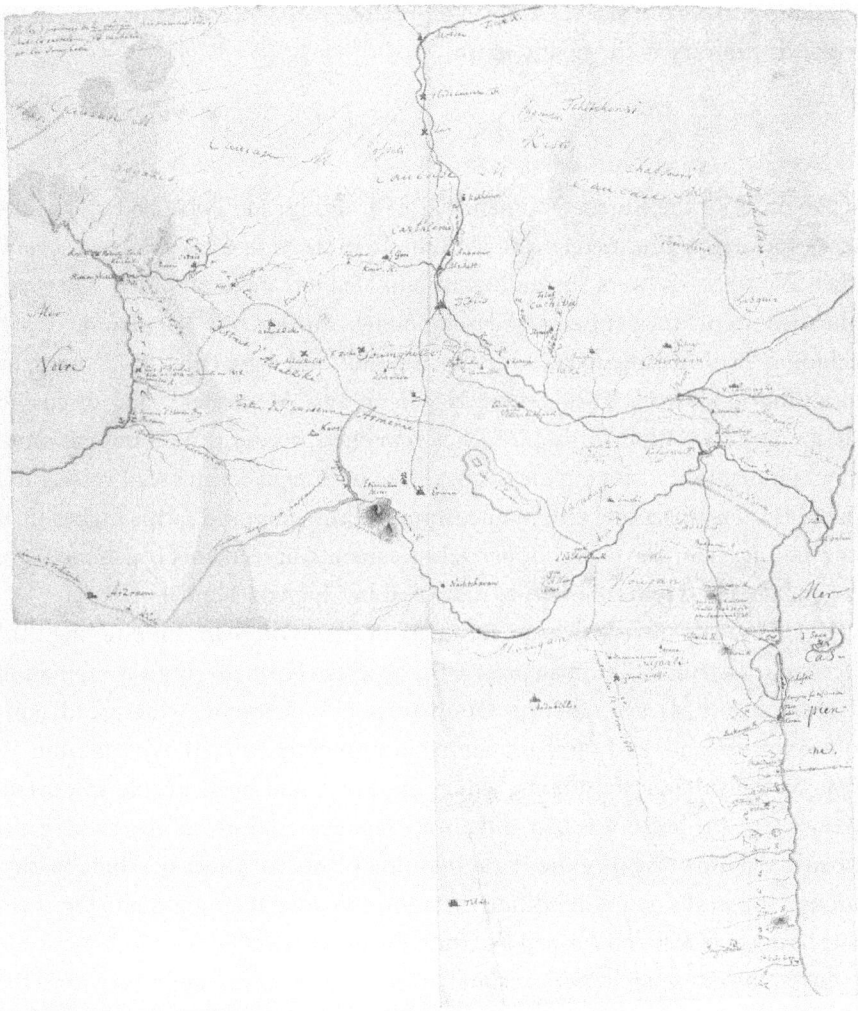

Map 4 Liston's Map of Georgia, Source: NLS MS 5579.

Ahmet Zeki, he strove to persuade the Ottoman commissioner to renounce them. He tried to explain to Zeki the 'true contents of the treaty', maintaining that the islands on the Danube would be held in common and remain uninhabited according to the 1812 settlement and that the frontier line was to be drawn along the large islands. Ahmet Zeki was unyielding – and, in the eyes of Harting, blatantly ignorant. He insisted on his demands, placing further strain on Russo-Ottoman relations. Peeved by the reports of Harting and Rumyantsev, d'Italinsky urged the Porte 'to forbid all Ottoman representatives or commissioners to make demands contrary to the treaty [again]'.[60]

§ § §

At the onset of the Russo-Ottoman War of 1806–12, the Porte had closed the straits to foreign commercial ships. Multiple protests from Russia and several other European powers, including Britain, fell on deaf ears. The Ottoman ministers were exasperated by developments during the Napoleonic Wars, including British campaigns targeting Istanbul and Egypt in 1807,[61] and the unsettling news from Tilsit, where Napoleon and Alexander I had discussed partitioning the Ottoman Empire. They remained steadfast in their decision to maintain neutrality, keeping the straits closed to foreign commercial vessels and warships.[62] Furthermore, Ottoman customs officers imposed tariffs higher than the amount set by previous commercial agreements, agreements which the Porte had endeavoured to recalibrate, as discussed in Chapters 3 and 4.

However, the severe wheat shortage in the Ottoman Empire in 1812 necessitated a shift in Ottoman policy. The shortage resulted from a combination of factors, such as the faltering Ottoman public economy, widespread non-cultivation of land, and rampant contraband (mainly British) exports from all parts of the sultan's dominions, which the Porte had been unable to curtail. Everywhere 'the bread was bad', d'Italinsky reported to the tsar, 'everywhere it is expensive'.[63] This was why the Porte permitted Russian merchant ships to pass through the straits on the condition that they unloaded their grain into Ottoman state barns at prices determined by Ottoman authorities.[64]

Given the Ottoman imperial capital's 'dire need' and the lengthy wait until the new harvest, Russian ships arriving from Russian ports with bread, barley and other grain were required to deposit half of their cargo in state stores.[65] Payment for these would be made in cash at the rate of five piastres per kilo, provided that the Commercial Treaty of 1783 was not infringed.[66] To ensure compliance, Russian ships were searched, and according to some captains, molested or

---

[60] Ibid., 364.
[61] See Chapter 5 of this book.
[62] BOA HAT 949/40816.
[63] A. Y. Italinsky to Alexander I, 13 February 1813, *VPR* I/VII, 46–50.
[64] Italinsky to Rumyantsev, 30 October 1812, *VPR* I/VI, 594.
[65] Ibid.
[66] BOA HAT 1165/46102; Italinsky to Rumyantsev, 30 October 1812, *VPR* I/VI, 594; Note from A. Y. Italinsky to the Ottoman Government, 17 January 1813, *VPR* I/VII, 16–18.

detained.⁶⁷ D'Italinsky protested to Ottoman authorities, maintaining that the previous agreements had set the rate at six piastres per kilo, which already represented a significant sacrifice on the part of the tsar. He warned that acting otherwise would prejudice the 1783 agreement and harm Russian commerce.⁶⁸

Seeing that a compromise was not within sight, the Russian envoy devised a plan to make an unexpected move and immediately supply the Ottoman government with 100,000 tchetverts of wheat, the quantity needed by the Porte for that year. D'Italinksy wrote to Alexander I about his plan, requesting the tsar to announce that Russia would willingly provide wheat annually, 'at the request of the Porte', for the supply of its capital. The Russian envoy argued that this would be an extremely magnanimous move on the part of the tsar. If the Russians came to the aid of the empire, it would produce 'the best effect' on the sultan, his ministry and the Muslim people. Such an act would allow for the resumption of Black Sea navigation without hindrance and the weakening of the so-called French party at the Porte.⁶⁹

The tsar sent to Sultan Mahmud II accordingly on 10 April 1813. 'At a time when providence has brought my victorious armies into the lands of my enemies,' he began:

> at a time when Warsaw, Berlin, Dresden, Hamburg, Lübeck, Lüneburg, and many other cities and provinces are occupied by my armies, ... and when the French army in Pomerania has been annihilated to the last man, ... at this time of glorious success for me, I wish to assure ... the sincerity of my friendship to you ... I approve in full force the regulation on the trade in bread ... for this current year only, for with the restoration of peace there will be abundance in your vast capital. I hope that your Sultan will accept this proof of my zeal for the preservation of your personal and your capital's tranquillity at the present price.⁷⁰

In his reply, the sultan expressed his gratitude for the friendly conduct of the tsar. Alexander I's offer was accepted but Mahmud II did not mention the resumption of commerce in the Black Sea.⁷¹ This omission prompted d'Italinsky to submit another note to the Porte, requesting that the impediments to Russian trade,

---

⁶⁷ Note from A. Y. Italinsky to the Ottoman Government, 17 January 1813, *VPR* I/VII, 16–18.
⁶⁸ Note from A.Y. Italinsky to the Turkish government, 11 March 1813, *VPR* I/VII, 83–4.
⁶⁹ A. Y. Italinsky to Alexander I, 13 February 1813, *VPR* I/VII, 46–50.
⁷⁰ Alexander I to Mahmud II, Trachenberg, 10 April 1813, *VPR* I/VII, 144.
⁷¹ BOA TS.MA.e 867/6, no date.

which were 'in contravention of the clear and precise stipulations of the [1783] treaty of commerce', be lifted.[72] Russian protests continued during the coming months.[73]

In early 1814 the Porte at first lifted all restrictions on Russian navigation between the Black Sea and the Mediterranean Sea. Due to opposition from French party ministers, however, it quickly reversed course and permitted only Russian commercial vessels carrying grain to pass the straits.[74] Liston also demanded passage for British ships, but neither he nor the Spanish or Austrian agents who had made similar claims received a satisfactory response.[75] Without permission from the Porte for the passage of their ships into the Black Sea, Russian, British and other merchants were compelled to smuggle.[76] This subject resurfaced at the Congress of Vienna at the end of the year.

§ § §

Meanwhile, a congress had convened in Prague in the summer of 1813 and witnessed the signing of the treaties of Reichenbach. Although a general peace could not be achieved at Prague, the formation of the quadruple alliance, with Austria joining the combined Powers (Britain, Russia, Prussia, Spain, Portugal, Sardinia and others) during the war of the Sixth Coalition, was met with surprise and considerable disappointment by the Porte. Despite Austrian internuncio Baron Stürmer's assurances of Austria's continued support for the Ottoman Empire, Ottoman ministers were concerned that Austria's alliance had tipped the scales in Russia's favour in the war against France.[77]

In early August 1813, the Ottoman chargé d'affaires in Vienna, Yanko Mavroyeni argued that if the goal of the Prague gathering was to achieve a general peace in Europe, one based on a 'balance of power' and the 'reestablishment of the former reciprocal relations and proportionate strength of the nations of Europe', then the congress should restore the sultan's former possessions in Ottoman Europe.[78] Reis Efendi Küçük Ârif enquired whether British representatives

---

[72] 'Note from A.Y. Italinsky to the Turkish Government', 3 May 1813, *VPR* I/VII, 188–9.
[73] A. Y. Italinsky to K. V. Nesselrode, 26 March 1814, VPR I/VII, 624–6.
[74] A.Y. Italinsky to N.P. Rumyantsev, 14 July 1814, *VPR* I/VIII, 62–3.
[75] Robert Liston to Lord Castlereagh, 25 July 1814, NLS MS 5628, f. 51; A.Y. Italinsky to N.P. Rumyantsev, 14 July 1814, *VPR* I/VIII, 62–3.
[76] A.Y. Italinsky to N.P. Rumyantsev, 13 May 1813, *VPR* I/VII, 198.
[77] BOA HAT 1282/49718; BOA HAT 1206/47282; Robert Liston to Lord Castlereagh, 22 September 1813, NLS MS 5628, f. 147.
[78] Cevdet Paşa, *Tarih-i Cevdet* V, 2534; Robert Liston to Lord Castlereagh, 13 August 1813, NLS MS 5627, f. 133.

could support Ottoman claims in the ongoing Russo-Ottoman disputes at the Congress of Prague. Ottoman objectives included recovering the provinces beyond the Danube, securing full control around the Phasis Valley, and regaining sovereignty over the Republic of Ragusa. Smiling, Liston observed that, when it came to this last aim, it would be necessary for the Porte to apply directly to 'the usurper' of their rights – Bonaparte.[79]

After this conversation, the British ambassador grew concerned that 'the inattention of Russia' to Ottoman remonstrances 'might sooner or later lead to a rupture'.[80] Ottoman agents cautioned that 'if this course continued to be pursued [by Russia], we shall infallibly have another war'.[81] The ambassador promptly discussed the great risk with d'Italinsky. But these dialogues were not well received in the court of Saint Petersburg.

The hardline Russian foreign minister, Rumyantsev, was incensed: 'I do not know, my lord', he wrote to Tsar Alexander I, 'what to marvel at more: the simple-mindedness of the Porte, or the fact that your envoy shows neither surprise nor displeasure at this,' referring to the pacific language d'Italinsky had held until then. Rumyantsev suggested that the tsar should form an army ready to embark the Black Sea fleet, which would change the behaviour of the Porte immediately. It would make the sultan 'prudent and cautious, irrespective of the events of the present war'. Rumyantsev believed that, otherwise, the Porte might take advantage of the first failure of Russia in its war against France.[82]

Having received no instructions from the tsar for more than a month, Rumyantsev wrote to d'Italinsky at the end of October 1813. He acknowledged that the 1812 treaty required Russia to return lands conquered in the 1806–12 war to the Porte. But, Rumyantsev argued, the tsar's court had already 'completed the fulfilment of its obligations' by returning the fortresses of Anapa, Poti and Akhalkalak. Claims made by the Porte concerning the people and provinces not covered by the treaty were moot, for those provinces 'were not conquered by force of arms, but voluntarily submitted to the Russian sceptre, some even before the outbreak of war'. The people and rulers of those provinces were 'entitled to decide their own fate'.[83] After the signing of the peace treaty between Russia and Persia on 24 October 1813, Russia had obtained control of all the mountainous

---

[79] Robert Liston to Lord Castlereagh, 13 August 1813, NLS MS 5627, f. 133.
[80] Robert Liston to Lord Castlereagh, 2 November 1813, NLS MS 5627, f. 153.
[81] Robert Liston to Lord Castlereagh, 9 October 1813, NLS MS 5627, f. 149.
[82] N.P. Rumyantsev to Alexander I, 30 September 1813, *VPR* I/VII, 386–7.
[83] Rumyantsev to A.Y. Italinsky, 28 October 1813, *VPR* I/VII, 426–7.

principalities lying between the Caspian and the Black Seas.⁸⁴ According to Rumyantsev, this secured the Phasis Valley and the adjoining districts as Russian property.⁸⁵ He warned that, if the Porte kept making objections, it would lead to war.

'Another victory over France'

In February 1814, even after Mehmed Galib, the signatory of the 1812 peace with Russia, became the new Reis Efendi in place of the late Küçük Ârif, Liston did not expect a change in the Porte's neutral diplomatic stance.⁸⁶ Galib was a man of considerable talents and experience, Liston reported after an audience with him, but the new Reis Efendi also suspected that the ultimate designs of the tsar were to retain permanent possession of the coast of Mingrelia in the Phasis Valley. Galib feared that Alexander I could use the region as a staging post, to facilitate his plans of encroachment and conquest when an opportune moment came.⁸⁷

Liston reminded Galib that the Reis Efendi had himself consented to the cession of the land in question in 1812, by a secret article of the treaty. The tsar was 'excusable for still looking forward to the possession of the disputed post', because, in agreeing to ratify the treaty without the secret article, he had 'expressly proposed that the point should be referred to further discussion'. But Galib was unimpressed. He believed that the affair had by now been placed on a new and more suspicious footing, especially when the court of Saint Petersburg asserted that not only the disputed spot but the whole district around the Phasis Valley belonged to Russia.⁸⁸

Two days later, Galib held a meeting with d'Italinsky, during which both parties reiterated their claims. D'Italinsky assured Galib that the tsar had 'not the most distant idea of making conquests and encroachments on the Turkish territories'. Russia, he insisted, only intended to retain what it had acquired by force of arms and legitimate contract. Galib, however, disputed the legality of Russia's actions, leading to a breakdown in the talks.⁸⁹

---

⁸⁴ 'Treaty of Peace and Friendship between Russia and Persia, Gulistan', 24 October 1813, *VPR* I/VII, 403.
⁸⁵ Robert Liston to Lord Castlereagh, 26 February 1814, NLS MS 5628, f. 7.
⁸⁶ Şânî-zâde Mehmed 'Atâ'ullah Efendi, *Şânî-zâde Târihi* I, 659; *Câbî Târihi* II, 1048.
⁸⁷ Robert Liston to Lord Castlereagh, 10 February 1814, NLS MS 5628, f. 3.
⁸⁸ Ibid.
⁸⁹ Robert Liston to Lord Castlereagh, 26 February 1814, NLS MS 5628, f. 7.

§ § §

With the progress of the forces of Russia and her allies into France since December 1813, and notably with the provision of Russian grain and the temporary ousting of the leaders of the so-called French party, such as Halet Efendi, from the imperial council, the tides momentarily turned in the Ottoman imperial capital. One and a half years after his arrival in Istanbul, d'Italinsky was finally granted an audience with the sultan in March 1814. The customary ceremony had been postponed until then due to the reluctance of the Porte to enter into official talks with Russia, and due to the schemes of the French ambassador General Andréossi and the French party.

'[T]he very lateness of the delay gave the greater significance to the decision finally taken to fulfil this formality,' d'Italinsky reported.[90] Something that in ordinary times would barely have been noticed became one of the major events in the life of the Ottoman imperial capital. By the day of the audience, there were more than thirty Russian ships in the harbour of Istanbul: 'our cannons were sounded twice, Russian flags and pennants were flying over the ships ... and in general everything looked as if Constantinople had become a Russian port'. The Russian envoy was followed by grateful crowds, from Pera to the heart the capital itself. D'Italinsky considered the audience 'another victory over France'.[91]

In point of fact, at this moment of rapprochement with Russia in March 1814, the imperial council (*Divan*) resolved to apply to the anticipated general congress to settle peace in Europe. They hoped that their affairs with Russia could be discussed and arranged favourably for them.[92] Galib Efendi informed Liston of their hopes. But by the time the Congress of Vienna began in September 1814, further dramatic changes had occurred in the Ottoman imperial capital.

General Andréossi's influence on these events is noteworthy. A veteran of Napoleon Bonaparte's Italian campaigns and the Egyptian expedition, Andréossi remained a loyal follower of the emperor, undertaking a series of diplomatic missions in London and then Vienna before his appointment to the Istanbul embassy in 1812. His primary task in the Ottoman imperial capital was to urge the Porte to continue its war with Russia and to invite the sultan into an alliance against their common enemy.[93] However, as we have seen in previous chapters,

---

[90] A.Y. Italinsky to K.V. Nesselrode, 26 March 1814, *VPR* I/VII, 624.
[91] Ibid.
[92] Robert Liston to Lord Castlereagh, 26 March 1814, NLS MS 5628, f. 15.
[93] Géraud Poumarède, '1814 vue de Constantinople: Le général-comte Andréossy et la chute de l'Empire', in Laurent Coste (ed.) *Le Sud-Ouest, la France et l'Europe à la fin de l'Empire napoléonien* (Bordeaux: MSHA, 2015), 55–68, at 55.

by the time Andréossi arrived in Istanbul in late July 1812, the Russo-Ottoman peace treaty had already been signed and ratified.[94] Despite his efforts, Andréossi could not reignite the Russo-Ottoman War.[95]

After Prussia's defection at the end of 1812 and Austria's alignment with Russia and Britain following the Congress of Prague, Andréossi found himself cut off from almost all communication with Paris – the Vienna route had been suspended by Austria, the Balkan route was prohibited after the loss of the Illyrian provinces in 1813, and the sea route was blocked by the British navy.[96] Facing significant financial difficulties, Andréossi sent several letters to Paris and retaliated against the Austrian 'betrayal' by abruptly terminating the temporary tenancy of the Austrian internuncio Baron Stürmer at the Dutch Palace in Istanbul – a French possession at the time – and forcing him to leave the premises.[97]

Against all odds, Andréossi's communication with the Porte became more frequent and intimate in the spring of 1814. Although Liston expected that the victories of the allied courts would prompt more friendly conduct from the Porte, Ottoman agents chose 'the opposite system' once again.[98] This was partly due to the return of Halet to the imperial council, which saw the so-called French party regain power. Additionally, Ottoman ministers dreaded that the total destruction and degradation of France would deprive them 'of an old friend' and 'a powerful ally', while the increasing glory and power of Russia inspired them with 'jealousy and dread'.[99] At the same time, Andréossi's suggestions that European peace was still 'at a great distance' encouraged certain ministers, such as Halet and Halil Efendi, as well as the sultan, to continue military preparations against Russia.[100]

The French ambassador was elated by the momentary advantage gained by Napoleon Bonaparte over Marshal Blücher's Army of Silesia at Brienne-le-Château in late January (due to absence of telegram system at the time, the news arrived weeks later).[101] He told Ottoman ministers that the approaching congress in Vienna was only meant to please the people of France and to gain time, that the war had become a national one and that Napoleon would ultimately triumph

---

[94] *Câbî Târihi* II, 943.
[95] Robert Liston to Lord Castlereagh, 4 September 1812, NLS MS 5627, f. 41.
[96] Poumarède, '1814 vue de Constantinople', 55–6.
[97] 'De Frontiers de Turquie', *Journal de Francfort*, 29 March 1814; Ozan Ozavci, 'Intrigue at the Dutch Palace', The Security History Network Blog, 24 April 2023.
[98] Robert Liston to Lord Castlereagh, 25 April 1814, NLS MS 5628, f. 19.
[99] Robert Liston to Lord Castlereagh, 9 April 1814, NLS MS 5628, f. 17.
[100] Robert Liston to Lord Castlereagh, 25 April 1814, NLS MS 5628, f. 19.
[101] Ibid.; Mikaberidze, *Napoleonic Wars*, 577–8.

over all his enemies. He spread rumours in Istanbul about 'the ruinous situation of the allied armies in France', that the allies were completely defeated, that the Russian army had abandoned the Austrian army to its fate, and that the Swedish crown prince had abandoned the allies.[102] The French ambassador made considerable progress in gaining the confidence of the Porte, Liston admitted, so much so that he had several secret audiences with the sultan: there were now too few 'staunch friend[s] of the good cause' in the Ottoman cabinet. The Porte was 'proceeding blindly in a course which must terminate in a rupture'.[103]

Upon learning of the shift in the Ottoman cabinet's disposition, the court of Saint Petersburg grew anxious. Karl V. Nesselrode (1780–1862), state secretary and the head of the Russian delegation to Vienna, wrote to d'Italinsky that 'if the [Ottoman] Diwan takes the wrong path in politics, then it alone will be responsible for the possible consequences of such decisions'. As the war with France neared its end, 180,000 Russian soldiers on the Vistula, the Bug and on the borders of the province of Podolia had been freed up, with 200,000 more soon returning home. 'These remarks, Mr. Envoy, are not empty phrases,' Nesselrode warned.[104]

Just about the same time, news of Napoleon Bonaparte's removal from the throne of France and the approaching restoration of the Bourbon royal family arrived in Istanbul on 9 May 1814. It led to 'astonishment and dejection' within the Porte, Liston reported. The Ottoman ministers were 'indeed completely thunderstruck with the intelligence'.[105] The British ambassador was hopeful that the sultan would now dismiss the French party.[106]

§ § §

With Napoleon's exile to the Island of Elba in the spring of 1814, in fact all diplomatic corps in Pera anticipated the imminent downfall of the so-called French party at the Porte.[107] Contrary to these expectations, the French party gained even more power. 'Not only have the expectations of the public ... been disappointed', Liston wrote in June 1814, but Galib Efendi, 'the minister whose

---

[102] A.Y. Italinsky to K.V. Nesselrode, 26 March 1814, *VPR* I/VII, 624–6.
[103] Robert Liston to Lord Castlereagh, 25 April 1814, NLS MS 5628, f. 19.
[104] K.V. Nesselrode to A.Y. Italinsky, 18 April 1814, *VPR* I/VII, 656–7.
[105] Robert Liston to Lord Castlereagh, 11 May 1814, NLS MS 5628, f. 26.
[106] Ibid.
[107] Robert Liston to Lord Castlereagh, 10 June 1814, NLS MS 5628, f. 37.

talents, information and experience rendered him the most formidable rival' to the French party, had been abruptly sent into exile.[108]

In *Şânizâde Tarihi*, the Ottoman observer and historian Şânizâde Mehmet Ataullah Efendi (1769–1826) maintains that the dismissal and exile of Galib Efendi (and his associates in the Porte such as Sani Hamid Bey and Emin Efendi) resulted from his reckless actions.[109] In *Tarih-i Cevdet*, the historian Cevdet Paşa argues that in his view the real reason for his dismissal was that Galib's conduct had riled Halet Efendi.[110] Liston's reports from the time corroborate both accounts.

On 10 June, the British ambassador informed Lord Castlereagh that the probable reason for Galib's dismissal was that, at an imperial council meeting, he had spoken 'too freely of the inability of the Porte' to fight Russia and 'exposed with such eloquence the folly of hazarding a rupture for trifling interest'. He confounded his antagonists, particularly Halet and Halil while also offending the sultan 'whose ears have not been accustomed to hear disagreeable truth'.[111]

Two weeks later, Liston detailed what he believed to be the 'real causes' of Galib's 'disgrace'. He gathered this from the chief dragoman Pisani and *kahya bey* Mazhar, with whom he had long maintained confidential relations. According to their accounts, Galib had been dismissed after Halet's conspiracies, which arose when Galib began to acquire a decided influence over the sultan.[112] Mahmud II had recently sent for Galib and asked his views on the two main objects occupying the attention of the Porte – the foreign affairs of the empire and its internal state, 'where serious discontents prevail on account of the sultan's supposed intention to review the project of introducing a new discipline in the army'.[113]

Even though the sultan had repressed the mutinous spirit of the Janissaries with considerable severity and successfully detached them from the *ulema*,[114] Galib counselled the sultan that the time was not right for initiating any measures

---

[108] Robert Liston to Lord Castlereagh, 25 June 1814, NLS MS 5628, f. 37.
[109] Şânî-zâde Mehmed 'Atâ'ullah Efendi, *Şâni-zâde Tarihi* I, 668.
[110] Cevdet Paşa, *Tarih-i Cevdet* V, 2550.
[111] Robert Liston to Lord Castlereagh, 10 June 1814, NLS MS 5628, f. 37.
[112] Robert Liston to Lord Castlereagh, 25 June 1814, NLS MS 5628, f. 37; A.Y. Italinksy to K.V. Nesselrode, 29 May 1815, VPR I/VIII, 354–8.
[113] Robert Liston to Lord Castlereagh, 25 June 1814, NLS MS 5628, f. 30; 'Sur la Turquie', par Comte Andréossi, April 1815, AMAE 50MD/31, Correspondance Politique Turquie, 1808–1819, f. 145.
[114] Religious Islamic scholars and advisers.

that might heighten their anxiety. He urged prudence, emphasizing that caution in this matter was 'more than ever necessary' given the current state of Ottoman relations with the European states, which required the Porte to act 'with perfect civility and attention'.

According to Liston, Galib's arguments produced a temporary conviction in the mind of the sultan, who announced his resolution to make a corresponding change. But his adversaries, Halet and Halil, were astonished to hear this. They felt their continued political existence was at stake and hastened to counteract the influence of Galib by a memorandum in which they stated:

> [T]he sultan could not have been induced to swerve for an instant from the right and dignified system of conduct he had so long pursued but by the treacherous information given by such a man as the maker of the last peace with Russia [i.e. Galib Efendi], and who had always been a determined friend of the Janissaries. A man whose partiality to Foreign Nations was demonstrated by the whole course of his administration, a man who in private life affected to imitate … the manners of the Franks; who authorized a culpable and indecorous conduct in his dependents (… a noisy entertainment, with dancing and music, given by his confidential secretary) … A Man who in short carried his imitation of Christian ministers so far as not to appear at his office till after the third hour of the day (11 o'clock), neglecting thus the management of the most urgent business of the State.[115]

Halet and Halil further maintained that the affairs of France were still far from being settled. Information transmitted by Yanko Mavroyeni suggested that the ultimate resolution of the war remained uncertain due to the quarrels among the allies and the formidable partisans of Bonaparte who could still turn the tide. To Halet and Halil, neither the external nor internal affairs of the empire gave any cause for alarm. They argued that 'only by firm resolution and an uninterrupted perseverance in the same system' that the sultan had been pursuing could they 'hope to arrive at results consistent with [the] dignity and worthy of the high destinies of the Ottoman Empire'.

Since the reasoning of the two flattered the sultan, Mahmud II, with little hesitation, adopted their propositions and dismissed Galib Efendi, assigning in his place Mehmet Seyyidâ (also known as Mehmed Seyyid) Efendi.[116] A

---

[115] Ibid.
[116] Şânî-zâde Mehmed 'Atâ'ullah Efendi, *Şânî-zâde Tarihi* I, 668; Robert Liston to Lord Castlereagh, 25 June 1814, NLS MS 5628, f. 30.

week later, Halet was reappointed as the butler of the sultan.[117] That is, just as Napoleon fell from power in France, the so-called French party, which was intent on sequestering the Porte from European politics, gained supremacy in Istanbul. This would heavily influence the Porte's decisions when a new international order came into being at the Congress of Vienna in 1814–15.[118]

---

[117] Şânî-zâde Mehmed 'Atâ'ullah Efendi, *Şânî-zâde Tarihi* I, 698.
[118] De Graaf, *Fighting Terror after Napoleon*; Glenda Sluga, *The Invention of International Order*.

8

The Vienna moment

Two proud nations

The day after receiving the news of the Bourbons' return to power, the French ambassador to Istanbul, General Andréossi, removed the *tricoleur* and the eagles from the French Palace and hoisted the *fleur-de-lys*.[1] On 12 July 1814, Liston and the other inhabitants of Pera received intelligence of the first Treaty of Paris (concluded on 30 May 1814), which sealed the peace between the Allied Powers and France. To celebrate this, Andréossi, once a loyal follower of Napoleon, organized a dinner, inviting over his once adversaries. At the dinner, he made a toast to the new king Louis XVIII, 'to the peace he has given us and to the firmness he has shown'.[2]

Upon the advent of the new regime, Andréossi was promptly tasked with the delicate mission of restoring friendly relations between France and the Ottoman Empire, alongside fostering goodwill with other embassies in Istanbul, 'formerly enemies or subjects, now allies'.[3] The aim was to convey to the Porte that the traditional friendship between the courts of Paris and Istanbul had been disrupted by the preceding government. The dispatch to Andréossi highlighted that in 1798 Napoleon had unjustifiably attacked Ottoman territories in Egypt, aiming to embroil 'the Turks in his first war against Russia'. After spurring them into military action, he ultimately 'sacrificed them' by the Franco-Russian peace at Tilsit in 1807. The time had come to restore normalcy in diplomatic relations.[4]

The narrative presented in Andréossi's communication to the Porte must have struck Ottoman ministers as both reassuring and alarming. While it aligned with their perception of recent interactions with France, it also evoked memories of

---

[1] Robert Liston to Lord Castlereagh, 25 May 1814, NLS MS 5628, f. 27.
[2] Poumarède, '1814 vue de Constantinople', 61.
[3] Ibid., 65; Andréossi to Liston, 23 July 1814, NLS MS 5626, f. 64–5.
[4] Ibid.

vulnerability. It signalled the end of an era. The revolutionary French regime, which had long served to counterbalance the Ottoman position against Russia, had ceased to exist. This was in itself a source of concern for Mahmud II.

As the attention of Europe turned to the peace congress that would be held in Vienna, the new Reis Efendi Mehmed Seyyidâ sought Liston's counsel on the policy that the Porte should adopt.[5] Initially hesitant to express any opinion on the matter, Liston was persuaded when he was told that the sultan might adopt 'a part of the measure' he might suggest. Consequently, in July 1814, the British ambassador dispatched an 'unsigned', 'perfectly secret' and 'confidential note' in Turkish through his dragoman Pisani.[6] In it Liston invited the sultan to send a minister, of respectable rank and character, to Vienna, not to sit in the congress, – for probably only those who took a share in the war will be admitted, but to be within reach of the assembly to give explanations if required – to watch over the interests of the Ottoman Empire.[7]

Liston opined that the courts of Saint Petersburg and Istanbul, as 'two proud nations', were unlikely to come to a lasting peace. '[T]wo powerful Sovereigns have no superior but God, no Court of appeal but Heaven,' he noted:

> [A]s between man and man a dispute may without hurting the honour of either be submitted to common impartial friends, so it seems that between crowned Heads their differences might be safely referred to the decision of another Sovereign or other Sovereigns whose sentiments and interests are of a nature to lead them to justice ... The affairs of the Porte may naturally become an object of discussion [at the Congress of Vienna]; for her tranquillity and independence are nearly connected with a system of general and permanent peace which is said to be the ultimate object of the meeting.

Liston proposed that Sultan Mahmud II should write letters to the principal crowned heads, requesting their acceptance of his minister and the inclusion of his disputes with Tsar Alexander I in the congress discussions. The sultan should assure them that he would 'abide by their award'. This was a substantial concession, but the essential interests of the Ottoman Empire would not be jeopardized under the mediators' guidance, Liston added, because the Sublime Porte had long shown 'no disposition to conquer or invade her neighbours', demonstrating less jealousy and illiberal views on commerce than European nations had been displaying towards each other. The one exception was 'a

---

[5] Robert Liston to Lord Castlereagh, 25 July 1814, TNA FO 78/82, f. 72.
[6] BOA TS.MA.e 243/16, 6 July 1814.
[7] 'Unsigned Note', 18 July 1814, NLS MS 5628, f. 55.

disregard to certain articles of ancient treaties, a refusal of trifling favours and even sometimes a denial of justice', according to Liston. He was referring to the aforementioned suspension of Black Sea trade and the unwillingness to honour commercial agreements since 1806.

Despite these issues, European powers had not 'proceeded the length of a wish to see any other nation established at Constantinople'. On the contrary, they had a vested interest in maintaining 'the Porte as a great and independent Empire'. Liston also conceded the possibility of returning the district in the Phasis Valley to Russia, recognizing that 'the Porte has a clear and incontrovertible right to demand' it. 'Cool and imperial men' might not regard it 'as a matter of essential concern', he argued given that the Porte had agreed to cede that territory to Russia by a secret article in the Treaty of Bucharest.

It now fell on the Ottoman ministry to deliberate on whether the prospect of permanent peace and security would indeed 'compensate the disappointment arising from the supposable loss'. If the differences 'unfortunately terminate in a quarrel, it is not unimportant to have to say to the world that every step was taken that could tend to a reconciliation'.[8] Liston's was an explicit request from the sultan to secure representation for his empire at the forthcoming congress in Vienna, entrusting the resolution of his differences with Russia to the mediating European powers.

§   §   §

At the Congress of Vienna, Tsar Alexander I's policy aimed, among other goals, to preserve the frontiers in Asia and Europe adjacent to the Ottoman Empire, while seeking expansion on the western side through the acquisition of the Duchy of Warsaw.[9] As for his territorial disputes with the Porte, the tsar seemed disinclined to enter into any discussions, preferring to maintain the status quo for the time being.[10] Concurrently, he justified Russia's territorial claims in Poland 'as a compensation for the sacrifices she has made and as a guarantee of her security for the future'.[11] For the tsar, this was a precondition for establishing a new European equilibrium.

---

[8] Ibid.
[9] Note by K.V. Nesselrode, 12 August 1814, *VPR* I/VIII, 87–8.
[10] Tim Chapman, *The Congress of Vienna: Origins, Processes and Results* (London, New York: Routledge, 1998), 23–4.
[11] 'Instructions from Alexander I to K.V. Nesselrode', 13 August 1814, *VPR* I/VIII, 89.

Alexander I's demands regarding Poland and the issues involving the Porte in the Balkans (the 'Serbian question') and the Caucasus (the 'Asiatic question'), collectively formed the core of the 'Eastern Question' at the time. These issues were considered alongside other matters concerning Saxony, Bavaria and Italy, among others.[12]

Even before the Congress of Vienna commenced on 18 September 1814, Russian revisionism was viewed as a potential cause of conflict between Russia and Austria. While Russia was firmly demanding the acquisition and incorporation of all the former provinces of the Kingdom of Poland, the sultan's ministers received regular updates on developments in Europe from the Ottoman chargé d'affaires Yanko Mavroyeni, and through John George Caradja (1754–1844), prince of Wallachia.[13] Caradja communicated frequently with Friedrich von Gentz (1764–1832), the Austrian secretary of the congress and Chancellor Prince Metternich's confidant, who placed great importance to the persistence of the Ottoman Empire for European security.

As a matter of fact, under his counsel, placing the territorial integrity of the Ottoman Empire 'under the guarantee of the new order' had become a cornerstone of the Austrian Near Eastern policy, and particularly for Prince Klemens Metternich (1773–1859).[14] To maintain general peace and tranquillity throughout Europe, it was of utmost importance to ensure stability in their backyard in the Balkans.[15] In July 1814, around the same time Liston invited the Porte to send a minister to Vienna, Metternich had made the exact same request from the Reis Efendi.[16]

For its part, the Porte was anxious about the advantages Russia might gain through negotiations over the reconstruction of Europe.[17] At the start of

---

[12] Stein to Alexander I, 21 June 1814, VPR I/VIII, 25; K.V. Nesselrode to G.O. Stackelberg (secret), 22 June 1814, VPR I/VIII, 26; G.O. Stackelberg to K.V. Nesselrode, 21 July 1814, VPR I/VIII, 67; K.V. Nesselrode to Alexander I, 25 September 1814, VPR I/VIII, 103; Italinsky to the Court of Saint Petersburg, 15 January 1815, AVPRI f. 133, o. 468, d. 2303, l. 21–9; 'Articles sur lequels les Plénipotentiaires de Russie doivent recevoir des instructions: Rapports du Comte Nesselrode', AVPRI f. 133, o. 468, d. 11781, l. 3–13, l. 25–30, l. 43–7; Halil İnalcık, 'Tanzimat Nedir?' in Halil İnalcık, Mehmet Seyitdanlıoğlu (eds.), *Tanzimat Değişim Sürecinde Osmanlı İmparatorluğu* (Ankara: Türkiye İş Bankası Yayınları, 2012), 48.

[13] 'Précis de la lettre écrite au Drogman de la Porte par le Chargé d'affaires Ottoman à Vienne, et expédiée avec le courier de la Sublime Porte Souleiman Tatari', 14 Juin 1814, AVPRI f. 133, k. 1814, o. 468, d. 2295, l. 415–16; BOA HAT 953/40926; BOA 1277/49536; BOA HAT 1278/49568; Dépêches inédites du Chevalier de Gentz aux Hospodars de Valachie pour servir à l'histoire de la politique européenne (1813 à 1828), I, ed. Anton Prokesch-Osten (Paris, 1876) [hereafter *Dépêches*].

[14] Miroslav Šedivý, *Metternich, the Great Powers and the Eastern Question* (Pilsen: TYPOS, 2013), 56.

[15] Metternich to Stürmer, 5 October 1814, HHStA, StA, Türkei VI, 10, cf. Sedivy, *Metternich*, 40.

[16] Sedivy, *Metternich*, 40.

[17] Italinsky to Nesselrode, 22 June 1814, AVPRI f. 133, o. 468, d. 2295, l. 292.

the congress, however, more than two months after Liston delivered his note to the sultan, there was still no response from the court of Istanbul. 'I must almost assume', Gentz wrote to Caradja, 'that there is no intention in Constantinople to take any steps with regard to any guarantee clause of the Ottoman possessions'.[18]

Two weeks later, as the conference progressed, Gentz became increasingly uneasy. He asserted that it was 'a matter of urgent necessity that the Porte should take a step, if not a solemn one, at least a very positive and very pronounced one to urge the principal Powers to guarantee its rights and possessions by some formal act'. Gentz feared that even if the congress concluded 'in the least alarming manner' without causing new upheavals, it was 'inevitable' that Russia, the Porte's 'most dangerous enemy, the only one it has to fear today', would emerge with enormous advantages. This would leave the political position of the Porte more precarious and 'more threatened than it has ever been'. For Gentz, it would be 'neither wise, nor proper, nor even very decent on the part of a great Power like the Ottoman Empire, not to raise its voice, and to make, as it were, its political existence forgotten'.[19]

Ottoman chargé d'affaires Mavroyeni also believed it was necessary to appoint a minister plenipotentiary at the Congress of Vienna because he would not be allowed to attend many of the gatherings as a 'member of the fourth class' in the diplomatic rank. Without any money and 'deprived even of the necessities of life, my zeal and my eagerness to serve the S[ublime] P[orte]' would not be 'sufficient', he feared.[20]

§ § §

The Porte's response, which came three months later in November 1814, took Liston, Gentz, Mavroyeni and many other European statesmen and diplomats by surprise. The sultan refused to send a plenipotentiary to Vienna. Ottoman historian Cevdet Paşa contends that the reason for the Porte's prolonged silence and eventual rejection of the powers' invitation stemmed from its focus on internal affairs as well as the lack of capable men to represent the Porte at the congress.[21] Although it was true that talented delegates such as Vahid and Galib

---

[18] Gentz to Caradja, 24 September 1814, *Dépêches*, 105.
[19] Gentz to Caradja, 6 October 1814, *Dépêches*, 117–8.
[20] 'Précis de la lettre écrite au Drogman de la Porte par le Chargé d'affaires Ottoman à Vienne, et expédiée avec le courier de la Sublime Porte Souleiman Tatari', 14 June 1814, AVPRI f. 133, k. 1814, o. 468, d. 2295, l. 415–16.
[21] Cevdet Paşa, *Tarih-i Cevdet V*, 2558–9.

efendis had been dismissed by the sultan, and that Mahmud II was preoccupied with a dangerous quarrel with local notables and the janissaries over army reform, there were other reasons for the Porte's decision, as I have shown elsewhere.[22]

First of all, with the intelligence they received from Vienna, Ottoman ministers were aware that Russia and the other powers were at odds over issues such as the future of Poland and Saxony.[23] They believed that peace in Europe was far from settled. According to Liston, some of the ministers still harboured great admiration for Napoleon, remaining inclined to think that the former French emperor would ultimately extricate himself from all his difficulties, even placing bets on this outcome.[24]

The sultan was loath to accept a lower status for his minister, who was to 'be within reach of the assembly to give explanations if required, and act as an observer [*karardâdeye rızadâde*]'. The subordinate position accorded to his empire was an affront to his pride.[25] Perhaps most importantly, the Ottoman sultan and his ministers' distrust of European 'politicking' led the Porte to maintain its policy of isolation from European affairs. Of these ministers, Halet and Halil, who still harboured hopes for further instability in Europe, had the greatest influence on the sultan.[26]

Liston's dispatches to Foreign Secretary Castlereagh at the end of 1814 are notably silent on the Porte's policy towards the congress. However, Austrian secretary Gentz wrote to Caradja that his cabinet recognized in the Ottoman decision 'the same spirit of moderation and wisdom, which has characterized the conduct of this Power throughout the great troubles of Europe'. The Austrian cabinet pledged that 'without waiting for a formal invitation', they would do all in their power at Vienna for 'the entire satisfaction of the Porte' in its dispute with Russia, despite Prince Metternich's belief that making active efforts in this direction would be 'useless and unfocused today'.[27]

In October and November 1814, the situation in Vienna was tense. The tsar rejected accusations of having aggressive designs on Poland, arguing that his territorial acquisitions were strictly defensive and insisting that he would

---

[22] Ozavci, 'A Priceless Grace'.
[23] BOA HAT 1151/45698, 7 July 1814; Robert Liston to Lord Castlereagh, 10 August 1814; 25 November 1814; 30 December 1814, NLS MS 5628, ff. 67, 121, 143.
[24] Robert Liston to Lord Castlereagh, 30 December 1814, NLS MS 5628, f. 143.
[25] BOA TS.MA.e 243/16, 6 July 1814.
[26] Ozavci, 'A Priceless Grace', 1462.
[27] Gentz to Caradja, 7 November 1814, *Dépêches*, 119–21.

give Prussia what he ought to, but 'I will not cede a single village to Austria'.[28] Metternich was furious with the tsar's rhetoric: '[T]he language of truth and justice is no longer the language that Russia understands.' The Austrian statesman believed that any démarche for the restitutions that the Porte demanded from the tsar now would only weaken the 'well-understood interests' of the sultan.[29]

Metternich made it clear to the Ottoman chargé d'affaires, Mavroyeni, that he had proposed guaranteeing the territorial integrity of the sultan's dominions as early as October 1813 and would not abandon the idea. If the tsar continued in his obstinacy and became the crowned king of Poland, his neighbours, and Europe with them, would refuse to accept it. The congress would dissolve without having established a general peace and 'we shall be heading for a sad future'.[30] Despite his cynicism, in a separate audience with Mavroyeni, Metternich remarked that Austria would not leave the congress without first establishing and guaranteeing the independence and integrity of the entire Ottoman Empire.[31]

Mavroyeni was equally perturbed by the behaviour of Alexander I in Vienna. 'It seems that the Emperor Alexander wants to imitate Napoleon, without having the talents of the latter,' he reported. '[The tsar] only talks about his armies and his plans to come, he must have said more than once that he will employ thereafter part of his army to hold her in exercise against the Turks.'[32] Such reports likely reassured the Ottoman ministers of the wisdom of their 'principled conduct' in sequestering themselves from European politics.

The proposals

On 3 January 1815, Austria, France, Britain and Bavaria signed a secret agreement to contain Alexander I's ambitions, which, indeed, proved effective.[33] As Count Nesselrode, the head of the Russian delegation to the Congress of Vienna, apprehensively wrote: 'The misbehaviour of the Austrian ministry, the intrigues of France, the misplaced jealousy of Britain, and finally the hesitation

---

[28] Alexander I to Castlereagh, 30 October 1814, *VPR* I/VIII, 122, Castlereagh to Liverpool, 25 November 1814, *VPR* I/VIII, 133.
[29] Gentz to Caradja, 7 November 1814, *Dépêches*, 120–1.
[30] Ibid., 121–2.
[31] 'Rapport du chargé d'affaires ottoman à Vienne', 16 December 1814, AVPRI, f. 133, o. 468, d. 2303, l. 73–4.
[32] Ibid.
[33] Brian Vick, *The Congress of Vienna: Power and Politics after Napoleon* (Cambridge, MA and London: Harvard University Press, 2014), 279; [Vienna] to Stürmer, 4 January 1815, HHSta, Türkei VI 10.

of the Prussian cabinet' caused a departure from the initial Russian revisionism. Yet still, Saxony was dismembered, a confederation was established in Germany and a semi-autonomous Kingdom of Poland, attached to the tsar, was founded.[34]

As for the disputes with the Porte, Metternich, Lord Castlereagh and Charles Talleyrand decided that before his departure on 14 February 1815, Castlereagh should present this issue to Tsar Alexander I and urge him to consent to their mediation. '[T]his is the moment', Metternich assured the Ottoman agent Mavroyeni in February 1815, 'when we are going to take care of [your interests]'.[35] As a result, Castlereagh held two lengthy conversations with the tsar and one with Nesselrode.

Nesselrode had recently asked Castlereagh to take a joint step with the Porte 'to grant the European powers more freedom of trade on the Black Sea'.[36] Nesselrode's plan was to conclude a pact among the Great Powers against the Porte regarding the exercise of 'existing [capitulatory] rights'.[37] Castlereagh shrewdly used this request to benefit the general cause. In mid-February, he told Nesselrode and Alexander I that the joint representations of the powers for the liberalization of Black Sea commerce would be more effective if they wanted to give the Porte 'visible proof that they were interested in the integrity of the Ottoman Empire'.[38]

Just hours before his departure, Castlereagh informed the Ottoman chargé d'affaires in Vienna of the details of his conversation with the tsar. According to his account, Alexander I replied to him that he would be 'quite willing to guarantee with the other Powers the preservation of the Ottoman Empire and its integrity'.[39] Castlereagh underscored that 'with [Russia's] great forces on a war footing', and to ensure they would not attack the Ottoman Empire and not 'disturb the rest in Europe', the tsar ought to 'kindly agree to consult with the other Powers, the friends of the Ottoman Porte, on the means of guarantee, and on this subject, without opposition'. The tsar gave the British foreign secretary his word. '[Alexander I] would even accept the intervention of England, and that of France and Austria' with respect to the differences in the Caucasus.

---

[34] 'Note by K.V. Nesselrode', 4 March 1815, *VPR* I/VIII, 207–8.
[35] BOA HAT 951/40846; [Vienna] to Stürmer, 19 January 1815, HHSta, Türkei VI 10.
[36] Castlereagh to Liston, 14 February 1815, August Foukniee (ed.). *Die Geheimimpolizeiauf dem Wiener Kongßess: Eine Auswahl aus iheen papieren* (Wien: F. Tempsky, 1913), 410; [Vienna] to Stürmer, 4 February 1815, HHSta, Türkei VI 10.
[37] 'A Note from E.O. Richelieu' (Vienna), 29 October 1814 r., *VPR* I/VIII, 119–21; Castlereagh to Liston, 14 February 1815, *Geheim Polizei Wien*, 410.
[38] Castlereagh to Liston, 14 February 1815, *Geheim Polizei Wien*, 410.
[39] Mavroyeni to the Porte, 16 February 1815, TNA FO 139/26; 'Precis de la conversation de Lord Castlereagh avec M. du Mavrojeny', n.d., HHSta, Türkei VI 10.

Castlereagh advised the Ottoman chargé d'affaires that 'it is necessary [for the Porte] not to be difficult about an arrangement with Russia, and ... to give her something to her claims in order to satisfy her'. He had in mind commercial issues. 'I must confess to you at the same time', he continued, 'the Government of England is not very happy and it takes a great interest in the singular manner in which the Sublime Porte is proceeding towards our trade ... in the Black Sea, quite in opposition to the treaties and regulations existing between England and the Porte'. While there was 'no question of sailing warships in the Black Sea', the trading vessels of 'the friendly Powers of the Porte' had a right to free passage under the aforementioned capitulatory treaties.[40]

Metternich, Talleyrand and the duke of Wellington, who had taken over from Castlereagh, made similar remarks in their talks with Mavroyeni over the following days. Metternich assured the Ottoman chargé d'affaires that the mediation of the three powers would not harm the interests of the Porte.[41] Talleyrand confirmed that the tsar had consented to the guarantees on the territorial integrity of the Ottoman Empire. The tsar also told the French foreign minister that, before signing up to these guarantees, the question of the Phasis Valley and the 30,000 people living there had to be resolved in his favour.[42]

The truth is that neither Talleyrand and the duke of Wellington, nor Mavroyeni himself knew much about the Russo-Ottoman differences in 'Asia', as they all admitted. But Mavroyeni believed that Russia's calculations might be more far-sighted than was realized, because the tsar could not undertake a new war in Europe against the Ottomans 'without disturbing the general peace and quiet'. The tsar was still hoping to extend his frontiers and power over the Ottoman Empire. He might be looking to undermine the rule of the sultan on one side of Asia, specifically the Phasis Valley,

> while on the other side ... operate a diversion by extending his powerful influence in Persia and in the Persian Gulf, and there put himself in contact with India, in order to be able sooner or later to balance the trade of England and the great influence in these distant countries under the dependence of the latter power, of which Russia is jealous and the rival.

---

[40] Ibid. See Chapter 4.
[41] BOA HAT 286/17183, 21 February 1815.
[42] 'Raport Italinskogo ob audiencii Taleirana', 3 March 1815, AVPRI f. 133, o. 468, d. 2303, l. 360–6; BOA HAT 961/41197; Metternich [?] to Stürmer, 4 March 1815, HHSta, Türkei VI 10.

Metternich, Talleyrand and the duke of Wellington assured Mavroyeni that they considered the guarantee to be given to the dominions of the sultan as 'a capital' problem and that they 'absolutely want them to be guaranteed' before the congress adjourned.[43]

§ § §

At the end of February 1815, Liston received instructions dispatched by Castlereagh before he left Vienna. Castlereagh noted the tsar's acceptance of 'including the Ottoman Porte in the general Guarantee' and also that Russo-Ottoman differences would be resolved after the congress with the mediation of Britain, Austria and France. A general application to the Porte would be made concurrently 'to facilitate a more liberal Commercial intercourse of the nations of Europe with the Black Sea.'[44] The court of Istanbul was requested to authorize Mavroyeni to respond to the Powers' proposal 'so favourable to the general tranquillity and to the particular interests of the Ottoman Porte.'[45] Liston was entrusted with communicating these requests to the Porte.[46] His instructions reached Istanbul together with Mavroyeni's dispatches detailing his audiences with the representatives of the Powers.[47]

Liston made at first a verbal announcement to the Reis Efendi. But Ottoman ministers urged him to present this proposition in writing to enable the Porte to explain the exact proposal to the sultan.[48] He duly penned and delivered the note to the Reis Efendi on 13 March 1815, making 'two small alterations' in the contents of Castlereagh's instructions. He did not mention the suggestion that Mavroyeni might be accredited to discuss the guarantee proposal, because a Greek had never been given a commission of this nature – that is, to act as the sole representative and voice of the Ottoman Empire – and the request might offend the Porte.

Secondly, '[i]n stating the right which the nations of Europe have to a more liberal commercial intercourse', Liston took 'the liberty of expressing the demand in general terms, instead of confining it to the navigation of the Black Sea', referring to the 'variety of restraints and encroachments [on European trade] which demand equal redress', in accordance with the treaties. He made

---

[43] 'Raport Italinskogo ob audiencii Taleirana', 3 March 1815, AVPRI f. 133, o. 468, d. 2303, l. 360–6.
[44] Lord Castlereagh to Robert Liston, 14 February 1815, AVPRI f. 133, o. 468, d. 2303, l. 356.
[45] Ibid.
[46] Metternich [?] to Stürmer, 18 February 1815, HHSta, Türkei VI 10.
[47] BOA HAT 961/41197.
[48] Robert Liston to Duke of Wellington, 23 March 1815, NLS MS 5629, f. 36.

this adjustment in response to complaints from British merchants who claimed that Ottoman customs officers were not adhering to the 3 per cent customs tariff rule in other parts of the empire either.

The written note Liston submitted to the Porte stated that the Congress of Vienna had already settled the principal territorial arrangements:

> But this system of union and peace would be defective if public tranquillity were subject to be interrupted by disputes which might arise between any European Power and the Sublime Porte. For the system to be complete, general security would also have to embrace the integrity of the Ottoman States. And indeed the great sovereigns, including the Emperor of Russia, are prepared to give this extension to their guarantee.

Since the possession of the territories around the Phasis Valley was still disputed, it also had to be settled before a guarantee could be established.

> To this end it is proposed that the Sublime Porte agree to end its dispute amicably by submitting it to the decision of the three friendly Powers, Austria, France and England; and [Tsar] Alexander has already declared that he is ready to give his hands to this compromise. If the Sublime Porte takes this course, ... it will be necessary for her to give notice of it to the Allied Powers, to appoint forthwith a Minister Plenipotentiary to manage her affairs on this occasion, and to agree upon the time and place when she will be ready to enter into the matter.

Because resolving the issue could take a considerable time and the dissolution of the Congress of Vienna was approaching, the Allied Powers proposed 'to pass without delay the act of guarantee in favour of the Ottoman States'.

> By spontaneously giving the Ottoman Government this unequivocal mark of their friendship and of the interest which they can take in its welfare, the Allied Powers are not stipulating anything for themselves, but they confidently expect that the Sublime Porte for its part will be more than ever disposed to confirm and maintain the rights and privileges which it has granted them, and that it will above all not allow the subordinate officers of the Turkish Government to abuse their position in order to interfere with the perfect freedom of navigation and commerce which is assured to them by the Treaties.[49]

After the translation of Liston's note and Mavroyeni's dispatches from Vienna, the Ottoman imperial council held two meetings on the sultan's orders to deliberate on their response.[50] In his reports to Istanbul, Mavroyeni reiterated

---

[49] Robert Liston to Duke of Wellington, 25 March 1815, TNA FO 139/26, f. 40; BOA HAT 956/41003.
[50] BOA HAT 956/41006.

his views about British interests in Asia, and noted that, after peace was settled in Europe, Russia was planning an assault on Persian dominions, intending to annex its lands and thus encroach (*itâle-i dest-i taârruz*) on Indian trade, thereby endangering British interests.[51] Ottoman ministers suspected that Britain aimed to establish its influence over both Persia and the Ottoman Empire. However, they observed that Liston had not done anything to lead them to suspect Britain of harbouring such a plan.[52]

In the note (*hatt-ı hümâyun*) he appended to the margins of the initial proposal, Sultan Mahmud II remarked that the proposal did not indicate to him any sign of friendship from Britain. In the eyes of the sultan, the only thing the Porte had asked for was the implementation of the Treaty of Bucharest, above all a Russian evacuation from the Caucasus. He was concerned that Britain was complaining about free trade in Ottoman dominions, which, in his view, emboldened Russia's position. Indian trade was a separate matter. The sultan ordered his ministers not to make any hasty decisions and not to act without his approval, as either acceptance or rejection of the proposal could be perilous.[53]

The Ottoman imperial council further evaluated the subject and advised refusing the proposal. The sultan's ministers believed that accepting the arbitrage of the three powers would risk losing possession of lands they believed were rightfully theirs.[54] They also feared that if Russia gained control of the Phasis Valley and Georgia, it would leave the sultan's dominions vulnerable to new attacks from the tsar's forces. Their discussions reveal that Austrian and British representatives in Istanbul had made verbal communications with the Ottoman ministers. The Austrians had 'secretly' warned the Porte of Britain's intentions, suggesting that Britain might act in Russia's interests, while Liston pledged that as soon as the Porte entrusted the settlement of Russo-Ottoman differences to the Powers, he would 'take the whole matter into his own hands'. These accounts, along with the fear that the mediation could be a Russian ploy to gain time and so maintain her troops in the Caucasus, left the Porte uneasy.[55]

The distrust of Ottoman ministers, particularly Halet and Halil efendis, towards European politics, international law and on this occasion also towards

---

[51] BOA HAT 1274/49419.
[52] BOA HAT 956/41006.
[53] Ibid.41006.
[54] Also in Ozan Ozavci, 'A Priceless Grace'.
[55] BOA HAT 956/41003.

Liston, proved to be the main cause of their rejection of the proposal. Sultan Mahmud II was satisfied with the 'thorough' deliberations of his ministers and ordered them to communicate their decision to Liston in person. He also suggested considering the subject of commercial liberties further, as he appeared to be aware that as long as the treaties were in force, 'even the Russians' (*Rusyalıya dahi*) had to be offered such liberties. Exploiting the precarious state of peace and diplomacy in Europe, the Porte preferred to implement the unequal commercial treaties only after its own territorial demands were fulfilled.

The Reis Efendi communicated the sultan's decision to Liston on 31 March, stating that 'there was no question between the two courts, of Saint Petersburg and Constantinople, which needed to be discussed, nor any other which required the intervention of a third party'. The evacuation of certain districts was formally stipulated by the Treaty of Bucharest, and Russia had not fulfilled this. Assuming for a moment that the Porte agreed to arbitration, if the decision were contrary to its wishes, its adherence would be harmful and its refusal would cause great umbrage. The Reis Efendi suggested that it would be 'a real service to both parties' if the friendly Powers would use their good offices to persuade the tsar to fulfil the article promising the evacuation of the districts in question.[56]

To Liston, the Ottoman answer was a 'civil rejection'; the Porte's difference with Russia was not 'of a nature to admit of a compromise'. He had expected this because 'no member of the Government, indeed no well informed and patriotic Musulman', could risk Russia establishing herself in an almost unassailable position by controlling the region between the Caspian Sea and the Black Sea. Ottoman ministers feared that such an establishment, 'so formidable in the eyes of all', would likely be the outcome if the Porte submitted their differences to the arbitrage of the Powers, as the mediating powers would not wish to enter into war with Russia or offend Alexander I for such a 'trifling object'.[57]

Liston also suspected that the 'unexampled prosperity' of its treasury lay behind the Porte's rejection. Though it was always difficult and even dangerous to make enquiries in this area, Liston admitted, he had the good fortune to procure a general statement he believed was the 'near truth'. According to this, the government's expenses were minimal in peacetime, while its income considerably exceeded the sultan's expenditure due to annual savings, extraordinary profits, confiscations (from the local notables) and numerous escheats resulting from the extinction of families by the plague. The sultan had been able to deposit between

---

[56] 'Iz depeši Italinskogo', no date, AVPRI f. 133, o. 468, d. 2303, l. 420.
[57] Robert Liston to Duke of Wellington, 4 April 1815, TNA FO 78/84, f. 69.

seven and eight million sterling in the treasury. Even though several of these resources might not be permanent, the 'present superabundance' confirmed the sultan's determination to reject terms of compromise with Russia and to pursue his plans to reform his army.[58]

Unfortunately, I was unable to verify whether Liston's account might be correct, as existing Ottoman sources and studies on the imperial treasury do not provide enough evidence on the situation of the Ottoman finances at the time, warranting further research.[59]

The most valuable fruit of civilization

Russian diplomats were not surprised by the Porte's decision either. Count Nesselrode believed that the 'unfavourable reception' of the proposal was hardly astonishing since it had been a 'premature offer'.[60] D'Italinsky was not surprised either. In fact, he had described the proposal as a 'priceless grace' to the Porte and remained 'an observer' both during its submission and the period leading up to the Ottoman decision.[61] The Russian envoy extraordinary believed that Ottoman ministers were 'in the grip of delusions and illusions' about their position in international politics, imagining their empire capable of sequestering herself from European politics. Even though the Porte appeared 'indifferent to the proposals of the Powers' now, he wrote to Nesselrode, there would come a time when it would feel 'compelled to seek their intercession'. He was looking forward to that moment when the tsar would 'present to the Turks ... [a] large bill'.[62]

Russian sentiments towards the Porte were bitter at this point, perhaps the more so because, after the offensive exactions of the Ottoman rulers, a revolt led by Hadži Prodan had erupted in Čačak in late 1814, prompting gruesome attacks by janissaries on several towns in Serbia.[63] Serbian chiefs had pleaded with Nesselrode for Russia to 'intervene mightily' before the Porte 'in order to

---

[58] Robert Liston to Lord Castlereagh, 10 April 1815, TNA FO 78/84, f. 75.
[59] Yavuz Cezar, *Osmanlı Maliyesinde Bunalım ve Değişim Dönemi: XIII. Yüzyıldan Tanzimata Mali Tarih* (Istanbul: Alan Yayıncılık, 1986); Ahmet Tabakoğu, *Osmanlı Mali Tarihi* (Istanbul: Dergâh Yayınları, 2016).
[60] K.V. Nesselrode to A.Y. Italinsky, 26 April 1815, *VPR* I/VIII, 282.
[61] A. Y. Italinsky to K.V. Nesselrode, 25 March 1815, AVPRI, f. 133, o. 468, d. 2303, l. 356.
[62] Ibid.
[63] Cevdet Paşa, *Tarih-i Cevdet* V, 2586–7; Şânî-zâde Mehmed 'Atâ'ullah Efendi, *Şânî-zâde Târîhî* I, 675, 680–1.

save them from total extermination'.⁶⁴ They implored Alexander I to induce the 'Christian monarchs to make a joint démarche to the Turkish government' to cease 'its atrocities motivated by feelings of revenge'. Russian state councillor Nedoba received daily reports from Serbia that the Ottomans had 'completely devastated many districts, slaughtered all the men, and taken the women and children into slavery …, while many women and children of both sexes have been raped'.⁶⁵

Indeed, Serbia overflowed with violence at a time when the janissary corps showed great unrest over Sultan Mahmud II's plans to reform the army. Liston reported that several leading janissaries who had vocally opposed the reform had disappeared one by one. It was widely believed that the sultan was using the Serbian 'revolt' as an opportunity to rid himself of those opposed to his reforms.⁶⁶

In November 1814, Nesselrode suggested that by ceding a number of fortresses on the Caucasian border to the sultan, the Russian government could get the Porte to honour articles of the Treaty of Bucharest regarding the rights and privileges of Serbia, as well as those regarding freedom of navigation on the Black Sea. However, Tsar Alexander I did not agree to these concessions. One month later, in December 1814, Archpriest Matija Nenadovic arrived in Vienna, with a letter signed by several Serbian elders and clergymen.⁶⁷ On the advice and with the participation of Kapodistrias, numerous petitions were drafted entreating the Austrian emperor and the Prussian and British plenipotentiaries at the congress to mediate a solution to their situation.

In February 1815, just about the time Castlereagh requested the aforementioned meeting with Alexander I and Nesselrode on the Powers' joint proposal to the Porte about the guarantees, the tsar and his chief delegate at Vienna were preparing a note on the Serbian cause, to circulate among the representatives of the Powers at Vienna.⁶⁸ Their plan was to urge the Powers to act collectively to induce the Porte to cease its 'acts of vengeance in Serbia', arguing that this would be a 'lawful intervention'.⁶⁹

---

⁶⁴ K.V. Nesselrode to Alexander I, 6 January 1815, *VPR* I/VIII, 156.
⁶⁵ Ibid.
⁶⁶ Robert Liston to Lord Castlereagh, 25 October 1814, NLS MS 5628, f. 113.
⁶⁷ *VPR* I/VIII, 632.
⁶⁸ 'Soobraženija po povodu noty otnositel'no Serbii, s kotoroj pervomu upolnomočennomu Rossii nadležit obratit'sja k kongressu', 15 February 1815, *VPR* I/VIII, 193–7.
⁶⁹ Ibid., 193.

Their note emphasized that the tsar was the natural protector of Greek Orthodox Christians under Ottoman rule, and the agreements he had made with the Porte gave him the right to 'supervise the maintenance of their advantage', while the Treaty of Bucharest 'specifically reaffirms all the provisions of the previous treaties and provides the full amnesty for Serbians'. The Ottoman government was 'grossly' violating the treaty, taking advantage of 'the critical situation of Russia'. The Porte had 'excited the resistance of [the Serbians] in order to be able to massacre them while maintaining some semblance of righteousness'.[70]

In view of this, the Russian ministry had 'an indisputable right to rebel against the rape committed by the Porte'. Neither the tsar nor the other European monarchs could 'tolerate scenes of carnage which would desecrate so sublime a moment [the Congress of Vienna] and might one day disturb the tranquillity of Europe', they argued. 'Humanity and nature' called 'all Europe' to the 'defence of the Christians in the East against desecrators', armed with the 'code of international law', which was the 'guardian of political order' and 'undoubtedly the most valuable fruit of civilisation'.

By virtue of this 'universally recognized law, a man captured in arms does not become for life the property of his victor ..., all wanton cruelty and arbitrariness are banished from the relations between nations ... [E]quality of rights was recognized for men of all races ...', which is why the slavery question (the original Russian text reads 'the negro question',) had been brought before the sovereigns at Vienna. The same principles required the heads of the European family of nations to demand from the Porte 'an end to such atrocities'. The note ended with a cautionary statement: 'Russia, having tried a mode of conciliation in accordance with her policy of universal pacification, and having subordinated her special claims against the Porte to European interests, will reserve to herself the right to act independently'.[71]

Archival sources and published materials give no indication that these documents were ever discussed at the congress. Admittedly, protocols and treaties at Vienna do not include any traces of other issues that we know were negotiated.[72] Ottoman sources suggest that Britain, Austria and Prussia refused joint intervention on behalf of the Serbs, so as not to rile the sultan. In Istanbul and Paris, strong remonstrations were delivered to the sultan's chargé

---

[70] Ibid.
[71] Ibid.
[72] *VPR*, I/VIII, 641–2.

d'affaires and ministers by the Russian representatives, demanding an end to the violence against the Serbs.[73] Similarly, the Austrian internuncio expressed, in a less forceful tone, the anxiety of the court of Vienna about the developments in Serbia.[74]

One of the main reasons for the neglect of the Russian note and the failure to discuss the Serbs at Vienna appears to be that, with the settlement of the Polish question and especially with the prospect of ensuring joint action on Black Sea commerce, the Russian ministry did not wish to further strain its relations with the other Powers or the Porte, lest it remained further isolated. Nesselrode wrote to d'Italinsky that the tsar had in view 'cementing harmony and consolidating the equilibrium so necessary for the repose of mankind'. He was committed to the general cause, and to the 'spirit of conciliation which had been the conservative principle of the great alliance'.[75]

§ § §

Another reason for the omission of the 'Serbian question' was the shift in focus of all European monarchs to developments in France.[76] After Napoleon escaped from exile in Elba and regrouped his armies during the so-called 'Hundred Days', the issues of 'free commerce', the 'Serbian question' and the 'Asiatic question', that is, the Eastern Questions of the time, all dropped from the agenda at Vienna. In the new war on Napoleon, the Porte was urged in April and May 1815 to act 'in full accord with the high opinion of European sovereigns', to refuse negotiations with Napoleon's agents and not to admit his flag into Ottoman waters or ports.[77] The sultan was invited to 'to unite with the principles adopted by the Powers allied against Napoleon Bonaparte, and to take the most appropriate measures to achieve the goal they have set themselves'.[78]

Around the same time, the Russian ministry made a second proposal to the Porte, for the sultan's empire to '*join* [the European] system of guarantees

---

[73] BOA HAT 1097/44438; BOA HAT 1101/44532, 17 March 1815.
[74] BOA HAT 1196/46967.
[75] Ibid.
[76] [Metternich?] to Stürmer, 19 March 1815, HHSta, Türkei VI 10; [Metternich?] to Stürmer, 5 April 1815, HHSta, Türkei VI 10.
[77] [Vienna] to Stürmer, 8 April 1815, HHSta, Türkei VI 10; Copie d'une dépêche de S.E.M. de l'Italinski à S.E.M. le Comte de Nesselrode du 13/25 avril 1815, AVPRI, f. 133, op. 468, d. 2302, l. 448. 'Nota poslannika v Konstantinopole A. Ja. Italinskogo tureckomu pravitel'stvu', 3 May 1815, VPR I/VIII, 299–300; 'Memorial Submitted by Robert Liston to the Sublime Porte', 8 May 1815, TNA FO 78/84, f. 91.
[78] Baron Marshall to Stürmer, 8 April 1815, HHSta, Türkei VI 10.

and share in the benefits which it might derive from it for its preservation'[79] – a crucial development that has been overlooked in previous studies.[80] D'Italinsky informed the Porte that this was merely an attempt to prove to the Porte the 'sincerity and purity of [Russia's] intentions towards the Ottoman Empire', as well as its 'desire to make the present peace inviolable'. Their ongoing disputes concerning the frontiers of the two states in Asia and 'on certain other questions connected with the provisions of the Treaty of Bucharest' ought not be 'an obstacle to the acceptance of the proposed guarantees'.[81] It is debatable whether this proposal indicated the tsar's sincere desire to involve the Ottoman Empire in the general cause, or if it was an attempt to prevent the empire drifting towards Napoleon again.[82]

Following the submission of the note, d'Italinsky held an audience with Reis Efendi Mehmed Seyyidâ to persuade him, pointing out the difference between Liston's proposal in March and his own. According to d'Italinsky Liston's proposal wished 'to *guarantee* the inviolability of Ottoman possessions', which might have sounded 'offensive to Ottoman pride', whereas his way of expressing 'the same idea would spare their ego … and should flatter' the sultan, because Mahmud II was now invited to actively *join* a system rather than merely being protected by it.[83]

The Ottoman cabinet was again divided – not, however, on whether the Porte should accept the Russian proposal. Kahya bey Mazhar confidentially informed Liston that the majority of the sultan's ministers were inclined to 'let the Allies feel that the Porte did not regard herself as a member of the European system, and that [it] had never recognised the principles of the public law'.[84] In fact, despite Mazhar's opposing views, a strong current in the imperial council advocated declaring war against Russia and aligning the sultan's empire with Napoleon.[85] Described by Liston and d'Italinsky as a generally sensible man, Mazhar asked

---

[79] BOA HAT 1165/46092; 'Nota poslannika v Konstantinopole A. Ja. Italinskogo tureckomu pravitel'stvu', 19 May 1815, *VPR* I/VIII, 335–9. Emphasis mine.
[80] Including my 'A Priceless Grace'.
[81] BOA HAT 1165/46092; 'Nota poslannika v Konstantinopole A. Ja. Italinskogo tureckomu pravitel'stvu', 19 May 1815, *VPR* I/VIII, 335–9.
[82] Nesselrode to ?, May 1815, AVPRI, f. 133, o. 468, d. 11781, l. 82; Nesselrode to [unknown], 31 May 1815, AVPRI, f. 133, o. 468, d. 11781, l. 100.
[83] A. Y. Italinsky to K.V. Nesselrode, 29 May 1815, *VPR* I/VIII, 354–8.
[84] Robert Liston to Lord Castlereagh, 22 May 1815, TNA FO 78/84, f. 97; A. Y. Italinsky to K.V. Nesselrode, 29 May 1815, *VPR* I/VIII, 354–8.
[85] Robert Liston to Lord Castlereagh, 22 May 1815, TNA FO 78/84, f. 97.

Liston's advice on the subject, as he was afraid to express his opinions, dreading misrepresentations from the opposite party led by Halet and Halil efendis.[86]

Liston offered his advice in a curious guise, 'as the opinion of a certain Turk, a zealous defender of the interests of his native land', who viewed Russo-Ottoman relations 'from the angle most typical of a Turk who was the most ardent enemy of Russia'. In this note, the erudite *philosophe* in Liston came alive, blending his insights with those of Mazhar Efendi. Shortly after, he confidentially handed a copy to Mazhar and d'Italinsky.[87] Even though Liston requested that Mazhar read and then destroy the translation of the note, Mazhar asked to keep it, intending to pass them off as his own in the council, as they were 'quite close to his opinion'.[88]

Liston's note vividly portrays how, in his view, a moderate Ottoman minister might perceive international developments and the implications of the Eastern Questions for the Porte. 'As a good Mussulman and a faithful subject of the [sultan]', Liston's note began:

> I feel the deepest antipathy to Russia. I regard her as having formed a regular plan for the ruin of the Ottoman Empire; as having for near a century past sought pretexts for making war upon my country; as having concluded peace when she found it necessary, but with the resolution of recommencing hostilities when a favourable opportunity should occur.[89]

The hypothetical 'Turk' apprehended that Russia's non-evacuation of the Asiatic districts of the sultan signified long-term Russian plans 'to pour down armies from those mountainous tracks into the Turkish provinces of the lesser Asia' when the time came.

> There are perhaps moments when I think that national prejudices may have in some degree exaggerated the objects in my eyes, but such are my permanent sentiments as a good Mussulman, I burn with the desire of vengeance for the past; I shudder for the danger of the present; languish for an opportunity of recovering what has been lost; or at least of establishing security for future: I am inclined to hazard all in order to hasten that opportunity.

---

[86] Ibid.
[87] A. Y. Italinsky to K.V. Nesselrode, 29 May 1815, *VPR* I/VIII, 354–8.
[88] Robert Liston to Lord Castlereagh, 22 May 1815, TNA FO 78/84, f. 97; A.Y. Italinsky to K.V. Nesselrode, 29 May 1815, *VPR* I/VIII, 354–8.
[89] '"Would it be for the interest of Turkey at the present moment to declare war against Russia, and to connect herself with Bonaparte?" Answer by a Turk', 13 May 1815, TNA FO 83/74, f. 101.

The members of the imperial cabinet who 'regard the expected cooperation of the extraordinary man [Napoleon] as paramount to all other considerations' were politicians guided by prejudices, by the predilections and sanguine hopes of individuals, rather than the 'temperate deliberations of wise statesmen'. They were 'dazzled by the genius' of Napoleon, intent on throwing away the interest and the friendship of the European powers 'hitherto enjoyed by the Porte'. It was foolish for the Porte to hazard a contest with its rival, 'unless in one of the cases – either that she has regained her ancient superiority of skill, or that she can count upon the good wishes, the countenance, the eventual support of the principal Powers of Europe'. However, at the moment, its friends were in a strict alliance with Russia and jointly engaged with it in a cause 'which they regard as connected with their very existence as nations, there is danger that an attack upon her might be considered as an attack upon the whole'.[90]

It remains unclear whether and how Mazhar Efendi used this letter in the imperial council meeting a few days later. However, even though the French party was still 'fondly' hoping that Napoleon would triumph over the Allies, the Reis Efendi confirmed to Liston in an unofficial note that 'for the security of its friends', the Porte would not enter into negotiations with Napoleon. The sultan would not receive an envoy from him or acknowledge his tricoloured flag, adhering to its neutrality. In the same note, the Reis Efendi asked the Powers to persuade Russia to execute the Treaty of Bucharest and evacuate the sultan's Asiatic provinces.[91] Liston communicated this note to d'Italinsky immediately.

By July 1815, as news of Napoleon's failed final attempt to reassert dominance finally reached Istanbul, the Porte officially complied with the Allied Powers' requests regarding the ensigns of France. However, it declined to join the European system of 'reciprocal guarantees', rejecting, for the second time in six months, the opportunity to become a part of the new Vienna order.[92] Despite this, the Austrian court continued to advocate for the inclusion of the Ottoman Empire. In fact, during the negotiations for the second peace of Paris, concluded on 20 November 1815, Gentz even suggested guaranteeing the integrity of the sultan's dominions 'in spite of [the Porte's] own protests'.[93] Apart from the future of Parga and the inclusion of the (formerly Ottoman) Ionian Islands into the new

---

[90] Ibid.
[91] 'Literal Translation of a note transmitted by Reis Efendi to M. Liston', 20 May 1815, TNA FO 78/84, f. 105; Robert Liston to Lord Castlereagh, 26 May 1815, TNA FO 78/84, f. 112.
[92] BOA HAT 1313/51102; Robert Liston to Lord Castlereagh, 10 August 1815, TNA FO 78/84, f. 164; K.V. Nesselrode to A.Y. Italinsky, 16 August 1815, VPR I/VIII, f. 459–60.
[93] Gentz to Caradja, 24 September 1814, *Dépêches*, 1 January 1816, 199.

system of guarantees, the Eastern Question of the time, which embraced border disputes in the Caucasus and Bessarabia, the Serbian question and commercial liberalization, was not revisited in Paris.

In sum, while the Congress of Vienna redefined the political and diplomatic landscape following Napoleon's fall, forging a new system in Europe, the Ottoman Empire was not altogether excluded from the new international order. European Powers sought to mend fences with the Ottoman Empire. Liston encouraged the Ottomans to send a representative to the congress to safeguard their interests amid European reordering. Despite this counsel, Sultan Mahmud II and his ministers chose isolation over engagement. Their reluctance was also motivated by internal occupations such as administrative and military reforms.

Ottoman ministers remained wary of shifting European dynamics given the absence of a counterbalance against Russia, as they perceived it. However, in 1815, and the subsequent years, new practices such as conference diplomacy and permanent negotiation on issues that carried the risk of conflict, major or minor, gained more and more traction in European diplomatic practice, forging further a transimperial security culture. Yet the sultan's ministers did not immediately recognize or adapt to these changes.

At this hour, and in fact, through until the 1920s, the Ottoman perception of international law continued to be tinged with a lingering sense of inequity and mistrust. They viewed European legal frameworks, including those introduced at Vienna, as biased instruments that favoured powerful nations, perpetuating a system that compromised Ottoman independence. The disinclination to engage in European diplomacy was driven by a prevailing belief that international law (the practice, rather than the theory) failed to protect weaker states and often cloaked expansionist ambitions in legal obligations.

This was why, despite Liston's diplomatic efforts, the Porte rejected the Powers' proposals to include the Porte in the final act of the congress, *guaranteeing* its territorial integrity, as well as Russia's unilateral proposition for the sultan to *join* the European accord. Meanwhile the aspirations and security concerns of the Serbian people were accorded lesser importance. While the Powers brokered peace, the subjugated populations in the Balkans faced widespread slaughter. In the calculus of European diplomacy Serbian ambitions were abandoned, in the pursuit of a broader peace as well as the Powers' commercial interests in Ottoman dominions.

Had the Porte been formally integrated into the new European framework during the Congress of Vienna in June 1815, it could have been Liston's crowning achievement in his diplomatic career. The age of fickle alliances, land grabs and catastrophic wars in Europe may have ended, for now, at Vienna.

In early nineteenth century, the Powers learned to make concessions for the greater good and cooperate, a balance born out of their endless competition. Yet what this new European order meant for the rest of the world – especially the Ottoman Empire – remained a perplexing puzzle. How would diplomacy evolve between the European powers and the Ottomans moving forward? How would international law reconcile their many, often competing, interests? And most pressing of all, how would the subjugated peoples under imperial rules shield themselves from future oppression and bloodshed? The answers to these critical questions would begin to crystallize only with another revolution in the Ottoman world. It was during this turbulent period that they were collectively dubbed the 'Eastern Question'.

9

The phantom of Pera

Journey homewards

In October 1815, just as peace was once again restored in Europe, the Listons received the sad news of Robert's nephew's death. It was a shock for Robert because since his mother passed away, he had come to take a particular interest in his three nephews, 'those who are the nearest thing to my own children'.[1] The Listons set for Edinburgh hurriedly to attend the funeral and remained in Scotland for five months.

In the summer of 1816, the couple left the Milburn Tower once again, 'with infinite reluctance, uncertain when we should return to it'.[2] During their official leave from the Istanbul embassy, Henrietta found solace in her cherished conservatory. On 7 February 1817 the Prince Regent made Robert a Knight Grand Cross of the Order of the Bath, in recognition of his distinguished service as ambassador.[3] A few months later, the couple set sail once more for Istanbul, though they did so in the hope they would not remain there too long. Now aged seventy-five and sixty-six, they were determined not 'to leave [their] bones at Constantinople'.[4]

There was work still to do. Just as the Listons had taken their leave from the Porte in October 1815, Tsar Alexander I had departed Paris for Saint Petersburg, aware that his empire's domestic affairs demanded serious attention.[5] During and after the Hundred Days the tsar displayed 'a great and beautiful character', Friedrich Gentz wrote to the Ottoman agent Caradja, admiring the tsar's

---

[1] Robert Liston to Peggy Liston, 14 September 1791, NLS MS 5566, f. 79.
[2] Hart, *The Turkish Journals*, 207.
[3] *Evening Mail*, 23 October 1816; *Morning Post*, 7 February 1817.
[4] Petherbridge, 'Henrietta Liston', 16–17.
[5] Gentz to Caradja, 15 October 1815, *Dépêches inédites du Chevalier de Gentz aux Hospodars de Valachie pour servir à l'histoire de la politique européenne (1813 à 1828)*, I, Anton Prokesch-Osten (ed.) (Paris, 1876), 183.

peaceful rhetoric and commitment to the union of the powers. But Alexander I was 'a man, and his ideas may change', Gentz immediately cautioned. 'Many people in Russia favour the plans for a conquest of the Porte; a great part of the [Russian] army would certainly desire a new war, and would not be displeased to see it ignited on this side.'[6]

Gentz held that, with collective action becoming the norm in European politics of the time, a Russian campaign on the Porte would 'no longer be a simple and isolated project'. Should Austria and Britain commit the 'strange folly of associating themselves with Russia' in order to partition the Ottoman Empire, Prussia might invade half of Germany, and other powers seek to expand in turn. 'The immediate result would be the total upheaval of Europe.'[7] This scenario led Gentz to lament that the Porte had shunned the new Vienna order in 1815. It underpinned Lord Castlereagh's belief in the importance of Liston continuing his mission in Istanbul, to prevent a collapse of the fragile Russo-Ottoman peace.

The post-Vienna diplomatic strategies of Russia and the Ottoman Empire were nearly diametrically opposed. Even before the second Treaty of Paris was concluded, Alexander I sought to strengthen his ties with other powers by signing the 'Holy Alliance' with Emperor of Austria Franz I and the King of Prussia Friedrich Wilhelm III on 26 September 1815.[8] As historian Stella Ghervas notes, although it had 'no application from a diplomatic perspective', the Alliance underscored the 'intricate relationship between religion and politics on the continent' through its commitments to protect 'Religion, Peace, and Justice'.[9]

Many observers suspected the 'Holy Alliance' heralded a project against the Ottoman Empire.[10] According to Gentz, the tsar's 'secret wish' was to rally the 'first powers of Christianity by a solemn commitment', potentially leading to a kind of 'new crusade' masterminded in Saint Petersburg.[11] But the Austrian statesman believed that if Alexander I had truly pursued this plan, it would be the 'most foolish [action] that any monarch could ever have undertaken'.[12] Nonetheless, the Porte now needed to place its trust in the pacific powers of

---

[6] Ibid.
[7] Ibid., 184–5.
[8] Stella Ghervas, *Conquering Peace: From the Enlightenment to the European Union* (Cambridge, MA: Harvard University Press, 2021), 106–7.
[9] Ibid.
[10] Gentz to Caradja, 15 January 1816, *Dépêches*, 219–20.
[11] Ibid.
[12] Ibid.

Austria and Britain, with the latter's naval dominance in the Mediterranean serving as 'one of the first safeguards of the integrity of the Porte'.[13]

In stark contrast to the tsar, the sultan and his ministers shrank from any sort of negotiation with the other powers following their adversarial experiences during the Revolutionary and Napoleonic Wars. Gentz expressed his dismay in February 1816, writing that '[i]t is a system which [the Ottoman Empire] had never followed before'. The 'mysterious silence' of the Ottoman imperial council concerning European affairs was harmful to the empire. 'So little is known of her true intentions that one no longer knows how to act in her favour and to render her service'.[14] This was all the more unfortunate because a critical negotiation was soon to commence between the Porte and Russia, aiming for 'the definitive execution of the Treaty of Bucharest'.[15]

The Porte's persistent distrust and antagonism towards European courts, especially during the Napoleonic Wars, reinforced its belief that the Russo-Ottoman border disputes should not be subjected to mediation by other powers. These sentiments provided ample justification for an isolationist policy. While the Listons were away in Britain, the Anglo-Dutch bombardment of Algiers in 1816, which formed part of a post-Vienna anti-piracy campaign, exacerbated London's relations with the Porte.[16] The British had failed to consult or inform the Porte in advance about their campaign against the sultan's vassal. Furthermore, the Ottoman governments' reluctance to cede control of the Ionian Islands and Parga to Britain became new sources of friction.

Upon the Listons' return to Istanbul on 19 July 1817, the focus of Sir Robert's agenda quickly turned to Russo-Ottoman negotiations, alongside the issues of Parga and the future of the Ionian Islands.[17] Even though d'Italinsky had been replaced by the younger Count Grigorii-Alexandrovich Stroganoff (1770–1857) in 1816, Russo-Ottoman relations were still in a stalemate. They remained so for the next three years. By 1820, Ottoman ministers were convinced that, 'based on previous experiences', insistent Russian demands for further negotiations would ultimately 'lead to a day of confrontation'.[18]

---

[13] Gentz to Caradja, 25 February 1816, *Dépêches*, 225.
[14] Gentz to Caradja, 1 January 1816, *Dépêches*, 212–13.
[15] Ibid.
[16] Erik de Lange, 'From Augarten to Algiers: Security and "Piracy" around the Congress of Vienna', in *Securing Europe*, 231–48, at 238–46; Cevdet Paşa, *Tarih-i Cevdet* V, 2600; Şânî-zâde Mehmed 'Atâ'ullah Efendi, *Şânî-zâde Tarihi* II, 777.
[17] Robert Liston to Lord Castlereagh, 25 July 1817, NLS MS 5631, f. 3. For a detailed analysis of the negotiations around the Ioanian Islands, see esp. Aggelis Zarokostas, *Shadows and Whispers in the Mediterranean: Intelligence and the Ionian Protectorate, 1797–1831* (London: Routledge, forthcoming).
[18] Şânî-zâde Mehmed 'Atâ'ullah Efendi, *Şânî-zâde Tarihi* II, 976.

In fact, the Porte and Count Stroganoff had come close to settling their differences over the Treaty of Bucharest several times. Both parties agreed to modify the border at the mouth of the Danube, recognizing that the treaty's stipulations were both unintelligible and inexecutable. The tsar recognized that it was absurd for the treaty he had hastily ratified in 1812 'to take for a boundary a line drawn along the bank of a branch of the Danube which was never fixed but perpetually fluctuating since it overflowed the adjoining land for a great part of the year whereas the other branch was not subject to floods'.[19] Petty disagreements and the amour propre of both sovereigns repeatedly prevented a settlement.[20]

Stroganoff accused the Porte of injustices, extortion and treaty violations, particularly regarding the rights and privileges of the Serbs, as well as illegal requisitions and extortions in the Principalities of Moldovia and Wallachia. To substantiate these claims, the tsar sent agents to gather detailed reports of the exorbitant taxes imposed arbitrarily by Greek princes of these principalities.[21] Stroganoff asserted that the tsar's intentions were 'entirely pacific', and his orders were to seek justice through amicable representations. In his attempts to mediate between Russia and the Ottoman Empire, Liston suggested that concessions might be made in smaller matters 'reciprocally … for the sake of peace'. But Stroganoff pompously asked, '[W]here would be the consideration of the dignity of my sovereign, if he should consent to make concessions detrimental to the interests of his Empire and to the rightful claims of his subjects?'[22]

Sultan Mahmud II and his ministers remained resolute, refusing to make concessions without obtaining specific advantages in return. They were amenable to altering the Danube border, but only if it coincided with the Russian evacuation of the Phasis Valley, to which the Russian envoy would not agree. A sullen atmosphere enveloped the imperial council, exacerbated by young Stroganoff's tendency to let his pretensions escalate into threats during heated exchanges.[23]

---

[19] Robert Liston to Lord Castlereagh, 10 September 1817, NLS MS 5631, f. 11.
[20] Robert Liston to Lord Castlereagh, 10 September 1817; Robert Liston to Lord Castlereagh, 26 October 1817; 10 October 1817 NLS MS 5631, ff. 11, 35 and 47; Robert Liston to Lord Castlereagh, 3 January 1818; 10 January 1818; 15 October 1818; NLS MS. 5633, ff. 5, 7 and 202.
[21] K.V. Nesselrode to J.I. St. Aulaire, 26 April 1815, VPR I/VIII, 286–7; Robert Liston to Lord Castlereagh, 26 October 1817, NLS MS 5631, 35.
[22] Robert Liston to Lord Castlereagh, 26 October 1817, NLS MS 5631, f. 35.
[23] Ibid.

In the following years, the new Ottoman Reis Efendi Cânibi Mehmed Salih twice sought Liston's assistance, suggesting that the 1818 Congress of Aix-la-Chapelle – convened following serious disturbances in France in the wake of the withdrawal of the Allied forces – might address Russo-Ottoman tensions, with Britain potentially espousing the Ottoman cause.[24] He hoped 'the interference of England, the natural and best friend ... of the Turkish Empire, would induce the Emperor of Russia' to honour the Treaty of Bucharest by evacuating the Asiatic districts as promised.[25]

Liston abstained from intervening on this occasion, expressing a reluctance to meddle in the matter following the unsuccessful negotiations during the Congress of Vienna in 1814–15.[26] As subsequent meetings between Russian and Ottoman representatives proved fruitless, the peace between the two empires continued to be tenuous, perpetuating the instability that had greeted Liston upon his arrival in Istanbul in 1794 and again in 1812. Once again, it seemed a matter of 'when', not 'if', another war would erupt between the two empires.

§ § §

In 1817, Lord Castlereagh enquired about how long Liston preferred to remain in the Ottoman imperial capital.[27] Liston replied two, or at most three, years. Castlereagh found this agreeable. The foreign secretary consented to Liston's return once matters concerning the Ionian Islands and Parga were resolved, provided issues between Russia and the Porte were either settled amicably or postponed indefinitely.

By July 1819, the Parga affair had concluded with the town's cessation to Ali Paşa of Janina, returning it to Ottoman authority. The Parganotes were given the option to emigrate, many choosing to leave rather than live under Ottoman rule. The sultan relinquished his claims to the Ionian Islands, then under British protection.

In the summer of 1819, the Listons were eager to return home. Robert noted that there was 'reason to think that the discussions between the Turks and the Russians will ere long be adjourned *sine die*'. He informed Lord Castlereagh that within a year, he might ask to return to Britain, at least upon another leave of

---

[24] Robert Liston to Lord Castlereagh, 10 August 1818, NLS MS 5631, f. 144.
[25] Robert Liston to Lord Castlereagh, 26 September 1818, NLS MS 5631, f. 180.
[26] Robert Liston to Lord Castlereagh, 10 August 1818, NLS MS 5631, f. 144.
[27] Robert Liston to Lord Castlereagh, 10 July 1819, NLS MS 5635, f. 1.

absence, 'should no unforeseen obstacles arise'. He also requested (and received) Castlereagh's permission to spend the following winter on either an island in the Ottoman Empire or in the Mediterranean.[28] However, Henrietta fell ill at the end of 1819, which led the Listons to winter at the British Palace in Istanbul one last time.[29]

'Nothing interesting and important was passing in Constantinople', Sir Robert wrote to a friend in February 1820.[30] He had submitted his request to retire to the king.[31] Yet, as the Listons were preparing for their return journey, extraordinary developments unfolded. The first involved an exchange of letters between Tsar Alexander I and Sultan Mahmud II in March 1820. The two sovereigns addressed old controversies with 'good temper and perfect politeness', but without any immediate results.[32]

The second incident was more alarming. In April 1820, the uprising of Ali Paşa of Janina took a serious turn. Liston received intelligence that the Porte had become aware of crucial details, linking the rebellion to a larger Greek conspiracy.[33] A major revolution was brewing. Reports suggested that 'a very numerous association' had emerged among the Christian subjects of the Porte in the Morea, Albania and neighbouring provinces 'with a view to the liberation and independence of those countries'. Members of this association swore oaths of fidelity and secrecy, frequently assembling under the pretence of holding Freemasons' Lodges. A significant number of Ionian Islanders joined, showing fervent support particularly since Count Kapodistrias (then the tsar's foreign minister) visited Corfu in 1818. Their plans, the reports noted, were 'countenanced and supported by the Emperor of Russia'.[34]

This association was most likely the Philliki Etaria, founded in Odessa in 1814 for the liberation of Greece. It included notable figures such as Karadjordje, the aforementioned leader of the Serbian revolution, and Petros Itskos, a Greek merchant and diplomat, who had been involved in the Serbian revolution.[35]

---

[28] Ibid.
[29] Robert Liston to Lord Castlereagh, 25 October 1820, NLS MS 5635, f. 106.
[30] Robert Liston to Archibald Edmonstone, 16 February 1820, NLS MS 5663, f. 15.
[31] Robert Liston to [unknown], 20 April 1820, NLS MS 5663, f. 39.
[32] Robert Liston to Lord Castlereagh, 20 March 1820, NLS MS 5663, f. 43.
[33] Robert Liston to Lord Castlereagh, 10 April 1820, NLS MS 5663, f. 63.
[34] Robert Liston to Lord Castlereagh, 25 April 1820, NLS MS 5663, f. 69.
[35] Ozan Ozavci, 'The Ottoman Imperial Gaze: The Greek Revolution of 1821–32 and a New History of the Eastern Question', *Journal of Modern European History*, 21, no. 2 (2023), 222–37.

Only months before the bedlam of revolution engulfed Istanbul and various other Ottoman provinces, Liston announced his retirement to the Porte, stating that Bartholomew Frere would serve as British minister plenipotentiary until the arrival of the new envoy Percy Clinton Sydney Smythe, Viscount Strangford (1780–1855).[36] Following some delays from the Ottoman authorities, Sir Robert was granted permission to leave, with the gift of 'a box handsomely set with diamonds' from the sultan. Henrietta was presented 'four superb shawls of cashmere as a mark … of the Turkish government's approbation of my husband's conduct during his embassy'.[37]

On Friday, 7 July 1820, the Listons departed from their 'handsome palace at Pera', having received visits from their many friends and paid off their dependents and domestics.[38] 'The house, the garden, every local object in and around our dwelling became interesting to me, by the painful idea of seeing them for the last time,' Henrietta wrote in her diary. Their family and mission, British merchants, and all their friends and acquaintances in Pera accompanied them 'to the sight of the never to be forgotten beautiful Bosphorus'.[39]

The Listons' pleasure of returning to Milburn Tower was damped by revolutionary activity in Spain and Italy as well as 'reports of disturbances' in France. Both Sir Robert and Henrietta had a strong aversion to revolutions. Henrietta observed that the French nation was not prepared for 'the present happiness of their situation'. 'Those born, and those particularly brought up during the Revolution', she noted, 'have their minds so distorted and depraved that the mild and liberal system of government adopted by Louis the Eighteenth irritates instead of claiming their obstinate minds'.[40]

Ironically, just forty-eight hours later they boarded the frigate *Révolutionnaire*, which had been waiting for them in the Dardanelles. Wherever they went, revolutions seemed to trail them. Upon landing in Genoa at the end of July, they learned of revolutionary activity in Naples and Palermo.[41] There, rumours circulated that they had fled from a revolution in Istanbul. Though untrue, these rumours foreshadowed actual events, for five months later, just as they arrived in London via France in February 1821, the Greek Revolution erupted.[42]

---

[36] Robert Liston to Reis Efendi, 10 June 1820, NLS MS 5663, f. 75.
[37] 'Departure from Constantinople', 7 July 1820, MS 5712, f. 3.
[38] Ibid., f. 3–4.
[39] Ibid.
[40] Ibid.
[41] Ibid., 4.
[42] 'Fashionable Arrivals', *Morning Post*, 26 February 1821.

Spectral illusions

The Listons observed the Greek Revolution from afar, primarily through journals and newspapers, as well as through letters from their many correspondents. Among these correspondents were Robert Liston Elliot, Sir Robert's polyglot protégé (he could speak Turkish, Arabic and Persian), who now served as secretary of the Orient at the Istanbul embassy, and their former chief dragoman, Pisani.

Soon after the revolution broke out, the perceived 'betrayal' and 'treachery' of the Greeks, coupled with the mass killing of Muslims and Jews in the Morea, sparked great fury and consternation among Sultan Mahmud II and his ministers. They harboured an unshakeable belief that the revolution was orchestrated by the Russians as a strategic ploy to attack Istanbul.[43] The Ottoman ministers suspected that the tsar had adopted a new strategy due to the unresolved Russo-Ottoman differences over the Treaty of Bucharest. 'Had [the Russians] not promised to help and interfere', stated the sultan, 'the Greeks could not dare [to revolt]'.[44] This belief was fuelled by the memory of the 1770 revolt in the Morea, when the Greeks had risen with Russian support, and by the events of the 1800s and 1810s, when the Serbs received Russian encouragement in their revolution. Moreover, the revolutionary leaders' declarations, particularly those of Alexander Ypsilantis, aimed at re-erecting a Byzantine empire in Istanbul, further aggravated the sultan.[45]

The Porte gathered a substantial number of provincial troops in the vicinity of the capital. Eight thousand men were encamped at Büyükdere, with larger forces (around 12,000 each) quartered at Üsküdar and Silivri.[46] A formidable battery was erected at Belgrade village.[47] 'All Turks from the sultan down to the lowest porter go about armed with pistols, muskets, swords and by order of government,' reported Pisani. Anyone found without arms was accused of disobedience and punished accordingly. Several paşas were ordered to be ready to cross from Asia to Europe at a moment's notice.[48] On the surface, everything suggested a country in a state of war, 'yet no enemy comes forward to attack

---

[43] Şânî-zâde Mehmed 'Atâ'ullah Efendi, *Şânî-zâde Tarihi* II, 1065, 1068.
[44] Şükrü Ilıcak, 'The Revolt of Alexander Ipsilantis and the Fate of the Fanariots in Ottoman Documents', in P. Piziniars (ed.), *The Greek Revolution of 1821: A European Event* (Istanbul: ISIS Press, 2011), 225–39, there at 225–6.
[45] Ozavci, *Dangerous Gifts*, 119.
[46] Robert Liston Elliot to Henrietta Liston, 10 July 1821, NLS MS 5665, f. 30.
[47] B. Pisani to Robert Liston, 25 September 1821, NLS MS 5665, f. 202.
[48] Ozavci, 'The Ottoman Imperial Gaze', 227.

the Turks and justify the measures pursued as if a great foe were galloping this way from the Danube', Pisani observed.[49] He added that 'a scene so singular was never witnessed in this country'.[50]

In Istanbul, the Greek and Armenian 'riffraff' had been disarmed.[51] The situation was much worse in Izmir (Smyrna), where the greater part of the European population had taken refuge on ships and 'the massacre of the Greeks appears to have been very extensive'. The violence escalated and spiralled out of control, prompting the sultan to issue orders to alleviate the 'distressing situation' of his Christian subjects.[52]

The Russian envoy Stroganoff was exasperated by this, as the Greeks enjoyed Russian protection according to the 1774 Treaty of Küçük Kaynarca. He was infuriated by the Porte's accusations that the tsar had incited the 'treachery'. By July 1821 he was openly quarrelling with the Ottoman government, and the Porte denied his dragoman access to ministers.[53] A few weeks later, Stroganoff left Istanbul with his entire mission, breaking diplomatic ties with the Ottoman Empire.[54]

§ § §

The following year, in 1822, during the Congress of Verona, the term 'Eastern Question' emerged as a semantic category. Eager to defuse the risk of a new Russo-Ottoman War, Austrian chancellor Metternich wrote to his minister Ludwig von Lebzeltern (1774–1854) in Saint Petersburg that '[t]he revolt of the Greeks ... directly originated in the plots of the disorganised faction which menaces all thrones and all institutions'. Austria's approach to 'the Eastern question' was built upon the 'peculiar position of the Russian monarch with regard to the Porte, both in a political and religious point of view'. In using this term, Metternich had in mind 'the impression that must be made on the Ottoman government by the ... insurrection' of its Greek subjects, the insurrection's tone from the outset, the untiring efforts of the diverse Greek groups, 'religionists, political radicals, atheists as well as visionaries', and the 'stupor of the Turkish government, its weakness, its jealousy, its fanaticism, supported by the fanaticism

---

[49] B. Pisani to Robert Liston, 25 September 1821, NLS MS 5665, f. 202.
[50] B. Pisani to Robert Liston, 10 August 1821, NLS MS 5665, f. 100.
[51] Ozavci, 'The Ottoman Imperial Gaze', 227.
[52] Robert Liston Elliot to Henrietta Liston, 10 July 1821, NLS MS 5665, f. 30.
[53] Ibid.
[54] B. Pisani to Robert Liston, 25 September 1821, NLS MS 5665, f. 202.

and barbarism of the Mussulman people'.⁵⁵ His understanding of the Eastern Question epitomized its multilayered nature, discerning and conflating at once the interactions between the sultan and the Powers, among the Powers themselves, and between the sultan and his subjects.

At Verona, the Powers initially agreed on a policy of non-intervention in Ottoman affairs. This consensus shifted with the change in Russian stance, driven by various motivations – humanitarian, religious (due to the violent oppression of the Greeks), commercial (the disruption of trade in the Aegean caused by mounting piracy) and geopolitical (the prospect of establishing a satellite kingdom in Greece). Despite strenuous Austrian and Prussian protests and calls for non-intervention, Britain and France aligned with Russia. Their decision was influenced by both the desire to prevent Russia from dominating the field and humanitarian, religious and philhellenic public pressure at home. For nearly half a decade, Sultan Mahmud II had resisted the demands of the intervening Powers to grant autonomy to the Greeks, perceiving such demands as unwarranted intrusions into his domestic affairs.⁵⁶

While it might seem teleological to argue that almost every episode of the Eastern Question was directly or indirectly linked to its predecessor, peeling apart the Question's multiple layers reveals how historical actors saw a continuity. In 1826, Sultan Mahmud II finally gave in and agreed to discuss with Russia their disputes in the Balkans and the Caucasus arising from the 1812 Treaty of Bucharest. He acquiesced to Alexander I's demands only after the tsar assured him that the Greek Revolution would subsequently 'die of neglect'.⁵⁷ However, in October 1827, despite no formal declaration of war, the fleets of the Triple Alliance (Britain, France and Russia) annihilated the Ottoman imperial navy, supported by Egyptian, Algerian and Tunisian forces, in Navarino Bay. This incident only deepened Ottoman bewilderment with international law, and disgust for its duplicity. Navarino finally made Ottoman authorities realize that their policy of isolation was detrimental to their interests.

When a new Russo-Ottoman War broke out in 1828–9, its disastrous course compelled the Ottoman government to plead with Austria and Britain to ensure their empire's territorial integrity under European public law, in a hopeless effort to reverse the Porte's decision during the Congress of Vienna a decade earlier.

---

⁵⁵ Metternich to Lebzeltern, 28 January 1822, in *Memoirs of Prince Metternich, 1815–1829*, vol III, (ed. Prince Richard Metternich), trans. Mrs Alexander Napier (New York: Charles Scribner's Sons, 1881), 601–2.
⁵⁶ Ozavci, 'The Ottoman Imperial Gaze', 222–3.
⁵⁷ Ozavci, *Dangerous Gifts*, 125.

But to no avail. The 1829 Treaty of Edirne (Adrianople) could have been even more devastating for the sultan if not for Russia's newly adopted 'weak neighbour' policy, initially propounded by none other than the aforementioned moderate Kochubei, who aimed at preserving Ottoman Empire as a feeble neighbour and a buffer zone, rather than dismembering it.

Sultan Mahmud II ceded the disputed territories around the Phasis Valley. The frontier in Asia was delineated by a line starting from the Black Sea and following the actual limit of the province of Guriel as far as Imeritia (Article IV). In the Balkans, the Prut River remained the boundary between the two empires, from where it reached the Moldavian territory to its junction with the Danube (Article III). The treaty granted Russian subjects complete freedom of commerce throughout the Ottoman Empire, safe from any prohibitions, restrictions or violence. Russian goods could be freely sold, stored or reloaded without notifying local Ottoman authorities, including Russian grain exports. Russian vessels would enjoy 'complete freedom of trade and navigation in the Black Sea', including free passage of the Straits (Article VII). The sultan agreed to pay compensation of 1.5 million Dutch ducats for the losses Russian merchants suffered due to commercial restrictions imposed by the Porte since the war of 1806 (Article VIII). The disagreements over the Treaty of Bucharest were thus resolved, by force and in favour of Russia. Finally, the sultan granted partial autonomy to the Serbians (Article VI) and agreed to the demands of the Triple Alliance in resolving the Greek Revolution (Article X). This would pave the way for Greek independence in 1832.

Shortly thereafter, the rise of Mehmed Ali Paşa of Egypt drew inspiration from the successes of the Greek revolutionaries and the failures of the Porte. During the empire-wide civil war between Cairo and Istanbul that lasted from 1832 to 1841, the term 'Eastern Question' became prevalent in international thought, coinciding with the growing traction of the idea of 'civilization'.[58] It was also in the late 1830s that the Ottoman Empire agreed to sign new commercial agreements with all major European Powers, starting with Britain, which aimed at securing the same advantages Russian merchants had gained through the 1829 treaty. The commercial agreements of the 1830s and 1840s ensured the abolition of all monopolies and the further opening of Ottoman territories to global free trade.[59]

[58] Ozavci, *Dangerous Gifts*, Chapters 6–7.
[59] Ibid., 192–7.

The Gülhane Edict of 1839, which marked a key moment in the history of the reform process dubbed the *Tanzimat*, was declared not under European pressure, but rather to pressure the European Powers to intervene in the 1832–41 civil war in favour of the sultan. Its authors strove to present Istanbul as the civilized face of the East and to redefine the empire's relationship with its subjects in order to prevent further revolutions like those in Greece and Serbia. The edict pledged to guarantee the liberty, property and perfect security of *all* Ottoman subjects.[60] Although the term 'equality' was absent in the edict, heavy play was made in diplomatic correspondence of the idea by one of the edict's authors, Mustafa Reşid, and by agents sent to Syria to call upon the locals – especially Catholic Maronites – to rise against the Paşa of Egypt.[61]

Promises of perfect security, liberty and equality were incompletely realized. Along with the adverse effects of free trade agreements on the Ottoman economy and finances, as well as multifarious political and social reasons, new civil wars and uprisings came into existence and triggered further European interference. The instability of the sultan's dominions led the Powers, especially Russia and to a lesser extent France, to contemplate partitioning the empire, which contributed significantly to the outbreak of the Crimean War. The first Great Power war post-1815, the Crimean conflict (1853–6) saw British and French finance houses issue the first Ottoman loans. The inability of the Porte to repay these and other foreign loans – or even keep up interest payments – elicited the financial turn of the Eastern Question. Thereafter, maintaining or reviving the Ottoman Empire had global financial implications.[62]

The 1856 Treaty of Paris which concluded the Crimean War formally admitted the Porte into the Concert of Europe and stripped Russia of many of its long-held advantages. Just two years later, however, Russian and French foreign ministers and diplomats were already negotiating the partition of the Ottoman Empire and the creation of a Balkan confederation and a free state in Istanbul.[63]

Two decades later, local uprisings, mistreatment of Bulgarians by Ottoman authorities as well as Russia's imperial aspirations precipitated another Russo-Ottoman War (1877–8). The resulting 1878 Treaty of Berlin partitioned a significant portion of Ottoman territories in the Balkans, granting

---

[60] Ibid., 216, 221.
[61] Pisani to Bulwer, 25 September 1839 and 17 November 1839, NOR BUL 1/17/1–63, 561X9; 'Exposé fait par Rechid Pacha à M. Desgranges', 21 September 1841, AMAE MD Turquie 44; C. White to Lord Ponsonby, 27 January 1842, DUR GRE/E/665/148.
[62] Ozavci, *Dangerous Gifts*, 330–1.
[63] Ibid., 288.

independence to Romania, Serbia and Montenegro, autonomy to Bulgaria, and guaranteeing the security of Ottoman Armenians and Romanian Jews under international law.

The 1878 partition left many national and ethnic tensions in the Balkans unresolved, creating a volatile environment and fuelling nationalist sentiments and ambitions for territorial expansion. The disputes among the newly founded Balkan states and the Ottoman Empire eventually led to two Balkan Wars between 1912 and 1913, setting the stage for the Great War. In what was then termed the Near East, the fighting persisted, accompanied by gruesome scenes of violence and genocide, until the Lausanne Conference of 1922–3.

The 1923 Treaty of Lausanne gave birth to a new imperial order in the Near and Middle East by sanctioning the mandate system, enabling Western European and American capital's increasing control of Middle Eastern oil resources and suppressing the aspirations for independence of many subaltern actors within Arab populations, as well as among victims of mass violence and genocide such as the Armenians.[64] With the de facto fall of the Ottoman Empire in November 1922, the Eastern Question might be said to have come to an end, yet the long shadow of this major puzzle – born from a tangle of foreign interventions, unequal treaties, financial collapse, brutal civil strives, inter-imperial and international wars, and colonial domination – has hardly stopped looming over post-Ottoman societies.

The Eastern Question was a dynamic, inter-subjective and inter-sectoral process. Initially centred on territorial aggrandizements and commercial disputes, and the non-implementation of unequal treaties, but later drawing in financial, religious and even medical ones, it evolved into a complex constellation. The vicious *berat* system, for instance, served as a trigger for tension and violence, not only among states but also among Ottoman subjects, while severely undermining the sultan's economy and finances. In the wake of the Anglo-Ottoman Treaty of 1809 numerous treaties signed with other powers ought to check the abuses of this system.[65] But the sale of *berats* continued well into the late 1860s.[66]

---

[64] Lerna Ekmekcioglu, 'Debates over an Armenian National Home at the Lausanne Conference and the Limits of Post-genocide Co-existence', in Jonathan Conlin and Ozan Ozavci (eds.), *They All Made Peace – What Is Peace? The 1923 Treaty of Lausanne and the New Imperial Order* (London: Gingko Library, 2023), 119–41.

[65] In 1823 with Sardinia; in 1827 with Sweden; in 1830 with the United States; in 1833 with Toscana; in 1838 with Belgium; in 1843 with Portugal. Rey, *La Protection*, 279–80.

[66] Ozavci, *Dangerous Gifts*, 293–4.

The Eastern Question acquired different connotations in different times at the hands of different historical actors. Until the late nineteenth century, while for Britain, Austria and Prussia (later Germany), it often referred to preserving the status quo, for Russia and France, it more often than not became a pretext for their ambitious revisionist plans to partition the Ottoman Empire, if not to maintain it as a 'weak neighbour'. For the Ottoman imperial elites, it was tied to efforts for reform and revival, but also wielded as speech act to shape European perspectives on Ottoman policy. As for Ottoman subject peoples, it offered potential lifelines, creating new links in the chains of influences with European Great Powers and raising hopes for greater freedom, autonomy or even full liberation. However, these transimperial connections and interactions frequently led to unprecedented violence and, in some cases, genocide. They formed a security paradox: an ever-increasing demand for security, despite its allegedly increasing supply by way of domestic reform and foreign interventions.[67]

Notwithstanding its inter-subjective nature, the Eastern Question has usually been associated with fear of the potential fall of the Ottoman Empire and the devastating conflict that this would trigger among the major powers. This was one reason why the self-defined Great Powers were so intent on extending the guarantees of European public law to the Ottoman Empire. In 1814–15, they strove to prevent Russo-Ottoman differences in the Balkans and the Caucasus (i.e. the 'Serbian' and 'Asiatic questions') from escalating into another catastrophic war.

Thenceforth, with a few exceptions and despite their differences and rivalries, the Powers tended to act collectively, if not always in concert, relying on the security of permanent negotiation when dealing with the perceived and relative weakness of the Ottoman Empire. A transimperial security culture was woven around it – a culture rooted in foreign interventionism, marked by appeals from Ottoman elites (at least in the beginning) and subject peoples (all along) for external involvement, yet also by their growing resentment towards unchecked foreign interference in their internal affairs.[68]

It is important to remember that the Eastern Question was first and foremost an Ottoman imperial question – a quest for security by way of (re-)defining the empire's position in the global imperial (dis)order and, perhaps more importantly, by reforming its army, navy and civil bureaucracy so that it could cope with internal and external 'enemies of the state' and ensure its maintenance.

---

[67] Ibid., 3.
[68] Ibid., 8.

But, at once, the Eastern Question came to constitute an insecurity memory or a 'syndrome' for many Ottoman imperial rulers – a deep-seated distrust of the European Powers' intentions, fears of foreign invasion and partition, as would indeed become the case with the Treaty of Sèvres in August 1920, when only a rump state remained of the once mighty empire.

Evident as early as the Russian annexation of the Crimea in the 1780s and consolidated during and after the Revolutionary and Napoleonic Wars (1792–1815), the insecurity memory and the syndromes precipitated by the Eastern Question long preceded what social scientists today call the 'Sévres syndrome' – the belief or, more recently, the spectral illusions that invisible external powers conspired to weaken, partition and terminate the Republic of Turkey by interfering in its domestic affairs, as they had actually done in the past.[69] It has also served in both late- and post-Ottoman eras as a means to justify (mass) violence against 'disloyal' and 'treacherous' subaltern groups and dismiss their grievances as the sock puppetry of foreign powers. The ghost of this past continues to haunt (post-)Ottoman polities, yoking to their often ultra-nationalist and/or ultra-conservative political cultures.

§ § §

The Listons also held on to the ghosts in their last years, which they spent in Milburn Tower on a pension of £2,056 per annum.[70] Henrietta devoted much of her time to cultivating her garden, filling it with plants brought from the Americas, the Ottoman Empire and Europe. Sir Robert, meanwhile, took on the role of contractor for the parish roads, finding joy in providing support to the elderly and infirm.[71] Observers noted that the Milburn Tower became a lively place, constantly receiving an 'unceasing round of visitors', who were as often foreign guests as friends from home.[72]

In his later years, Sir Robert mostly reflected on the true meaning of nobility rather than the 'airy phantom' of fame and distinction that he had once pursued.

---

[69] Baskın Oran, *Türkiye'de Azınlıklar: Kavramlar, Teori, Lozan, İç Mevzuat, İçtihat, Uygulama* (Istanbul: TESEV Yayınları, 2004); Ozan Ozavci, 'Cumhuriyetin Güvensizlik Hafızası: Doğu Sorunu ve Lozan Ânı', *Toplum ve Bilim*, 164 (2023), 6–32.

[70] Robert Liston to Captain Fleetwood Pellew, 3 July 1820; NLS MS 5663, f. 79; *The Sun*, 6 June 1833.

[71] Esq. James Craig, 'History of a Case of Spectral Illusions with Subsequent Loss of Memory of Words and Names, with the Appearances on Dissection', *Edinburgh Medical and Surgical Journal*, 46, no. 129 (October, 1836), 334–66, there at 336.

[72] Ibid.

'If you learnt this pride in the school of Babylon, look not to the beginning of the tower but to the end of the construction,' he wrote in an undated piece:

> not to the triumph of its vanity but to the chastisement of its audacity. If you think that hereditary nobility, the heraldry of your ancestors, the Escutcheon of your arms, are sufficient to oppress the virtue of this poor labourer, you are mistaken. For to be noble is to be so, but not to appear so … To be noble is to favour the humble, not the proud. To be noble is to defend the weak, not to assist the strong.[73]

At Milburn Tower, he offered assistance and advice to private individuals and became a steadfast supporter of any endeavour aimed at public – and especially local – improvement.[74] He became deeply engaged with an 'enlightened regard for the interests of the poor in his neighbourhood'.[75]

When Henrietta's health suddenly deteriorated in 1826, the couple had 'a great interruption' in their happiness. She was sorely afflicted with colds, coughs and asthma, 'almost without interruption', by which she was 'weakened and broken down'.[76] For change of air and climate, the Listons spent the spring of 1827 in Naples and the winter of 1828 in Devonshire, where Henrietta 'gained some degree of health and strength'.[77] However, by the following autumn, her condition worsened again. In the Friday afternoon of 3 October 1828, she was seized with a disorder of an inflammatory nature, which rapidly increased the next day. On Sunday, it spread to her brain, and on Monday, 6 October 1828, at 5 o'clock, it carried Henrietta off.[78]

Robert conveyed the sad news to family and friends in letters with very poor, unsteady handwriting, adding: 'I do not yet appreciate the extent of my loss, but I feel it enough to know that it is irreparable.'[79] As the reality set in and his grief deepened, his only solace was knowing that Henrietta 'breathed her last without a convulsion, without the semblance of a struggle'.[80] She was laid to rest at Gogar Kirkyard on Saturday, 11 October.[81]

---

[73] No title, no date, Sir Robert Liston, NLS MS 5720, f. 21.
[74] Craig, 'History of a Case', 336.
[75] 'Death of Sir Robert Liston', *Caledonian Mercury*, 21 July 1836.
[76] Robert Liston to Daniel M Cormick, 24 March 1828, NLS MS 5683, f. 61.
[77] Ibid.
[78] Robert Liston to Mrs Rich, 7 October 1828, NLS MS 5683, f. 71.
[79] Ibid.
[80] Robert Liston to Sir C.F. Bar., 15 October 1828, NLS MS 5683, f. 86.
[81] Robert Liston to Reverand D. Robert, 9 October 1828, NLS MS 5683, f. 81; *Pertshire Courier*, 21 October 1828.

Sir Robert lived on for another eight years, attending local society gatherings in Edinburgh and occasionally travelling south to London – once for the accession of King William IV and with hopes of negotiating the continuation of his pension, the potential reduction of which caused him considerable anxiety and unease.[82] His mental health deteriorated significantly in his last years, as he began to experience speech impairments, memory lapses and frequent vivid visions of phantasmic human figures. The spectral illusions had actually first emerged in 1819 while he was still residing in Pera.[83] But now, they became increasingly more common at Milburn Tower.

As noted by his physician Dr James Craig in *The Edinburgh Medical and Surgical Journal*, in one occasion after her death, Robert also claimed to have seen the form of Henrietta 'floating around the room, beckoning for him to follow, and ultimately appearing to depart at the window'. The vision was so realistic that he pursued her, 'jumped out of the window [...] and fell upon the grass', asking those around him, 'Did you see her? my own madame, my wife.'[84]

---

[82] *The Morning Post*, 21 April 1831; Craig, 'History of a Case', 336–7.
[83] Craig, 'History of a Case', 335.
[84] Ibid, 343. Also in Petherbridge, 'Henrietta Liston', 9.

Select Bibliography

Archives

Archives Ministère des Affaires étrangères et du Développement international, La Courneuve, Paris (AMAE)
Arxiv vneshnej politiki Rossijskoj imperii (Foreign Policy Archive of Imperial Russia), Moscow (AVPRI)
Başbakanlık (now Cumhurbaşkanlığı) Osmanlı Arşivi (Ottoman State Archives), Istanbul (BOA)
British Library Manuscripts, London (BL)
Edinburgh University Library (EUL)
Nationaal Archief (Dutch National Archives), The Hague (HETNA)
The National Archives, Kew, London (TNA)
National Library of Scotland, Edinburgh (NLS)
Österreichisches Staatsarchiv, Haus-, Hof- und Staatsarchiv, Vienna (HHStA)
Topkapı Sarayı Müzesi Arşivi (Topkapi Palace Museum Archives), Istanbul (TSMA)

Published Sources

Abermahlige Confirmation von dem Moscowitisch- und Türckischen dreytägigen Treffen, und die nach derselben auf beyden Seiten bedungene Friedensarticul zu ewigen Zeiten:worüber aber der König von Schweden mit dem Gross-Vezier in einen scharffen Disputat gerathen, Greifswald: Greiffswalde, 1711.
Abgenöthigte Kriegs-Erklärung Ihro Russisch-Kayserliche Majestät wider die Ottomannische Pforte, nebst den Berichten von den Operationen Allerhöchst Dero Armee wider die Türken, Riga: Bey Gottlob Christian Frölich, 1769.
Abou-El-Haj, Rıfaat A. 'The Formal Closure of the Ottoman Frontier in Europe: 1699–1703,' *Journal of the American Oriental Society*, vol. 89, No. 3 (Jul.–Sep., 1969), 467–75.
Adair, G.C.B., Sir Robery. *The Negotiations for the Peace of the Dardanelles in 1808–1809: With Dispatches and Official Documents*, vol 1. London: Longman, Brown, Green and Longmans, 1845.
Adanır, Fikret. 'Turkey's Entry into the Concert of Europe,' *European Review*, vol. 13, No. 3 (2005), 395–417.
Ahmad, Feroz. 'Ottoman Perceptions of the Capitulations, 1800–1914,' *Journal of Islamic Studies*, vol. 11, No. 1 (January, 2000), 1–20.

Akdes Kurat, Nimet. *Prut Seferi ve Barışı*, Ankara: AÜDTCF Tarih Enstitüsü Yayınları, 1951.

Aksan, Virginia. *An Ottoman Statesman in War and Peace: Ahmed Resmi Efendi, 1700-1783*, Leiden: Brill, 1995.

Aksan, Virginia. *The Ottomans 1700-1923: An Empire Besieged*, Second Edition, London and New York: Routledge, 2022.

Alloul, Houssine, and Auwers, Michael. 'What Is (New in) New Diplomatic History?,' *Journal of Belgian History*, vol. 48, No. 4 (2018), 112-22.

Amirell, Stefan E. 'New Diplomatic History and the Study of the Global Nineteenth Century,' *Global Nineteenth Century Studies*, vol. 1, No. 1 (2022), 27-36.

Anderson, Matthew S. *The Eastern Question, 1774-1923: A Study in International Relations*, London, Melbourne: Palgrave Macmillan, 1966.

Angell, James B. 'The Turkish Capitulations,' *The American Historical Review*, vol. 6, No. 2 (January, 1901), 254-59.

Anghie, Antony. *Imperialism, Sovereignty and the Making of International Law*, Cambridge: Cambridge University Press, 2005.

Ardeleanu, Constantin. 'Friedrich von Gentz and His Wallachian Correspondents: Security Concerns in a Southeastern European Borderland,' in *Securing Europe after Napoleon: 1815 and the New European Security Culture*, Beatrice de Graaf, Ido de Haan, Brian Vick (eds.), Cambridge: Cambridge University Press, 2019, 251-70.

Arsan, Andrew. '"There Is, in the Heart of Asia, ... an Entirely French Population": France, Mount Lebanon, and the Workings of Affective Empire in the Mediterranean, c. 1830-1919,' in *French Mediterraneans: Transnational and Imperial Histories*, Patricia Lorcin and Todd Shepard (eds.), Lincoln, NE: University of Nebraska Press, 2016, 76-100.

Artunç, Cihan. 'The Price of Legal Institutions: The Beratlı Merchants in the Eighteenth-Century Ottoman Empire,' *The Journal of Economic History*, vol. 75, No. 3 (September, 2015), 720-48.

Badem, Candan. *The Ottoman Crimean War (1853-1856)*, Leiden: Brill, 2010.

Bajov, A.K. *Russkaja Armija v Carstvovanie Imperatricy Anny Ioannovny: Vojna Rossii s Turciej, V, 1736-1739*, Saint Petersburg: n.p., 1906.

Başaran, Betül. *Selim III, Social Control and Policing in Istanbul at the End of the Eighteenth Century: Between Crisis and Order*, Leiden, Boston, MA: E.J. Brill, 2014.

Bély, Lucien. 'Un art de négocier,' *Revue des deux mondes*, No. 4 (April, 2004), 91-102.

Bilici, Faruk. *La politique française en mer noire, 1747-1789*, Istanbul: Les Éditions, 1992.

Blanning, T.C.W. *The Origins of the French Revolutionary Wars*, London and New York: Longman, 1986.

Bloxham, Donald. *The Great Game of Genocide Imperialism, Nationalism, and the Destruction of the Ottoman Armenians*, Oxford: Oxford University Press, 2007.

Blumi, Isa. *Foundations of Modernity: Human Agency and the Imperial State*, New York, London: Routledge, 2012.

Boogert, Maurits van den. *The Capitulations and the Ottoman Legal System: Qadis, Consuls and Beratlis in the Eighteenth Century*, Leiden: Brill, 2005.

Bostan, İdris. 'Rusya'nın Karadeniz'de Ticarete Başlaması ve Osmanlı İmparatorluğu (1700–1787),' *Belleten*, vol. 59, No. 225 (August, 1995), 353–94.

Brisku, Adrian. 'Ottoman-Russian Relations,' *Oxford Research Encyclopedia of Asian History*, 26 April 2019 (last access 1 December 2022).

Câbî Târihi (Târïh-i Sultân Selîm-i Sâlis ve Mahmûd-ı Sânî) Tahlîl ve Tenkidli Metin, I-II (Mehmet Ali Beyhan, ed.). Ankara: Türk Tarih Kurumu, 2003.

Case, Holly. *The Age of Questions or, a First Attempt at an Aggregate History of the Eastern, Social, Woman, American, Jewish, Polish, Bullion, Tuberculosis, and Many Other Questions over the Nineteenth Century*, Princeton, NJ, and Oxford: Princeton University Press, 2018.

Cevdet Paşa, Ahmed. *Tarih-i Cevdet*, I-VI. Dündar Günday and Mümin Çevik (eds.). Istanbul: Üçdal Neşriyat, 1994.

Cezar, Yavuz. *Osmanlı Maliyesinde Bunalım ve Değişim Dönemi: XIII. Yüzyıldan Tanzimata Mali Tarih*, Istanbul: Alan Yayıncılık, 1986.

Conlin, Jonathan, and Ozavci, Ozan (eds.). *They All Made Peace – What Is Peace? The 1923 Lausanne Treaty and the New Imperial Order*, London: Gingko Library, 2023.

Cunningham, Allan. *Anglo-Ottoman Encounters in the Age of Revolution: Collected Essays*. vol. 1, Edward Ingram (ed.), London: Frank Cass, 1993.

Davies, Brian L. *The Russo-Turkish War, 1768–1774: Catherine II and The Ottoman Empire*, London: Bloomsbury Academic, 2016.

'De Frontiers de Turquie,' *Journal de Francfort*, 29 March 1814.

De Graaf, Beatrice, Vick, Brian, and de Haan, Ido. 'Introduction,' in Beatrice de Graaf, Ido de Haan, Brian Vick (eds.), *Securing Europe after Napoleon: 1815 and the New European Security Culture*, Cambridge: Cambridge University Press, 2019, 1–18.

De Graaf, Beatrice. *Fighting Terror after Napoleon: How Europe Became Secure after 1815*, Cambridge: Cambridge University Press, 2020.

De Lange, Erik. 'From Augarten to Algiers: Security and 'Piracy' around the Congress of Vienna,' in *Securing Europe after Napoleon: 1815 and the New European Security Culture*, Beatrice de Graaf, Ido de Haan, Brian Vick (eds.), Cambridge: Cambridge University Press, 2019, 231–48.

Degoev, Vladimir. 'Diplomatija Petra I na zaključiteľnom ètape Russko-Tureckoj vojny 1686–1700 Godov VI,' *Rossija*, vol. 21, No. 6 (2016), 116–43.

Dépêches inédites du Chevalier de Gentz aux Hospodars de Valachie pour servir à l'histoire de la politique européenne (1813 à 1828), I, Anton Prokesch-Osten (ed.), Paris: Plon, 1876.

Duggan, Stephen Pierce Hayden. *The Eastern Question: A Study in Diplomacy*. Unpublished Doctoral Thesis, Columbia University, New York, 1902.

Ekmekcioglu, Lerna. 'Debates over an Armenian National Home at the Lausanne Conference and the Limits of Post-Genocide Co-existence,' in *They All Made*

Peace – What Is Peace? The 1923 Treaty of Lausanne and the New Imperial Order, Jonathan Conlin and Ozan Ozavci (eds.), London: Gingko, 2023, 119–41.

Ekrem, Reşad. *Osmanlı muahedeleri ve kapitülasyonlar 1300–1920*, Istanbul: Muallim Ahmet Halit Kitaphanesi, 1934.

Finkel, Caroline. '"The Clever Engineer Koehler": The Clandestine Activities of George Frederick Koehler (1758–1800) in the Ottoman Lands, 1791–93,' in *Ottoman War and Peace Studies in Honor of Virginia H. Aksan*, Frank Castiglione, Ethan Menchinger, and Veysel Şimşek (eds.), Leiden: Brill, 2019, 327–42.

Fisher, Alan W. *The Russian Annexation of the Crimea, 1772–1783*, Cambridge: Cambridge University Press, 1970.

Fleet, Kate. *European and Islamic Trade in the Early Ottoman State: The Merchants of Genoa and Turkey*, Cambridge: Cambridge University Press, 1999.

Foukniee, August (ed.). *Die Geheimimpolizeiauf dem Wiener Kongßess: Eine Auswahl aus iheen papieren*, Wien: F. Tempsky, 1913.

Frary, Lucien J., and Kozelsky, Mara. *Russian-Ottoman Borderlands: The Eastern Question Reconsidered*, Wisconsin, University of Wisconsin Press, 2014.

Ghervas, Stella. *Conquering Peace: From the Enlightenment to the European Union*, Cambridge, MA: Harvard University Press, 2021.

Grachev, V.P. 'Buxarestskij Mir 1812 G. I Serbskij Vopros,' *Slavjane i Rossija*, No. 1 (2013), 437–88.

Guskov, Andrey. 'Učastie Rossii v Karlovickom kongresse (1698–1699 gody): Russkaja diplomatija v rannee Novoe vremja,' *Novaja i novejšaja istorija*, No. 3 (2018), 119–41.

Hart, Patrick. '"Out of Your World": Liston's Turkish Travels,' in *Henrietta Liston's Travels: The Turkish Journals, 1812–1820*, Patrick Hart, Valerie Kennedy and Dora Petherbridge (eds.), Edinburgh: University of Edinburgh Press, 2020, 4–8.

Hitzel, Frédérick. 'Un ingénieur français au service de la Sublime Porte: François Kauffer (1751?–1801),' *Observatoire urbain d'Istanbul, Lettre d'information*, No. 6 (June, 1994), 17–24.

Ilıcak, Şükrü. 'The Revolt of Alexander Ipsilantis and the Fate of the Fanariots in Ottoman Documents,' in *The Greek Revolution of 1821: A European Event*, P. Piziniars (ed.), Istanbul: ISIS Press, 2011, 225–39.

İnalcık, Halil 'Tanzimat Nedir?' in *Tanzimat Değişim Sürecinde Osmanlı İmparatorluğu*, Halil İnalcık, Mehmet Seyitdanlıoğlu (eds.), Ankara: Türkiye İş Bankası Yayınları, 2012, 237–63.

İnalcık, Halil. 'İmtiyazat: Osmanlı Dönemi. Kapitülasyonların Karakter ve Mahiyeti,' *Türkiye Diyanet Vakfı İslam Ansiklopedisi*, 2000, 245–52 (last access 20 October 2024).

Ingram, Edward. *Commitment to Empire: Prophecies of the Great Game in Asia, 1797–1800*, Oxford: Clarendon Press, 1981.

Ismail, Fehmi. 'The Making of the Treaty of Bucharest, 1811–1812,' *Middle Eastern Studies*, 15, No. 2 (May, 1979), 163–92.

Karabıçak, Yusuf Ziya. 'Sultan's Clergy: The Orthodox Patriarchate of Constantinople between Serbian Communities and Ottoman Government, 1797–1813,' *Bulletin de correspondance hellénique moderne et contemporain* (online) 2 (2020), http://journals.openedition.org/bchmc/42.

Karadeniz, Ümran, and Bizbirlik, Alpay. 'Azak Kalesi'nin İşgali ve İstirdadı (1637–1642),' *Akademik Bakış*, 14, No. 27 (Winter, 2020), 221–41.

Karal, Enver Z. *Selim III'ün Hat-ti Hümayunları, Nizam-ı Cedit, 1789–1807*, Ankara: Türk Tarih Kurumu Basımevi, 1988.

Karal, Enver Ziya. *Osmanlı Tarihi: Nizam-ı Cedid ve Tanzimat Devirleri, 1789–1856*, Ankara: Türk Tarih Kurumu, 1983.

Kemal Beydilli, 'Mahmud II,' *TDV İslam Ansiklopedisi*, https://islamansiklopedisi.org.tr/mahmud-ii-osmanli (last access 12 August 2023).

Kurtaran, Uğur. 'Marquis Louis Sauveur de Villeneuve'nin İstanbul Büyükelçiliği ve Faaliyetleri (1728–1741),' *TAD* 41, No. 71 (2022), 276–323.

Kütükoğlu, Mübahat S. *Osmanlı-İngiliz İktisadi Münasebetleri (1580–1838)*, Ankara: Türk Kültürünü Araştırma Enstitüsü Yayınları, 1974.

Kyte, George W. 'Robert Liston and Anglo-American Cooperation, 1796–1800,' *Proceedings of the American Philosophical Society*, 93, No. 3 (June, 1949), 259–66.

Laidlaw, Christine. *The British in the Levant: Trade and Perception of the Ottoman Empire in the Eighteenth Century*, London, New York: I.B. Tauris, 2020.

Luchaire, M.A. *La Question d'orient*, Paris: Libraire Hachette, 1911.

Macfie, Alexander L. *The Eastern Question 1774–1923*, London, New York: Longman, 2013.

Marriot, J.A.R. *The Eastern Question: An Historical Study in European Diplomacy*, London: Clarendon Press, 1917.

Mazower, Mark. *Governing the World: The History of an Idea*, London: Penguin Press, 2012.

Mazower, Mark. *The Greek Revolution 1821 and the Making of Modern Europe*, London: Penguin Press, 2021.

Mémoires de l'amiral Tchichagov (1767–1849). Avec une notice biographique D'après des documents authentiques, Gollion: Infolio, 2012.

Ménage, V.L. 'The English Capitulation of 1580: A Review Article,' *International Journal of Middle East Studies*, 12 (1980), 373–83.

Menchinger, Ethan L. *The First of the Modern Ottomans: The Intellectual History of Ahmed Vasıf*, Cambridge: Cambridge University Press, 2017.

Meriage, Lawrence P. 'The First Serbian Uprising (1804–1813) and the Nineteenth-Century Origins of the Eastern Question,' *Slavic Review*, Vol. 37, No. 3 (Sep., 1978), 421–39.

Mikaberidze, Alexander. *The Napoleonic Wars: A Global History*, Oxford: Oxford University Press, 2020.

Mikaberidze, Alexander. *Kutuzov: A Life in War and Peace*, Oxford: Oxford University Press, 2022.

Mitzen, Jennifer. 'Ontological Security in World Politics: State Identity and the Security Dilemma,' *European Journal of International Relations*, vol. 12, No. 3 (2006), 342-70.

Mitzen, Jennifer. *Power in Concert: The Nineteenth Century Origins of Global Governance*, Chicago, IL: University of Chicago Press, 2013.

Mosley, Philip E. *Russian Diplomacy and the Opening of the Eastern Question in 1838 and 1839*, Cambridge, MA: Harvard University Press, 1934.

Nicholls, James C. 'Lady Henrietta Liston's Journal of Washington's "Resignation", Retirement and Death,' *The Pennsylvania Magazine of History and Biography*, vol. 95, No. 4 (October, 1971), 511-20.

Noradounghian, Gabriel Efendi, *Recueil d'actes internationaux de l'Empire ottoman*, vol. II (1789-1856) and III (1856-1878), Paris/Leipzig: Librairie Cotillon, 1900.

North, Louise V. *The Travel Journals of Henrietta Marchant Liston: North America and Lower Canada, 1796-1800*, London: Lexington Books, 2014.

Oreshkova, S.F. 'Osmanskaya imperiya i Rossiya v svete ix geopoliticheskogo razgranicheniya', *Voprosy istorii. Ezhemesyachnyj zhurnal*, vol. 3 (2005), 34-46.

Oreshkova, S.F. 'The Ottoman Empire and Russia in Light of Their Geopolitical Demarcation,' *Russian Studies in History*, 57, No. 2 (2018), 125-45.

Owen, Roger. *The Middle East in the World Economy, 1800-1914*, London, New York: Methuen, 1981.

Ozavci, Ozan. *Dangerous Gifts: Imperialism, Security, and Civil Wars in the Levant, 1798-1864*, Oxford, New York: Oxford University Press, 2021.

Ozavci, Ozan. 'A Priceless Grace? The Congress of Vienna of 1815, the Ottoman Empire and Historicizing the Eastern Question,' *The English Historical Review*, vol. 136, No. 583 (December, 2021), 1450-76.

Ozavci, Ozan. 'The Ottoman Imperial Gaze: The Greek Revolution of 1821-32 and a New History of the Eastern Question,' *Journal of Modern European History*, Vol. 21, No. 2 (2023), 222-37.

Özsu, Umut. 'Ottoman Empire,' in *The Oxford Handbook of the History of International Law*, Bardo Fassbender and Anne Peters (eds.), Oxford: Oxford University Press, 2012, 429-48.

Pamjatniki diplomaticheskikh snoshenij drevnej Rossii s derzhavami inostrannymi, vol. 9, Saint Petersburg: Tip., 1868.

Pamuk, Şevket. *The Ottoman Empire and European Capitalism, 1820-1913: Trade, Investment and Production*, Cambridge: Cambridge University Press, 2010.

Parry, Jonathan. *Promised Lands: The British and the Ottoman Middle East*, Princeton, NJ: Princeton University Press, 2022.

Perkins, Bradford. 'A Diplomat's Wife in Philadelphia: Letters of Henrietta Liston, 1796-1800,' *The William and Mary Quarterly*, vol. 11, No. 4 (October, 1954), 592-632.

Phillou, Christine M. *Biography of an Empire: Governing Ottomans in an Age of Revolution*, Berkeley, CA: University of California Press, 2011.

Pinon, René. *L'Europe et l'empire ottoman: Les aspects actuels de la Question d'Orient*, Paris: Libraire académique, 1917.

Plokhy, Serhii. *The Gates of Europe: A History of Ukraine*, New York: Basic Books, 2021.
Poumarède, Géraud. '1814 vue de Constantinople: Le général-comte Andréossy et la chute de l'Empire,' in *Le Sud-Ouest, la France et l'Europe à la fin de l'Empire napoléonien*, Laurent Coste (ed.), Bordeaux, MSHA, 2015, 55–68.
Rey, Françis. *La Protection diplomatique et consulaire dans les échelles du levant et de barbarie, avec des documents inédits tires des archives du ministère des affaires étrangeres*, Paris: L. Larose, 1899.
Richmond, Steven. *The Voice of England in the East: Stratford Canning and Diplomacy with the Ottoman Empire*, London, New York: I.B. Tauris, 2014.
Rodogno, Davide. *Against Massacre: Humanitarian Interventions in the Ottoman Empire, 1815–1914: The Emergence of a European Concept and International Practice*, Princeton, NJ: Princeton University Press, 2012.
Roider, Jr., Karl, A. *Austria's Eastern Question*, Princeton, NJ: Princeton University Press, 1982.
Salomon, Robert. *La Politique orientale de Vergennes*, Crimea: Les Presses Modernes, 1935.
Şânî-zâde Mehmed 'Atâ'ullah Efendi. *Şânîzâde Tarihi*, I-II, Ziya Yılmazer (ed.). Istanbul: Çamlıca Yayınları, 2012.
Sbornik Arxivnyx Dokumentov, Moscow: Russkaja Kniga, 1992.
Scharffenstein, M.J.F. *Acten-mässige Deduction derer zwischen dem russischen und türckischen Hof, neuerlich entstandenen Irrungen und dadurch veranlassten Kriegs:nebst einer accuraten Charte und geographischen Beschreibung des türckischen Kayserthums und aller angränzenden Reiche und Länder, wie auch dem Diario der kayserlichen Armee in Ungarn*, Frankfurt, Leipzig: Bey Felsseckers Seel. Erben, 1737.
Schroeder, P. W. 'The 19th-Century International System: Changes in the Structure,' *World Politics*, vol. 39, No. 1 (Oct. 1986), 1–26.
Šedivý, Miroslav. *Metternich, the Great Powers and the Eastern Question*, Pilsen: TYPOS, 2013.
Sharafutdinov, Denis R. 'Andrej Jakovlevič Italinskij – Diplomatičeskij Poslannik V Konstantinopole,' *Istoričeskie, filosofskie, političeskie i juridičeskie nauki, kul'turologija I iskusstvovedenie. Voprosy teorii i praktiki*, Vol. 1, No. 37 (2013), 204–7.
Shaw, Stanford J. *Between Old and New: The Ottoman Empire under Sultan Selim III, 1789–1807*, Cambridge, MA: Harvard University Press, 1971.
Simpson, Gerry. *Great Powers and Outlaw States: Unequal Sovereigns in the International Legal Order*, Cambridge: Cambridge University Press, 2004.
Sinoue, Gilbert. *Le Dernier Pharaon: Méhémet Ali (1770–1849)*, Paris: Pygmalion Gerard Watelet, 1997.
Sluga, Glenda. *The Invention of International Order: Remaking Europe after Napoleon*, Princeton, NJ, and Oxford: Princeton University Press, 2022.
Smiley, Will. 'War without War: The Battle of Navarino, the Ottoman Empire and the Pacific Blockade,' *Journal of the History of International Law*, vol. 18, No. 1 (2016): 42–69.

Smilianskaya, I.M. 'Razlozhenie feodalnikh otoshenii v Sirii I Livane v Seredine XIX v,' *The Economic History of the Middle East, 1800–1914: Book of Readings*, Chicago, IL: University of Chicago Press, 1966, 234–47.

Sonyel, Salahi R. 'Protégé System in the Ottoman Empire and Its Abuses,' *Belleten*, vol. 55, No. 214 (December, 1991), 675–86.

Sunar, Mehmet Mert. '1806–1812 Osmanlı-Rus Harbi'ni Çalışmaya Bir Girizgâh: Sefer İçin Asker Toplanması,' *History Studies / International Journal of History*, vol. 10, No. 2 (April, 2018), 239–56.

Tabakoğlu, Ahmet. *Osmanlı Mali Tarihi*, Istanbul: Dergâh Yayınları, 2016.

Taki, Viktor. *Russia on the Danube: Empire, Elites, and Reform in Moldavia and Wallachia, 1812–1834*, Budapest: Central European University Press, 2021.

Topal, Alp Eren. *Sürgünde Muhalefet: Namık Kemal'in Hürriyet Gazetesi*, Istanbul: Vakıfbank Kültür Yayınları, 2018.

Uygun, Süleyman. 'Sırp İsyanı ve Hurşid Ahmet Paşa,' *Uluslararası Sosyal Araştırmalar Dergisi*, Vol. 4, No. 17 (2011), 416–36.

Vinogradov, V.N. '"Strannaja" russko-tureckaja vojna (1806–1812) i Buxarestskij mir,' in V.N. Vinogradov (ed.), *Aleksandr I, Napoleon i Balkany*, Moscow: Nauka, 1997, 169–202.

Vneshnyaya politika Rossii XIX i nachala XX veka. Dokumenty rossijskogo Ministerstva inostrannyx del (Russian Foreign Policy Nineteenth until Early Twentieth Century. Documents of Russian Ministry of Foreign Affairs).

Wani, Kentaro. *Neutrality in International Law from the Sixteenth Century to 1945*, Abingdon, Oxon; New York: Routledge, 2017.

Wilson, General Sir Robert C. M. T., *Private Diary of Travels, Personal Services, and Public Events, during Mission and Employment with the European Armies in the Campaigns of 1812, 1813, 1814. From the Invasion of Russia to the Capture of Paris*, London: John Murray, 1861.

Wilson, General Sir Robert K.M.T., *Narrative of Events during the Invasion of Russia by Napoleon Bonaparte and The Retreat of The French Army*, Second Edition. London: John Murray, 1860.

Wright, Esmond. 'Robert Liston: Second British Minister to the United States,' *History Today*, vol. 11, No. 2, 2 February 1961 (last access 20 October 2023).

Yalçınkaya, Mehmet A. 'Robert Liston'un İstanbul Büyükelçiliği (1794–1795) ve Osmanlı Devleti Hakkındaki Görüşleri,' *Osmanlı Araştırmaları*, vol. 18, No. 18 (1998), 187–216.

Yaycıoğlu, Ali. 'Révolutions de Constantinople: France and the Ottoman World in the Age of Revolutions,' in *French Mediterraneans: Transnational and Imperial Histories*, Patricia M. E. Lorchin and Todd Shephard (ed.), Lincoln, NE: University of Nebraska Press, 2016, 21–51.

Yaycıoğlu, Ali. 'Karlofça Anı: Osmanlılar 18. Yüzyıla Nasıl Başladı?' *Tarih ve Toplum*, vol. 18 (2022), 8–56.

Yenidünya Gürgen Süheyla. *Devletin Kâhyası, Sultanin Efendisi: Mehmed Said Halet Efendi*, Istanbul: Dergâh Yayınları, 2018.

Yeşil, Fatih. 'Looking at the French Revolution through Ottoman Eyes: Ebubekir Ratib Efendi's Observations,' *Bulleting of the School of Oriental and African Studies*, vol. 70, No. 2 (2007), 283–304.

Yeşil, Fatih. 'İstanbul Önlerinde Bir İngiliz Filosu,' in *Nizam-ı Kadim'den Nizam-ı Cedid'e III. Selim ve Dönemi*, Seyfi Kenan (ed.), Istanbul: ISAM, 2010, 391–493.

Yıldız, Aysel. 'III. Selim'in Katilleri,' *Osmanlı Araştırmaları*, vol. XXXI (2008), 55–92.

Yıldız, Aysel. '"Louis the XVI of the Turks": The Character of a Sultan,' *Middle Eastern Studies*, vol. 50, No. 2 (2014): 272–90.

Yılmaz, Hüseyin. 'The Eastern Question and the Ottoman Empire: The Genesis of the Near and Middle East in the Nineteenth Century,' in *Is There a Middle East? The Evolution of a Geopolitical Concept*, Michael E. Bonine (ed.), Stanford, CA.: Stanford University Press, 2011, 11–35.

Yurdusev, A. Nuri. 'The Middle East Encounter with the Expansion of European International Society', in *International Society and the Middle East: English School Theory at the Regional Level*, Barry Buzan and Ana Gonzalez-Pelaez (eds.), Basingstoke: Palgrave Macmillan, 2009, 70–91.

Zarakol, Ayşe (ed.) *Hierarchies in World Politics*, Cambridge: Cambridge University Press, 2017.

Zelenina, L.V. 'Pervoe serbskoe vosstanie: Kul'minacija i tragedija,' in *Aleksandr I, Napoleon i Balkany,* V.N. Vinogradov (ed.), Moscow: Nauka, 1997, 215–24.

Zelenina, L.V. 'Pervoe serbskoe vosstanie: Načal'nyj ètap,' in *Aleksandr I, Napoleon i Balkany*, V.N. Vinogradov (ed.), Moscow: Nauka, 1997, 143–59.

Index

Abaza 108
Abbè François-Marie Choquart 12
Abkhazia 115
Academy of Sciences (Caen) 14
Adair, Robert 7–9, 105
Adriatic 112, 122, 127
Aegean 182
Ahmet Zeki Efendi 138
Ainslie, Robert (Sir) 15, 22, 29, 44, 51, 67
Akhalkalak 143
Aktiar/Sevastopol 41–2, 54
Albania, Albanian 112, 178
Aleppin 130
Alexander I (Tsar) 10, 91–3, 95, 97, 102, 107, 109–12, 118, 121–6, 140–4, 152–4, 157–8, 163, 165, 173–4, 178, 182
Alexandria 64, 90
Algerian 182
Algier 56, 175
Ali Paşa (of Janina) 112
Allied Powers 58, 132, 151, 161, 168, 170
Anapa 143
Anatolia, Anatolian 53, 115
Andréossi, Antoine-François (General) 122, 145–6, 151
Anglo-French War 42
Anglomanie 12
Anglo-Ottoman tariff 69
Anglo-Ottoman Treaty (of 1809) 118, 185
Antigua 81, 86
Arab 185
Arbuthnot, Charles 91, 95–6
Archipelago 39, 93
Argo 101, 116–17
Armenian 70–1, 92, 111, 130, 181, 185
Army of the Danube 112, 127
Army of Moldavia 111–12
Asia 110, 122, 137, 153, 159, 162, 168–9, 180, 183
Asiatic question 154, 167, 186
Astrakhan Khanate 32

Atlantic, 84, 98
Austria, Austrian 25, 31, 35–7, 41–2, 44–5, 49, 52, 57, 72–3, 80, 91, 94–5, 97, 109–113, 117, 125, 127, 129, 133–4, 136, 142, 146–7, 154, 156–8, 160–2, 165–7, 170, 174–5, 181–2, 186
autonomy 94–5, 123, 135, 182–3, 185–6
ayans 105, 131
Aynalıkavak 41
Aynalıkavak Convention 44, 65

Bagration, Peter I. 105
balance of power 20–1, 31, 43, 45–6, 142
Balat 129
Balkan Wars 185
Balkans 31–2, 40, 47, 93–5, 107, 118, 127, 154, 171, 182–6
Barrière St. Dominique 12
Batavian Republic 87
Battle of Jemappes 49
Battle of Valmy 49
Battle of Verdun 49
Bavaria 17, 154, 157
Belgrade 38, 93–5, 97, 114, 123, 136, 180
berat, *berat* system, *berat*-holder 39, 70–5, 79, 91–4, 97, 120, 185
Berlin 1, 16, 24, 141, 184
Bessarabia 39, 41, 107, 114, 138, 171
Black Sea 31–3, 38–44, 46, 50, 54, 94, 108, 125, 138, 141–4, 153, 158–60, 163, 165, 167, 183
Blücher von, Gebhartd Leberecht (Marshall) 146
Bonaparte, Napoleon 10, 87, 89–92, 97, 99, 102, 117–18, 132–3, 143, 145–7, 149, 167
Bosnia 44, 112
Boscawen, Edward (Admiral) 78
Bosphorus 39–40, 49, 53, 59, 65, 97, 179
Bougeant, Père 88
Bourbon 147
Bourbon War 42, 45

Bozcaada 95
Breila 105
Brienne-le-Château, 146
Britain, British 2, 12, 19, 22, 25, 28, 39, 41–4, 46, 51, 53–4, 59, 65–6, 68, 71, 74–80, 82, 84, 86, 90–1, 96–9, 101–3, 105, 112–13, 116, 118–20, 122, 125, 127, 133, 137, 140, 142, 146, 157–8, 161–2, 165, 174–5, 177, 179, 182, 184
British Palace 120, 178
British Royal Navy 75
Bruce, Thomas 120
Bucharest 126, 133
Budzhatsky 40
buffer zone 37, 183
Bug 147
Bulgaria, Bulgarian 50, 184–5
Burke, Edmund 88
Büyükdere 180
Byzantine empire 41, 180

Čačak 164
Cadiz 116
Caliph 40–1
Cambridge 105
Campbell, John 88
Campbell, Lawrance Dundass 88
Cape Lagos 78
capitulatory system, capitulations 6, 37, 39, 63–5, 67–8, 94
  capitulatory agreements 9
Captain Montgomery 77
Caradja, John George 154–6, 173
Cardinal de Retz 88
Carlston House 99
Caspian Sea 138, 144, 163
Catherine II (Empress) 2, 38, 40–2, 45–6, 52, 67–8
Catholic 25, 88
  Maronites 184
Çavuş Ağa 117
Çelebi Mustafa Reşid Efendi 134–5
Central Asia 122
Cerny, Djordje Petrovic (Karadjordje) 94–5, 123, 125, 134–6, 178
Cevdet Paşa 148, 155
chargé d'affaires 105, 109, 122, 142, 154–5, 157–9
Chichagov, Pavel Vassilievitch 112–13, 116–17, 119, 121–7, 133–4, 137

Chilia 39, 114
Christianity 32, 138, 174
Circassia, Circassian 59, 108, 115
Coalition 49–50, 91–2
Congress of Aix-la-Chapelle 177
Congress of Karlowitz 18, 33–6
Congress of Prague 143, 146
Congress of Utrecht 18
Congress of Verona 181
Congress of Vienna 5, 10, 142, 145, 150–7, 160–1, 165, 171, 177, 182
Constantin, Pavlovich (Grand Duke) 41
Continental System 118
Copenhagen 1, 87
Corfu 178
Court of Berlin 16
  of France 54
  of Lisbon 78
  of Turin 25, 42
Craig, James (Dr.) 189
Crimea, occupation of 3, 9, 26, 31–2, 37–44, 47, 65, 137, 187
Crimean Muslim 41
Crimean War 3, 184
Croatia, Croats 44, 122
Czartoryski, Adam 95, 111–12

Dalmatia, Dalmatians 93, 111–12, 122, 124, 127
Dalzel, Andrew 1, 11–12, 14, 23, 27, 51, 75, 80, 84, 87
Dalzel, Archibald 11
Damhead 29, 83, 87
Danube, 22, 44, 50, 68, 107–9, 112, 114, 117, 124, 127, 137–9, 143, 176, 181, 183
Danubian Principalities 72, 93, 96, 132
Dardanelles 39–40, 42, 53, 65, 96–7, 99, 116–18, 179
de Callières, François 79
de La Porta, Horace François Bastien Sébastiani 92
de La Rivière, Pierre-Paul Lemercier 20
de Mably, Gabriel 20, 89
de Mably, L'abbé 89
de Montesquieu, Charles 20–1
de Saujon, Marie Charlotte Hippolyte (Comtesse de Boufflers) 15
de Sémonville, Charles-Louis Huguet 52, 73
de Tocqueville, Alexis 3

de Vergennes, Charles Gravier 17, 45
de Wicquefort, Abraham 89
de-ayanization project 131–2
Delta of the Danube 117
Democratic-Republican Party 86
Denmark 25, 64, 87
Department of Laws of the Council of State 126
D'Escorches (Descorches), Marie Louis Henri 57–8, 73
Dick, Christian 12
Diderot, Denis 20
diplomacy, diplomatic service, history of diplomacy 3, 9–10, 16–19, 21–2, 25, 51, 55, 61, 88, 98, 103, 118, 137, 163, 171–2
D'Italinsky, Andrey Y. (Chevalier) 93, 108, 112–13, 116–20, 122, 125–6, 131, 133, 135–41, 143–5, 147, 164, 167–70, 175
diversion plan 118–19, 122, 125–7, 133–4
Dniester 47, 93
Don Cossacks 32
dragoman 34, 39, 70–1, 73, 91–2, 97, 108, 131, 148, 152, 180–1
Dresden 141
Duchy of Oldenburg 102
Duchy of Warsaw 153
Duckworth, John Thomas (Admiral) 96, 99
Dumont, Jean 89
Dutch 8, 35, 64, 68, 87, 175, 183
Dutch Palace 146
Dutch Republic 28
Dürrizade Ataullah Efendi (Shekh-ul Islam) 43

East Coast 85
Eastern Question, 2–9, 29, 37, 40–1, 62, 94, 98, 105, 171, 182, 185–7
Ebubekir Ratib (Reis Efendi) 80
Eden, Morton Frederick, 22, 28
Edirne /Adrianople 50, 107, 183
Edisan 40
Egypt, Egyptian 10, 64, 89–90, 96, 125, 132, 140, 145, 182–3
Eid al-Ahda 96
elector of Bavaria 17
Elliot, Hugh 15, 17, 21, 22–4, 26
Elliot, Gilbert (Sir) 12–15, 17

Elliot, Robert Liston 116, 180
Emin Efendi 148
England, English 8, 13, 15, 18, 35, 50, 64, 70, 74, 76, 80, 87, 110, 118, 138, 159
Enlightenment 12, 19
Epirus 112
Episcopal Chapel in Glasgow 81
Esma Sultan 56
Eternal Peace 35, 37
Ewart, Joseph 22

Falmouth 81
Fane, John 99
firman 50, 71, 74, 92
First World War (Great War) 3, 185
Firth of Forth 11
Flanders 50
Fonton, A. (dragoman) 131
Foreign Office 25, 28
France 15, 28–9, 42–5, 50, 52–3, 58, 64–5, 78, 89–92, 95, 98, 101–2, 108–10, 125, 132, 137, 145–7, 149, 151, 158, 161, 177, 179, 182
Franco-Ottoman tariff 90
Franks 77, 130, 149
Franz I (Emperor) 174
Frederick William II of Prussia (King) 50
Freemason 178
French 3, 8, 12–13, 16–19, 22, 29, 38–9, 42, 45, 49, 51–2, 55, 57–8, 61, 64–6, 73, 75–9, 82, 84, 87, 89–93, 96–9, 108–11, 113–14, 119–20, 122, 126–7, 132–5, 141–2, 145–7, 151–2, 156, 159, 179, 184
French Dalmatia 124
French party 132–3, 135, 141–2, 145–8, 150, 170
Frere, Bartholomew 116, 179
Friedrich Wilhelm III (King) 174

Galata 63, 129
Harting (Garting), Ivan Marcovici (General) 138
Geneva 15
Genoa, Genoese 63, 179
Gentz von, Friedrich 154–6, 170, 173–5
George III (King) 55, 80
Georgia, Georgian 39, 41, 47, 107–8, 113, 115–16, 162

German, Germany 8, 29, 35, 45, 158, 174, 186
Gibbon, Edward 88
Glasgow 1, 12, 16–17, 23, 81–3
Gogar Kirkyard 188
Golden Horde 31, 33
Golenishev-Kutuzov, Mikhail Illarionovich 53, 55, 61, 107–13
Gordon, George Hamilton (earl of Aberdeen) 99
Grande Armée 110, 118, 129
Great Game 122
Great Powers 6, 25, 73, 94, 158, 186
Greek Orthodox Christian 166
Greek Project 41, 45
Greek Revolution 10, 179–80, 182–3
Greeks 6–7, 72, 92, 111–12, 129–30, 180–2
Grenville, William Wyndham (Lord) 68, 75–6, 78, 84
Grotius, Hugo 89
Gülhane Edict 184
Gustav III (King) 28–9

Habsburg Empire 35–6
Hacı Halil Efendi 132, 146, 162, 169
Hagia Sophia 45
Halil Efendi (poet and imam) 46
Halil Hamid Paşa (Grand Vizier) 44
Hamburg 141
Hamid Efendi 108
Hamlet 14
Hammond, George 85–6
Hanse towns 102
haraç 70
Harris, James 16, 22
Hasan Paşa (Grand Admiral) 44
High Street 11
HMS Romney 75–6
Holy Alliance 174
Holy Roman Empire 32–3
hospodars 92–3, 132
Hume, David 12, 15, 21
Hundred Days 173
Hungary 36
Hurşid Ahmed Paşa (Grand Vizier) 136

Illyrian Provinces 111, 146
Illyrians 122
Imperial council (*divan*) 43, 69, 115, 125, 132, 145, 148, 161–2, 168, 170, 175
imperialism 7
independence 7, 16, 39, 41–4, 74, 94–5, 97, 112, 121–2, 134–5, 152, 157, 171, 178, 183, 185
India 90, 98, 122, 159
international law 6–7, 37, 76, 78, 162, 166, 171–2, 182–5
interventionism 186
Ioannovna, Anna (Empress) 37
Ionian Islands 90, 112, 170, 175, 177
Iran (Persia) 102, 113–16, 122, 143, 159, 162
Islam 4, 59
Island of Elba 147, 167
Islanders 76–8, 130, 178
Istanbul /Constantinople 1–2, 8, 10–11, 15, 22, 32, 37, 39–40, 43–6, 49–53, 57–8, 63, 68, 70, 79–80, 87, 91, 93, 96–100, 105, 111–13, 115–17, 119–20, 123–4, 126–7, 129–30, 132, 136, 140, 145–7, 151, 153, 155, 160, 162–3, 166, 173, 175, 177–81, 183–4
Italy 27, 118, 154, 179
Itskos, Petros 178

Jackson, James 81, 84
Jacobite Uprising at Culloden 21
Janina 112, 132, 177–8
Janissaries 54, 93–4, 96, 105, 108, 123, 129, 132, 148–9, 156, 164–5
Jay Treaty 86
Jenkinson, Robert (earl of Liverpool) 87
Jewish, Jews 70–1, 129–30, 180, 185
Joseph II (Emperor) 41–2, 45
Just-Pons-Florimond de Fay de La Tour-Maubourg 109

kadı 50, 95
Kamensky, Nikolai M. 107
Kapodistrias, Ioannis 111–12, 165, 178
Karaburun 78
kassabiye 70
Kauffer, François 61
Kazan Khanate 32
Kerch 33–5, 39
Kfili 137

Kilia 110
Kingdom of Poland 154, 158
Kingdom of Sardinia 26
Kirkliston 11, 13, 15–16
Knight Grand Cross of the Order of the Bath 173
Koehler, George Frederick 53–4, 61
Kraut, Charlotte 24, 83
Kuban 40, 47
Kuban River 47
Küçük Ârif Mehmed (Reis Efendi) 120, 133, 135, 142
Küçük Hüseyin Paşa (Grand Admiral) 56, 60

law of nations 6, 18, 78, 89
Laz Ahmed Paşa (Grand Vizier) 107–10, 113, 119–20, 126
Le Palais du Buen Retiro 28
Lebzeltern von, Ludwig 181
Leiden 118
Levant 45, 71, 74–5, 118
Liston, Henrietta 6, 9, 12, 81–7, 99–101, 116, 118–20, 129–30, 173, 178–9, 187–9
Liston, Margaret (Peggy) 29
Liston, Patrick 12
London 1, 12, 15–16, 22, 24, 27–8, 42, 46, 49, 51, 55, 76, 80, 97, 99, 101–2, 105, 113, 116, 118, 120, 145, 175, 179, 189
London Magazine 26
Louis XVI (King) 50, 73
Louis XVIII (King) 151
Lübeck 141
Lüneburg 141

Macdonald, J. (Sir) 14
Machin 105
Madrid 1, 23, 27–8, 82
Mahmud II (Sultan) 10, 105–9, 113, 120, 123, 125, 129–31, 136, 141, 148–9, 152, 156, 162–3, 165, 168, 171, 176, 178, 180, 182–3
Malta 117
Mamluk 90
Marchant, Ambrose 81
Marchant, Benjamin 81
Marchant, Nathaniel 81

Marmara Sea 96
Martens von, Georg Friedrich 89
Mavrokordatos, Alexander 34–36
Mavroyeni, Yanko 142, 149, 154–5, 157–161
Mehmed Ali Paşa 183
Mehmed Hüsrev Paşa (Grand Admiral) 120
Mehmed II (Sultan) 63
Mehmed Said Galib Efendi 108
Mehmed Said Halet Efendi 132, 145–6, 148–50, 156, 162, 162
Mehmet Seyyidâ (Seyyid) Efendi 149
Melek Mehmed Paşa (Grand Vizier) 56
Metternich, Klemens (Prince) 154, 156–60, 181
Metz 22
Middle East 185
Mihrişah Sultan 55, 59–60
Milburn Tower 87, 99–100, 173, 179, 187–9
Millot, Abbe 88
Mingrelia 114, 121, 138, 144
Moldavia, principality of 22, 39, 41–2, 45, 56, 68, 72, 107–9, 111–12, 126, 135, 176, 183
Mons Haemus 50
Montagu, Lady Mary Wortley 8, 25
Montenegro 185
Morea 36, 178, 180
Moscow 9, 32–3, 35, 37
Müftüzade Selim Efendi 108
mukataas 131
Munich 1, 17, 22–2
Murray, David (Lord) 26
Muruzi, George 56, 58, 92–3
Muscovite, Muscovy 31–2, 38, 46
Muslim 5, 59–60, 95, 141, 180
Mustafa II (Sultan) 36
Mustafa III (Sultan) 71
Mustafa IV (Sultan), 96
Mustafa Mazhar Efendi, 131
Mykonos/Miconi, Mykonos Affair 75–6, 79

Namık Kemal 3
Nanton, Henrietta 81
Nanton, Sarah 81
Naples 179, 188

Napoleonic Wars 2, 5, 10, 89, 91, 114, 116, 136, 140, 175, 187
National Library of Scotland 8
Navarino Bay 182
Nedoba, F. I. 133, 165
Nenadović, Jakov 94–5
Nenadovic, Matija (Archpriest) 165
Nesselrode, Karl Vasilyevich 147, 158, 164–5, 167
neutrality 6, 34, 56, 77–80, 87, 89, 91, 140, 170
new diplomatic history 9
New Order 61, 93, 154
New York 85
Nieman River 121
Niš 134
North America 86, 89
Northern Department 24–6
Northern European countries 25
Northwest Territory 86

Ochakov 31, 42, 45–6
Odessa 127, 178
Osborne, Francis Godolphin (duke of Leeds) 46
Ottoman decline 4
Ottoman Empire 4–7, 10, 31, 34, 41, 45–7, 53, 55, 59, 62, 65, 67, 70–1, 78–9, 89, 97, 102, 108, 110–14, 116, 118, 120, 124–5, 140, 142, 154, 158, 160, 168, 171–2, 174, 178, 183–7
Ottomans 2–3, 9–10, 31, 33–6, 39, 43, 45–6, 49, 53–4, 57, 60, 64–5, 69, 91, 93–4, 97, 109, 111–12, 114, 116, 125–7, 134, 138, 159, 165, 171–2
Oxford 22

Paget, William 76–7
Palermo 116, 179
Pall Mall 99, 101
Parga 170, 175, 177
Paris 1, 12–15, 17, 23–4, 37, 49, 52, 57, 73, 75, 108–9, 117, 124, 132, 146, 151, 166, 170–1, 173
Pashalik of Belgrade 93, 97
Pecquet, Antoine 89
Pera 2, 9, 49, 80, 120, 129, 145, 147, 151, 173, 179, 181, 189
Peter I (Tsar) 33, 35–6, 105

Phanariots 111, 132
Phasis River 122
Phasis (Rioni) Valley 133, 137–8, 143–4, 153, 159, 161–2, 176, 183
Philadelphia 1, 8, 84, 86, 88
philhellene 43, 182
Philliki Etaria 178
Pisani, Barthélemy 49, 131, 180–1
Pisani, Nicolas (dragoman) 148, 152
plague 10, 80, 101, 129–30, 163
plantocracy 81
Podolia 36, 127, 147
Poland, Poles 36, 38, 43, 50, 55, 57, 108, 153–4, 156–8
Polevu 123
Polish Confederation of Bar 38
Polish crisis 55
Polish question 36–7, 167
Polish-Lithuanian Commonwealth 33, 35–8
Polson, Ann 82
Pomerania 35, 141
Port of Leith 12
Portsmouth 116
Portugal 25, 142
Poti 143
Prague 142
Prilutsky district 118
Prince Regent 173
Privy Council/ Privy Counsellor 1, 100–1
Prodan, Hadži 164
Prussia, Prussian 24–5, 28, 38, 43, 47, 49–50, 64, 92, 110, 112, 132, 157–8, 165–6, 174, 182, 186
Prut River 37, 109–10, 114, 116, 183
Prut Treaty 37
Pufendorf 89
Pyrenees 28

Rammage, Alexander 12
Regensburg 1, 24
Reisülküttab 34
republics of Ragusa 112
Revolutionary Wars 47, 89
Rhodian knights 63
Riccoboni, Antoine François 13
Riccoboni, Marie-Jeanne 13
Roman Catholics 15
Romania 185

Romanovs 37, 47
Rome 32, 40, 187
Rousseau, Jean-Jacques 15, 21
Royal George (ship) 96
Royal Hotel 99, 101
Royal Society of Edinburgh 12
Rumelia 53, 134
Rumyantsev, Nikolai 107, 126, 133, 138–9, 143–4
Rumyantsev, Piotr Alexandrovitch 22
Ruschuk 22, 107–8
Russian campaign 10, 32, 99, 110–12, 121, 123, 132, 174
Russian Empire/Russia 2–3, 6, 9–10, 22, 26, 28, 31–2, 35–40, 42–3, 46–7, 57, 64–5, 67–8, 72–3, 80, 90–1, 95, 97, 99, 101–2, 108–14, 116, 118–25, 131–4, 136–8, 140–1, 143, 145–6, 148–9, 153–4, 156–7, 159, 162–4, 166, 168, 170, 174, 177, 182, 184, 186
Russo-French peace 97
Russo-Ottoman agreement 37
Russo-Ottoman disputes (tensions) 3, 9, 10, 45, 52, 69, 127, 143, 177
Russo-Ottoman peace 3, 55, 57, 65, 79, 99, 113, 117, 129, 133, 137, 146, 174
Russo-Ottoman relations 6, 32–3, 39, 139, 169, 175
Russo-Ottoman truce 35
Russo-Ottoman War 9, 22, 37–8, 45–6, 51, 53, 75, 93, 95, 140, 146, 181–2, 184
Russophile 46
Russo-Prussian pact 38

Saint Petersburg 9, 37, 39–40, 62, 67, 69, 92, 97, 109, 113, 118, 126, 136–7, 143–4, 147, 152, 163, 173–4, 181
Sani Hamid Bey 148
Şânizâde Mehmet Ataullah Efendi 148
Sardinia 25–6, 43, 142
Sauveur, Louis (Marquis de Villeneuve) 38
Saxony 158
Scotland 1, 8, 12–13, 16, 49, 83, 173
Scottish Enlightenment 12
secret Agreement, secret article 114–16, 122–3, 137, 144, 153, 157
security imperialism 7
Selim I (Sultan) 31

Selim III (Sultan) 47, 50, 53–6, 58–61, 73, 80, 89–96, 105, 109
Seraglio 55, 130
Serbian, Serbians 6, 95, 114, 121, 123, 127, 133–6, 164–6, 171, 183
Serbian Question 10, 133, 154, 167, 171
Serbian revolution 6, 94–9, 107, 125, 136, 178
Serbian Church 95
Seven Towers 119
Seven Years War 12
Seyyid Mehmed Emin Vahid Efendi 97
sheikh-ul Islam 43, 116
Shumen (Shumla) 107–8, 126
Silahdar Ali Paşa 134
Silesia 117, 146
Silistria 105
Silivri 117, 119, 122, 180
sipahis 94
Siret River 108
Slavic, Slavs 4, 95, 111–12, 123–5
Slobozia 108
Smith, Adam 12
Smith, Sidney 80
Smith, Spencer 80
Smyrna (Izmir) 76, 181
Smythe, Percy Clinton Sydney (Viscount Strangford) 179
Sofia 134–5
Southern Department 25, 28
sovereignty 6–7, 40, 70, 135, 143
Spain, Spanish 25, 27, 29, 50, 64, 100, 102, 142, 179
St. John, Henry (First Viscount of Bolingbroke) 89
Stewart, Robert, (Viscount Castlereagh) 103, 116–17, 120, 137, 148, 156, 158–60, 165, 174, 177–8
Stockholm 1, 28–9, 82–3
straits 2, 39–40, 93–4, 96–8, 107, 110–11, 114, 118, 137, 140, 142, 183
Stratford, Canning (viscount Stratford de Redcliffe) 92, 102, 105, 117, 119–20
Stroganoff, Grigorii-Alexandrovich (Count) 175–6, 181
Stuart, George 15–16
Stuart, Gilbert 15–16, 23, 86
Stuart, Henry 88
Stuart, John (Lord Mount) 25–7, 44, 88

Stürmer van, Baron Ignaz Lorenz Freiherr 109, 146
Sublime Porte 28, 40, 42–4, 51, 57–8, 60, 67–69, 72–3, 76–80, 91–3, 99, 107–10, 113–14, 117, 119, 121–3, 133, 135–38, 140–68, 170–1, 173–8, 180–1, 180–1, 183–4
Sweden, Swedes 25, 28–9, 35, 45–7, 57, 64, 91, 127
Switzerland, Swiss 15, 25, 52, 112
Sybylle 75–7

Talleyrand, Charles 90, 158–60
Tanzimat 184
tekalif-i örfiyye 70
Teşrifati Efendi 117
Tilsit 97, 140, 151
   agreement of 118
Tophane 120
Topkapı Palace 96, 136
treaties of Reichenbach 142
Treaty of Belgrade 38
Treaty of Berlin 184
Treaty of Bucharest 10, 93, 111, 119, 121–2, 124–5, 127, 133–5, 137–8, 153, 162–3, 165–6, 168, 170, 175–7, 180, 182–3
Treaty of Dardanelles 97, 118
Treaty of Edirne 183
Treaty of Jassy 47, 55
Treaty of Küçük Kaynarca 39, 181
Treaty of Lausanne 3, 185
Treaty of Paris 151, 174, 184
Treaty of Sèvres 187
Treaty of Sistovski 94
Triple Alliance 28, 46, 182–3
Tunisian 182
Turk, Turkish 8, 60, 66, 74, 92, 121, 124, 131, 144, 161, 165, 169, 177, 179–81
Turner, William 116
Tuscany 25, 64
Twickenham 12, 17
Tyrol 112

Ukraine 9, 32, 36
United States 12, 25, 51, 84, 86
Üsküdar 180

Vattel de, Emmerich 89
Venetians 63, 66
Vezir Port 117
Vidin 136
Vienna 5, 23, 26, 37, 40, 44, 95, 109, 124, 136, 142, 145–7, 151–8, 160–1, 165–7, 171–2, 174–5
   order 170, 174
Vistula 147
Voltaire, François-Marie Arouet 88
Vorontsov, Mikhail Illarionovich 38

Wallachia, principality of 107, 176
Wallachians 124
War of the First Coalition 49, 51, 76, 84, 89
War of the Second Coalition 87, 90, 94
War of the Sixth Coalition 142
War of the Third Coalition 91
Warsaw 141, 153
Washington, George 86
Wellesley, Arthur (Duke of Wellington) 100
Wellesley, Henry 100
Wellesley, Richard Colley (Marques of) 98–103
West Asia 122
West Indies 81
Western Europe 10, 89, 185
Whitworth, Charles 22
William IV (King) 50
Wilson, Robert Thomas (Sir) 116, 120, 126–7, 130
Wurtemburg 25

Ypsilantis, Constantine 92–3
Yusuf Agah Efendi 55
Yusuf Paşa (Grand Vizier) 55

www.ingramcontent.com/pod-product-compliance
Ingram Content Group UK Ltd.
Pitfield, Milton Keynes, MK11 3LW, UK
UKHW020621040326
468569UK00009B/58